This is a unified account of all quantity changes affecting English stressed vowels during the Early Middle English period. Dr Ritt discusses Homorganic Lengthening, Open Syllable Lengthening, Trisyllabic Shortening, and Shortening before Consonant Clusters. The study is based on a statistical analysis of the Modern English reflexes of the changes. The complete corpus of analysed data is made available to the reader in the appendices.

All of the changes are shown to derive from basically the same set of quasi-universal tendencies, while apparent idiosyncrasies are shown to follow from factors that are independent of the underlying tendencies themselves. The role of tendencies – probabilistic laws in the description of language change – is given thorough theoretical treatment. In his aim to account for the changes as well as trace their chronology, Dr Ritt applies principles of Natural Phonology, and examines the conflict between phonological and morphological 'necessities'.

CAMBRIDGE STUDIES IN LINGUISTICS

SUPPLEMENTARY VOLUME

General Editors: J. BRESNAN, B. COMRIE, W. DRESSLER,
R. HUDDLESTON, R. LASS, D. LIGHTFOOT, J. LYONS,
P. H. MATTHEWS, R. POSNER, S. ROMAINE,
N. V. SMITH, N. VINCENT

Quantity adjustment

In this series

Earlier issues not listed are also available

QUANTITY ADJUSTMENT

VOWEL LENGTHENING AND SHORTENING
IN EARLY MIDDLE ENGLISH

NIKOLAUS RITT

University of Vienna

CAMBRIDGE
UNIVERSITY PRESS

Published by the Press Syndicate of the University of Cambridge
The Pitt Building, Trumpington Street, Cambridge CB2 1RP
40 West 20th Street, New York, NY 10011–4211, USA
10 Stamford Road, Oakleigh, Melbourne 3166, Australia

© Cambridge University Press 1994

First published 1994

Printed in Great Britain at the University Press, Cambridge

A catalogue record for this book is available from the British Library

Library of Congress cataloguing in publication data

Ritt, Nikolaus.
Quantity adjustment: vowel lengthening and shortening in early middle English /
Nikolaus Ritt.
    p.   cm. – (Cambridge Studies in Linguistics)
Includes index.
ISBN 0 521 46232 0 (hardback)
1. English language – Middle English, 1100–1500 – Vowels.
2. English language – Middle English, 1100–1500 – Quantity.
I. Title.   II. Series.
PE553.R58   1994
427'.02–dc20 94–7605 CIP

ISBN 0 521 46232 0 (hardback)

Contents

Preface

This study had its origins in my doctoral dissertation on Early Middle English changes of vowel quantity. Since I was a student at Vienna University, it is no big surprise that my thesis took the great Viennese philologist Karl Luick's treatment of the topic as a starting point. In some way, even, it started out as an attempt to translate the story Luick had told of the changes into the language of historical linguists of our time. As often happens with translations, however, mine turned out to become an interpretation, a deconstruction and eventually an almost complete recreation of the text it set out merely to 'make understandable'. The obvious reason for this was, of course, that many of the Neogrammarian concepts Luick had employed have come to be refuted by the linguistic community and that even the very existence of sound laws that had long counted as well established has come to be questioned in brilliant and convincing ways by modern historical linguists. Most eye-opening to me, in this respect, was Donka Minkova's radical re-interpretation of Middle English Open Syllable Lengthening in her 1982 paper in *Folia Linguistica Historica*. At some stages during my work, then, I thought that the purpose of my study was to discover 'errors' in the stories of Luick and my other predecessors, to set them right and to make their accounts more 'true'. Certainly, while I was working on my dissertation, such a heroic search for 'truth' appeared as a noble and worthy task to me and motivated me greatly. Afterwards, however, and particularly during the phase in which I reworked my thesis for publication, my attitudes towards 'God's truth' and what I may believe to have grasped of it underwent the unavoidable change and became considerably more modest. Now, I feel that the essential difference between my version of Early Middle English quantity changes and the accounts Luick and other scholars after him have given is not one of truth. Rather than answering the question of Early Middle English changes of vowel quantity 'once and for all' I hope to have highlighted some relevant aspects concerning this question and shown how concepts and methods of contemporary linguistic science can be applied to them to yield surprising results and to make new sense of old stories.

Apart from my friends and colleagues from the English department of Vienna university, I owe great thanks to the following people: *Dieter Kastovsky* for suggesting Early Middle English vowel quantity as a topic to me and for supervising my thesis; *Harald Mittermann* for showing me what it really means to ask scientific questions, for honestly pointing out to me whenever I was on a really false track, for suggesting literature to me of which I never would have dreamed that it could be relevant for my topic and, generally, for applying his sharp mind to the task of straightening out my sometimes confused way of thinking; *Donka Minkova* mostly for her outstanding work in the field of Middle English vowel quantity, but also for her careful reading of earlier versions of this study and for her useful comments and corrections; *Wolfgang Dressler* for introducing me to natural linguistics; *Ádám Nádasdy* for his meticulous reading of my thesis, as well as for representing in my eyes a reincarnation of Karl Luick himself; finally *Roger Lass* for his great encouragement, for his careful and sympathetic reading of my thesis, for pointing out its rough edges and suggesting ways of smoothing them, as well as for adjusting my perspective of what it was that I was really doing, and for flooding me with interesting questions to pursue.

What I owe to Laura, Jakob and Julian, Marille, Ernie and all other family members (particularly *zio* Pierre Giorgio with his impressive moustache) as well as to all my friends is expressed only inadequately by the word form *thanks*.

1 *Approaching the changes*

1.1 The standard descriptions

It is widely acknowledged among historical linguists that between the ninth and the thirteenth centuries English stressed vowels underwent widespread quantity changes. The established way of describing these alterations is in terms of four distinct sound changes. The first of them, which has become known as **Homorganic Lengthening** (from now on HOL), seems to have made short vowels long, if they were followed by certain consonant groups (namely: *mb, nd, ng, ld, rd, rs, rn, rð*) – unless those groups were themselves followed by a consonant. It turned *bindan* into *bīndan*, *cild* into *cīld*, or *climban* into *clīmban*, to give a few examples. The second change is supposed to have made long vowels short, if they were followed by a group of two consonants. (Homorganic groups did not trigger the change, however; nor did groups that occurred at the beginning of words, such as: *pl, pr, cl* or *tr*.) This change, which is called **Shortening before Consonant Clusters** (SHOCC), is taken to have been behind such changes as that of *kēpte* into *kepte*, *dūst* into *dust* or *fīfta* into *fifta*. By the third change, then, long vowels are supposed to have been shortened if they occurred in the antepenultimate syllables of wordforms: *superne* and *erende* are thus said to have replaced *sūperne* and *ērende*, for example. This change is commonly called **Trisyllabic Shortening** (TRISH). The fourth process, finally, is believed to have lengthened short vowels, if no consonant followed them within the same syllable. It is said to have turned *maken* into *māken*, *weven* into *wēven* or *hopen* into *hōpen* and is known as **Open Syllable Lengthening** (OSL).

Ever since this type of account was first brought forth linguists have felt that it was not really adequate. In particular, it has been felt that the changes had more in common with each other than their description in terms of four independent rules makes explicit. After all, it was always the quantity of vowels that was altered and all changes seem to have occurred during the period that can be regarded as the transition between Old and Middle English. This, it was assumed, had to be more than just coincidence.

Indicatively, it was the scholar who was mainly responsible for the description that has become the acknowledged standard who first attempted to overthrow it. He proposed the view that all the four changes were just reflections of a single underlying tendency, namely the adjustment of a vowel's quantity to its prosodic environment.[1]

Luick proposed two factors. The first was that English stressed syllables adjusted their size to the number of unstressed syllables with which they had to share the 'space' of one word: thus, if a syllable had a word of its own to inhabit, it would grow to fill it out completely; if it had a 'roommate', so to speak, it would have to watch its waistline more carefully, but could still afford to grow to a certain size; if it had to share a word with two or more syllables, however, it was not allowed to grow but, on the contrary, would even have to lose weight. The second factor was that the length of vowels depended – in a similar way – on the number of consonants that followed them within the same syllable: a vowel would tend to lengthening, unless there were one or more consonants squeezed between it and the beginning of the next syllable. Of course, Karl Luick did not express himself quite as metaphorically when he proposed his theory,[2] but in essence it was the same. Clearly, Luick's proposal appears to be a very clever and elegant answer to our problem: each of the quantity changes can be derived from one of the two underlying principles: TRISH could be regarded as following from the first, while SHOCC, and OSL could be interpreted as effects of the second. Although HOL does not quite seem to fit (the neighbourhood of two consonants would suggest shortening), it can be argued – as did Luick – that the apparently biconsonantal clusters that caused it did in fact not weigh more than a single consonant.

1.2   Why unification has failed so far

In spite of its ingenuity, however, Luick's attempt at unifying the description of English changes of vowel quantity did not make it into the handbooks.[3] The main reason for this was, I believe, that Luick's ideas were incompatible with the linguistic theory he himself followed, namely that of the Neogrammarians. There, phonological change had to be handled by so-called sound laws that applied to sharply delimited classes of speech sounds and altered them under strictly defined phonological conditions. Hold this theory, then, against the tendency that Luick proposed for unifying the description of English vowel quantity changes: first, the class of sounds that were affected was not homogeneous (it included both long and short vowels, second, it involved two types of change (lengthening and shortening), and third, there was no class under which the highly heterogeneous environments that triggered the quantity changes could possibly be subsumed. In other words, it simply could not be expressed in terms of such a single law. Within the Neogrammarian paradigm, therefore, the four changes that I described at the beginning were simply as far as one could get.

However, while this explains why Luick did not manage to translate his ideas into a theory in his days, it begs the question why his ideas were not taken up when Neogrammarianism became outdated. There are two reasons for that, it seems to me.

First, shortly after Luick's hypothesis had been proposed most of the concepts on which it rested came to be questioned and re-interpreted radically during and after the structuralist revolution of linguistic theory. Soon none of them had the meaning it had had in Luick's days anymore. In fact, some have been re-approached and redefined in so many different ways that today one cannot use them without making clear within the framework of which version of which theory one wants them to be understood.

The concept that has probably suffered most in this way is the **syllable**.[4] Defining it has always been problematical, and most of the early definitions were so intuitive and ad hoc that for some time it was even thought best to eliminate the concept from phonological theory altogether.[5] Although recently the syllable has been re-admitted to phonological descriptions, the ways in which the concept is approached differ markedly from the views held in Luick's days.

The fates of other, apparently basic concepts have been similarly turbulent, although they were never really wiped off the terminological map. Thus, the concepts **speech sound**,[6] **(vowel) quantity**[7] or **sound change**[8] have been redefined so often that Luick, or anybody who takes the terms to have their common-sense everyday meanings, would fail to understand what contemporary linguists are referring to when they use them.

I shall of course have to cope with this problem myself when I employ – rather than only mention – the terms. Meanwhile, just one point will be made: if one subtracts those concepts from Luick's brilliant proposition, all that remains is the uncomfortable feeling that Luick might have hit upon some truth and that we are unable today to decipher the symbols in which he encoded it. At the same time, deciphering Luick's code, or trying to carry his approach over into a contemporary theoretical framework, would amount to at least as much work as tackling the problem from a new angle, altogether. Therefore, a new attempt to answer the question whether and how the four great changes of vowel quantity that occurred in the transitional period between Old and Middle English were related to each other, may as well start from scratch.

The second reason why I think that Luick's proposal has never been successfully modernized might appear almost paradoxical after what has just been said. It lies in the fact that in spite of all theoretical innovation there are ways in which Neogrammarian ideas do govern contemporary linguistic thinking, after all. Since most post-structuralist linguistic theories were devised, in the first place, for synchronic purposes and since few survived for a long enough period without being either seriously modified or dismissed, those theories that have made it into historical linguistics have been few and those that have established themselves in this area of research even fewer. Consequently, many historical linguists have come to develop a suspicious attitude towards theoretical linguistics altogether and have focussed their energies on empirical work employing conceptual tools that are theory unspecific and compatible with linguistic common sense. Thus, diachronic correspondences between phonological entities are innocently described in terms of sound changes and recorded in terms of *A became B* rules. Intuitive and plausible as this approach might seem, however, it is often neglected that it is, in fact, theory laden and reflects straightforwardly the Neogrammarian 'sound law' approach, even though it has been stripped of its explicit theoretical status. Not figuring as a theoretical term, then, the concept tends to govern the way in which historical phonologists view their data very implicitly.

Concerning the changes of Early Middle English vowel quantity that I am investigating this means that the four sound changes that were devised in the days of Karl Luick are often regarded as the most intuitive way of organizing the data for further investigations. In fact, they are almost viewed as the pattern that the data seem to form by themselves. They are rarely interpreted as parts of a Neogrammarian theory and are therefore hardly ever questioned in principle. Taking the four sound changes for granted, however, means buying all the disadvantages of the Neogrammarian approach in a bag with the data. It follows, therefore, that a unified description of the changes of Middle English vowel quantity must necessarily turn out to be impossible for the same reasons as in Luick's days. The only difference is that the impossibility will seem to lie in the 'data' themselves rather than in the theory.

To avoid this trap, I have therefore already tried to exercise great caution at the stage of problem definition. Instead of defining my task as trying to find the relation among four quantity changes that affected stressed vowels in Early Middle English, I have tried to find a more neutral format in which to view my data.

In the following section, then, I will analyse representative handbook accounts of OSL and try to reveal what theory-specific assumptions about sound changes are implicit in them.

1.3   Looking beyond the established accounts: OSL deconstructed

Established handbooks normally describe OSL as following: 'In the first half of the 13th cent. – in the North already in the 12th cent. – *a, e, o* (vowels without high tongue position) in open accented syllables of disyllabic words were lengthend to /aː/, /ɛː/, /ɔː/' (Jordan and Crook 1974: 47); or 'ME short vowels, of whatever origin, were lengthened in open syllables of disyllabic forms during the thirteenth century' (Wright 1928); or 'In disyllables, if the accented syllable was open, the short vowels a, e, o lengthened into ā, ē, ō' (Mossé 1952: 17).

The entities and processes which these descriptions hypostatize suggest that there existed in the thirteenth century some entities A, E and O, and that they changed their shape and were made longer. Although the process through which the change was effected is not given any definition, formulations such as 'lengthened' or 'were lengthened' suggest something uniform and simple instead of a complex interplay of different types of events. If one considers the types of events that might be concealed in the idea of sounds changing through processes, however, one will perceive a more complex picture.

The configuration of phenomena which the concept might refer to could be viewed in the following way, for example. Suppose that at some point in time before the thirteenth century, there existed a community of people who spoke (Middle) English with each other. Sometimes they would use words such as *maken* 'make', *hopen* 'hope' or *bede* 'bead'. Using the words implied, of course, that they should be pronounced so that listeners could judge, from the sounds they heard, which words (or rather: meanings) were intended. It is, of course, difficult to say exactly what conditions had to be met in order for a pronunciation of *maken* 'make', *hopen* 'hope' or *bede* 'bead' to be successful. But one can safely make a couple of general assumptions: speakers of Middle English were quite ordinary human beings. They would, when communicating, perform sequences of articulatory gestures, and, by the performance of these gestures, they would produce strings of sounds that could then be clearly identified as the intended linguistic signs. When they wanted to say *bede*, for instance, they would direct their articulatory organs to perform a gesture (among others) that caused the sound corresponding to the ⟨e⟩ to come out as something like an [e], or rather, as something that could be interpreted as an /e/. The performance of this gesture fulfilled the function of guaranteeing that listeners would really understand that *bede* 'bead', rather than *bidde* 'bid', *bede* 'announce' or something else was meant. Naturally, speakers could choose how exactly they would produce this /e/-like sound, but they could not afford to deviate too far from a certain prototype (Lüdtke (1980a: 12) calls that prototype 'ideale[s] artikulatorische[s] *target*'). If they did, they would be misunderstood. If, for example, they failed to raise their tongues to a certain height while articulating the vowel in the middle of *bede*, they would produce a string of sounds that others might interpret as *badde* 'bad'. If, alternatively, they pushed them upwards a bit too much, their utterance might have been received as *bidde* 'beg, command'. And if they blundered completely by pulling their tongues backwards while simultaneously raising them (and unwittingly rounding their lips, maybe), some listeners might have understood *budde* 'bud'. Also, they might have been tempted to make the intended /e/-like sound last just a little too long. Then, some listeners might have thought that they wanted to say *bēde* 'bid, announce (1st sg. ind. pres.)', instead of *bede*. Thus, to avoid such misunderstandings, speakers of Middle English (just like all speakers of natural languages) had to make sure that the sounds they produced had enough distinctive quality to guarantee that they would not be interpreted as some different sound. Thus, the /e/-like vowel sound produced in the articulation of *bede* had to have a sufficient amount of /e/-ness, or in other words: it had to have enough of those features that distinguish it from /i/, /a/, /u/, /eː/ and so on. It had to be pronounced with the tongue in a distinctly **front** position of distinctly **middle** height and had to be maintained for a distinctly **short** span of time. In terms of contemporary phonological notation, the /e/ of *bede* had to be:

(1) $\begin{bmatrix} -\text{back} \\ +\text{front} \\ -\text{high} \\ -\text{low} \\ -\text{long} \end{bmatrix}$

Then, at some point after the thirteenth century, the situation seems to have altered: there was still a community of speakers of (Middle) English, albeit composed of different members; they still would sometimes intend to mean 'make', 'hope' or 'bead', and they would then use words similar to those which their predecessors had used about a hundred years earlier; but in the articulation of those words they would perform different actions to make sure that they were understood properly: particularly, when it came to the articulation of the vowels in *maken, hopen* or *bede*, they would try to maintain the gestures producing them for a distinctly *long* period, rather than for a distinctly *short* one. In other words, they would aim at an articulatory target that was different from the one their ancestors had aimed at. To put it formally, the vowels in words such as *maken, hopen* or *bede* would have the feature [+long] rather than [−long].

In this view, then, the concept of sound change – or the concepts behind such expressions as '(were) lengthened' – refers to the following phenomenon: at one time one group of people pronounce certain words of their language in one particular way, while other people at a different time use similar words to convey similar meanings but pronounce them in a different way. A change can be said to have occurred whenever in a language a certain role is played by one articulatory target at one time, and by a different target at another time.[9] Finally, this view can be broken up to yield the following more specific interpretations of 'sound change'. In the first, it stands for the *mere fact* that the latter target can be regarded as the functional equivalent and thus the temporal successor of the former. In the second interpretation, which is much stronger, 'sound change' stands for *all the factors that caused* the functional correspondence between the two elements.[10]

In the case of OSL, which could formally be represented as

(2) $[-\text{long}] \rightarrow [+\text{long}] / \{\text{in vowels of stressed open penults}\}$,

the 'change' (represented by the arrow) may either stand for the *observation* that the feature [+long] came to play the role of the feature [−long] under the mentioned conditions or for the factors that might have been behind this. In both readings, OSL is a cover term for a large set of interrelated events. It represents a high-level abstraction and is definitely not a good starting point for an investigation that tries to be neutral with regard to theory.

1.4   The data problem

One must go back to square one, in other words, and start with the data that caused Luick and his colleagues to establish OSL and the other changes in the first place. But which data? The obvious choice would be to compare the situations before and after the events which made up the four 'quantity changes'. The starting points of an investigation would thus be the phonological systems of English as spoken before and after the period in which HOL, TRISH, OSL and SHOCC are supposed to have occurred. Specifically speaking, one would compare the phonological shapes – and particularly the quantities of stressed vowels – of corresponding lexemes and wordforms. This way, one would study the correspondences normally expressed by the four quantity changes rather than the 'changes' themselves. In a second step, then, one would try and reconstruct the nature and the effects of the processes which could have brought the correspondences about. Whether a picture of four sound changes would emerge at all from that could obviously not be known beforehand.

The question is, however, exactly which language systems one should compare. As will be shown, this problem is again closely related to the interpretation given to the notion 'sound change'. Taken as it is, my interpretation of sound change is so global as to potentially cover more than one type of situation. In particular, it is vague with regard to both the size and the nature of the speech communities that are related, and with regard to the spatio-temporal distance between the corresponding situations. For a diachronic comparison, it therefore allows one to choose from several geographical dialects and different historical stages of English.[11]

Take OSL again: in system (1) (I shall call it **pre-OSL English**) the penultimate vowels in words such as the following were pronounced so that they would come out as distinctly short. They had the feature [–long].

(3)   a.   *aken* 'ache', *aker* 'acre', *akern* 'acorn', *ale* 'ale', *ape* 'ape', *bacon* 'bacon', *baken* 'bake', *bale* 'bale', ...
...*waken* 'wake', *wale* 'wale', *wanien* 'wane', **war* 'ware', *waven* 'wave', *whal* 'whale';

b. (*bi*)*neopen* 'beneath', *bede* 'bead', *bere 'bear', *beren* 'bear', *besme* 'besom', *bever* 'beaver', ...

... *wele* 'weal', *wenen* 'wean', *wer 'weir', *werien 'wear', *wesle* 'weasel', *weven* 'weave', *wreken* 'wreak', *þefe* 'thieve'

c. *bodien* 'bode', *bole* 'bole', *borin 'bore', *broke* 'broke', *caf* 'cove', *cheoke* 'choke', *cloke* 'cloak', ...

... *stole* 'stole', *stove* 'stove', *thode* 'thode', *thole* 'thole', *trone* 'throne', *þrote* 'throat'

d. *wicu* 'week', *yfel* 'evil'

e. *duru* 'door'

Then, in system (2) (**post-OSL English**), the counterparts of those words had the feature [+long]. In other words, they were intended to come out as distinctly long. Now, the question is, which systems pre-OSL English and post-OSL English are supposed to represent.

At first sight it would seems that one should take as 'pre-OSL English' the last stage of English in which speakers intended the stressed vowels of words such as those in (3) to be [–long]. Analogically, 'post-OSL English' would be defined as the first stage of English in which they were intended to be [+long]. After all, it seems obvious that the events which amounted to the lengthening must have taken place in the transitional period between the two systems. The shorter this period is, the greater are our chances of pinning those events down. In addition, this sort of approach has been common in historical linguistics for about a century, and still underlies most contemporary studies.

However, such an approach runs into the following difficulties. First, just like any conceivable natural language, English has at no point in time been anything like a uniform system. It has always been characterized by regional, social, personal, situational and probably other sorts of variation. The transition between pre-OSL English and post-OSL English will therefore have been smooth at best, with no clear boundaries to be found. It can be safely assumed that for a long period speakers who pronounced the words in (3) with their stressed vowels as [+long] would coexist with others, who had a [–long] vowel in those words. Furthermore, there will probably have been many speakers who used both pronunciations alternatively, their choice depending on such factors as speech, register, etc.[12]

Second, it cannot be told with any reasonable certainty how pre- or post-OSL phonologies were distributed at any point of time earlier than maybe the twentieth century. This is due both to the near impossibility of re-constructing historical pronunciations and, in particular, to the difficulties encountered when it comes to vowel quantity. There, spelling evidence is so inconclusive that hardly more than an approximate reconstruction is possible even on the phonemic level. As far as OSL is concerned, the only thing that can be said at all from the evidence that we have (spelling, metrical poetry, comparative reconstruction) is that at some stage before the thirteenth century the words in (3) were normally intended to be pronounced as [–long], and that at some later stage the [+long] pronunciation had become common. Although one knows that the post-OSL pronunciation first spread among speakers in the north of England, it is not known when it first turned up, nor when it started to be used more generally than the pre-OSL pronunciation.

Evidently, one cannot expect to find either an immediate pre-OSL stage of English, or a post-OSL one. What data, then, is one to choose? An interesting and daring suggestion was made by Minkova (1982). In a study of the question why some parts of the English vocabulary reflected OSL, while others did not, she compared Late Old English to Modern English. In other words, she held two language systems against each other that are separated by more than eight (!) centuries.

This approach seems counterintuitive at first and Minkova herself was aware that it was not unproblematic. What she regarded as the greatest drawback of studying long-term instead of short-term correspondences was that both Middle English dialectal detail and variation in general were ignored (cf. 1982: 40f.), and that therefore 'only a bird's eye view of ... successive stages of the language, treated as homogeneous within their respective time spans' (Minkova 1982: 41). could be gained.

However, reconstructions of Middle English dialectal detail are notoriously unreliable with regard to vowel quantity anyway. Ignoring them is therefore hardly worse than basing one's investigations on them. Furthermore, intermediate stages between Late Old English and Modern English are not attested very well either. It would at least be extremely difficult and maybe impossible to say how pre- and post-OSL pronunciations were distributed over the varieties of English at any point of time between the thirteenth and the twentieth centuries. It was this difficulty, it seems, that motivated Minkova to turn to Modern English for evidence, because she observes that 'so far, details about the development of the forms within Middle English have not been productive in providing an answer to the puzzle [of OSL]' (Minkova 1982: 41). Therefore, her decision to ignore what cannot be reliably reconstructed was the most reasonable step that could possibly have been taken.

There is, however, criticism of another type that could be launched against Modern English data as evidence for such historical processes as we are investigating. It is connected to the problem of dialect mixture. Since it seriously threatens the position which was taken by Minkova it deserves a more detailed discussion.

1.5   Long-term reflexes and dialect mixture

It is of course well known that, diachronically speaking, Modern Standard English must be regarded as a mixture of many historical dialects and is directly related to none of them. Therefore, if Modern Standard English is held against some hypothetical variety spoken before the thirteenth century any particular difference between the two may principally be due to *one* of *two* things: *either* it was caused by processes directly affecting the transmission of the language system from generation to generation; *or* the respective element of Modern Standard English was not passed down at all from the variety in question but from some other Middle English dialect. Clearly, this possibility makes it problematic to use Modern English data as evidence of processes that might have affected only some of the many historical varieties of English.

Take, for example, the fact that the diphthong in Modern English *make* reflects a long $\bar{a}$, while the apparent counterpart of that vowel in most of the known varieties of Late Old English can be assumed to have been short. Now, this fact allows the conclusion that at some stage there were processes at work affecting the replication of the vowel by ever-changing generations of speakers so that eventually the counterparts of the *a* came to be long $\bar{a}$s. On the other hand, the fact that the Modern English counterpart of Late Old English *latin* has a short vowel, does *not* allow the conclusion that the *a* was not affected by the same processes as the *a* in *maken*. It might theoretically also be possible that the Modern English short vowel in *latin* simply goes back to a different variety of Old English: a variety in which the vowel of *make* was not lengthened either. Therefore, the short vowel in Modern English *latin* does not prove that its Old English counterpart was never lengthened. Rather, the only thing that may be assumed is *either* that the vowel in *latin* was not lengthened in the same way as in *maken*, *or* that dialect mixture has taken place. The point is that the latter possibility can never be ruled out completely.[13]

In other words, the only thing that can be recovered from Modern English data seems to be the mere fact that some sound-changing process must have taken place. Nothing may be derived on the scope and effect of such a process. It could therefore be argued that Modern English data should not be taken as evidence in investigations such as this after all.

However, it can be shown that 'dialect mixture' is not necessarily as disturbing a factor as it might seem. Take another look at OSL. As stated above, the term stands for the fact (and/or the processes resulting in that fact) that the [–long] vowels in such Early Middle English words as those in the left column of table (4) correspond to [+long] vowels in the later counterparts of the words.[14] This is illustrated in the right column.[15]

(4)   **EME**   **ModE**[16]

EME	ModE
labor	labour
basin	basin
barin	bare
whal	whale
waven	wave
waden	wade
tale	tale
starin	stare
stapel	staple
stede	steed
bleren	blear
repen	reap
lesen	lease
efen	even
drepen	drepe
derien	dere
dene	dean
-stoc	stoke (X-)
sole	sole
mote	mote (of dust)
mote	moat
hopien	hope
cloke	cloak
smoke	smoke
broke	broke
ofer	over[17]

As the name suggests, it has always been acknowledged that the process central to OSL must have been some type of 'lengthening'.[18] The objects of this 'lengthening' have traditionally been assumed to be vowels, i.e. speech 'segments'.[19]

Apart from involving lengthening, OSL is assumed to have the following characteristics:

(a) The first syllables in words that were affected by the change are regarded as 'open' or 'unchecked'. (Roughly, this means that they end immediately after the vowel.) The following consonants are regarded as the beginnings, or 'onsets' of the final syllables, because they are also found at the beginning of words. However, I will show below (see p. 50ff.) that much can be gained if this view is given up.

(b) The Middle English and the Modern English vowels that correspond to each other belong to the syllables on which the main stress falls, when the words are pronounced.

(c) All the Middle English words are composed of exactly two syllables, so that the syllable bearing the main stress is always penultimate.

All these qualities are expressed in the formula:

(5)

$$[-\text{long}] \rightarrow [+\text{long}] \; / \; \#x\begin{bmatrix} --- \\ +\text{voc} \\ +\text{stress} \end{bmatrix}§y\#$$

where # stands for a word boundary, § stands for a syllable boundary, *voc* marks vowels, and *x,y* stand for any string of sound segments that does not contain a syllable boundary.

In the days of Karl Luick, however, it was implied that every word that met those conditions would *always and inevitably* have its stressed vowel lengthened, without any exceptions being possible. In other words, it was assumed that OSL was a 'sound law' entailing a prediction like the following:

(6)　If a word from pre-OSL English consists of two syllables, of which the first one is stressed, open and has a short vowel as its nucleus, then its post-OSL counterpart, if there exists one, will have a long vowel in the syllable with main stress.[20]

At the same time, it has always been known that there are many apparent 'exceptions' that seem to contradict this prediction. Example (7) contains some of them.

(7) | EME | ModE |
|---|---|
| adlen | addle |
| aler | alder[21] |
| alum | alum |
| anet | anet |
| anis | anise |
| aspen | aspen |
| azür | azure |
| baron | baron |
| barrat | barrat |
| baril | barrel |
| | |
| bet(e)r(e) | better |
| besant | bezant |
| brevet | brevet |
| celer | cellar |
| devor | endeavour |
| desert | desert |
| ether | edder |
| edisch | eddish |
| feþer | feather |
| felon | felon |
| | |
| bodig | body |
| bonnet | bonnet |
| boþem | bottom |
| broþel | brothel |
| closet | closet |
| koker | cocker |
| cokel | cockle |
| cofin | coffin |
| colar | collar |
| colop | collop |

As pointed out above, these Modern English exceptions are open to more than one interpretation: *either* OSL did not 'lengthen' all vowels equally, *or* OSL did lengthen all vowels in some dialects, while in others the process did not occur, and the Modern English 'exceptions' simply going back to one of the latter varieties.[22]

Within the theoretical framework within which OSL was first proposed, however, the question how its Modern English exceptions should be interpreted was given a clear answer. It was inherent in the Neogrammarian theory of language change and its view of the processes which caused such changes. 'Sound laws' were assumed to apply to basically uniform dialects. They were thought to change the gestures which the speakers of such a dialect performed when aiming at a given target gradually and imperceptibly. Eventually, then, the position and other features of that target were altered as well. Having no exceptions apart from those that were due to the fact that sound laws applied only at certain places and at certain periods, 'sound laws' were taken to resemble such laws as those of physics. This view implied that all apparent exceptions to a sound change were regarded as *necessarily* due to such disturbing factors as dialect mixture. The possibility was inconceivable on theoretical grounds that Modern English 'counter-examples' to OSL could be due to the fact that the sound change did not affect all items equally.

For my purposes, of course, this type of approach will not do, quite apart from the fact that it has long been superseded by different and probably more adequate models of language change (see, for instance, Weinreich, Herzog and Labov 1968). In particular, Modern English exceptions to OSL would only be interesting if they told one anything about OSL itself rather than about the historical interaction of different varieties of English. After all, in light of the difficulties of reconstructing historical quantity, Modern English seems to provide the only data against which any hypothesis about OSL and the other quantity changes can be tested at all.[23] Therefore, if Modern English reflexes of OSL contain no information as to how they have been brought about, they are useless for the purposes of this study. If they admit of no conclusion beyond the general observation that at some time a process that lengthened vowels must have taken place, one might as well admit that any attempt to reconstruct the processes behind OSL will have to remain speculative.

I will try to show in the following, however, that the way in which the lexicon of Modern Standard English reflects OSL might potentially be more revealing than one would think. To do so, I will first sketch a very simple and – so I hope – uncontroversial model of the steps that it might have taken for a sound change such as OSL to occur. It involves the assumption that OSL was the diachronic implementation of an originally synchronic process in Early Middle English phonologies. In terms of natural phonology (as represented, for example, by Stampe or Dressler) the process behind OSL could be thought of as a foregrounding process, whose ultimate purpose might have had something to do with the facilitation of perception. However, this will not be my concern here. In any case, the application of this process will have been constrained by various factors: one group of them socio-stylistic, the other language-internal or structural. As to the former, the lengthening process behind OSL may be assumed to have applied more frequently in slow, hyper-correct speech and in more formal registers than in fast, casual speech and informal registers – although the exact nature of the restrictions is irrelevant for my purposes. On the other hand, however, the application of the lengthening will also have depended on the phonological environment of the affected vowels.

Thus, the phonological process which eventually resulted in OSL must be kept apart from the diachronic correspondences that actually constitute the change. It was just a necessary condition for the actual change to occur. For the change itself, the following set-up is conceivable: pre-OSL English included a lengthening process of the type outlined above. It would have substituted *maːken* for intended, or underlying, *maken*, *beːver* for underlying *bever*, and so on. Then post-OSL phonologies were derived from the *outputs* of pre-OSL phonologies – and thus from lengthened outputs such *maːken* or *beːver*. So, they may have incorporated the lengthened items as underlying representations instead of generating them through lengthening. This type of **target re-interpretation**, then, can be viewed as the diachronic implementation of the lengthening process at the heart of OSL.[24] It represented the step that brought the actual change about.

However, while the diachronic change was not identical with the process it implemented, it can be assumed to reflect it and, in particular, the factors by which that process was constrained synchronically.[25] More specifically, the constraints will be mirrored in the way in which re-interpreted targets are distributed over the lexicon. This hypothesis is based on the assumption that the chance of an item's phonological representation to be re-interpreted correlates with the relative proportion of outputs affected by the synchronic process against outputs not affected by it.[26] In the case of OSL, this might have looked as follows.

First, constraints on the application of the lengthening process behind it will have resulted in the coexistence of outputs ranging – in phonetic terms – from [maken] over [maˑken] and [maːken] to [maːrken], for example. Obviously, not all of them will have suggested a phonological re-interpretation as [+long].

At the same time, the variation will not have been unsystematic: in slow speech the vowels will have tended to be longer than in fast speech, irre-spective of the formality of the speech situation, while they will have tended to be longer in formal than in informal registers, irrespective of other factors. Similarly, vowel lengthening will have occurred more often in some phonological environments than in others.

Crucially, such influences do not interfere with each other, unless they are in some way correlated. This is as true as it is tautological. However, the point is essential for the following argument, and therefore I have taken the liberty to state the obvious. In the case of the suggested influences on OSL, then, one may assume that they were indeed not correlated. Thus, the influence which the phonological environment of a vowel exerted on its chance of being lengthened was not altered or reversed by the fact that lengthening also depended on other factors, such as style or tempo. The following thought experiment will elucidate the point and show what it entails.

Imagine that lengthening was constrained by the following three factors:

(a)   **Speech tempo**: assume that in slow speech lengthening was twice as likely as in regular speech and that in fast speech it was half as likely as in regular speech.[27]

(b)   **Register**: assume that in formal speech lengthening was twice as likely as in neutral speech and that in casual speech it was half as likely as in neutral speech.

(c)   **Type of consonant following the vowel**: assume that the chance of vowel lengthening was 4/5 before sonorants, 2/5 before non-sonorant fricatives and 1/5 before stops

Now, imagine that the following lexical items were potential targets of lengthening:

(8)   {xal, xel, xil, xul} {xaf, xef, xif, xuf} {xat, xet, xit, xut}

First, let us look at the impact of the following consonants: in accordance with the probabilities stated above, we could expect 160 out of 200   x l tokens to be lengthened, 80 out of 200 x f tokens and 40 out of 200 x t tokens, as shown in the following chart:

(9)

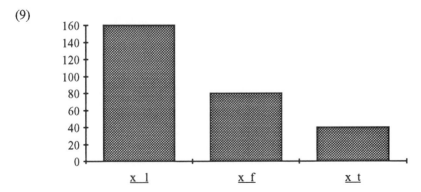

Diachronically, then, we could expect, very roughly, to find most lengthened vowels within the x̲ l̲ group, fewer within the x̲ f̲ group, and still fewer within the x̲ t̲ group. We could, in other words, expect the diachronic reflexes of the processes to reflect the way in which the environment of the vowels constrained the application of the synchronic lengthening process.

It may be argued, however, that such a simple and straightforward case is extremely unlikely, since, of course, there are many different factors constraining such processes as vowel lengthening. On might fear, therefore, that their influences will obscure each other's effects to the degree of unrecoverability, so that the historical impacts of a change will not tell us anything anymore about the factors that constrained the process behind it. Well, the point I am making here is that, as long as the factors are uncorrelated, such fears are ungrounded and that uncorrelated constraints might mellow each other's impacts but will leave them essentially traceable.

Let me go back to my example and show what happens if a factor other than phonological environment enters the scene: for instance, speech tempo. First, there is no reason to believe that speech tempo and the phonological shape of an item are correlated factors. Items with fricatives are no more likely to be spoken rapidly than items with stops, for example. This means that speech tempo can be expected to constrain vowel lengthening equally among each of the three phonological types established above. Furthermore, let us assume – for the sake of this experiment – that the chance of an item to occur in fast, normal or slow speech is 1/3 in all cases. This means that vowels in items of the x̲ l̲ type, whose phonological structure gives them a 4/5 chance of being lengthened, will now be lengthened with a probability that equals the average of a doubled 4/5 (i.e. a 8/9) chance, a 4/5 chance and half a 4/5 (i.e. a 2/3) chance. In order to calculate this lengthening probablity, one has to apply the general formula

(10)
$$\bar{x} = \frac{\sum\limits_{i=1}^{i=n} x_i}{n}$$

In our special case, this yields a lengthening probabilty of

(11)
$$\bar{x} = \frac{\frac{8}{9} + \frac{4}{5} + \frac{2}{3}}{3} = \frac{40 + 36 + 30}{45 \times 3} = \frac{104}{135} = 0.77$$

For vowels in items of the x̲ f̲ type the probability of lengthening would then equal the average of a doubled 2/5 chance, i.e. a 4/7 chance, a 2/5 chance and half a 2/5 chance, i.e. a 1/4 chance, i.e.:

(12)
$$\bar{x} = \frac{\frac{4}{7} + \frac{2}{5} + \frac{1}{4}}{3} = 0.41$$

and for vowels in items of the x t type the probability of lengthening would then equal the average of a doubled 1/5 chance, i.e. a 1/3 chance, a 1/5 chance and half a 1/5 chance, i.e. a 1/9 chance, i.e.:

(13)
$$\bar{x} = \frac{\frac{1}{3} + \frac{1}{5} + \frac{1}{9}}{3} = 0.21$$

Among 200 occurrences of x l items we could thus expect to find 154 lengthened vowels, among the same number of x f items 82 lengthened vowels and among 200 x t items 42. Again, this can be illustrated in a chart that shows the distribution of lengthened vowels with regard to the phonological environments in which they occur:

(14)

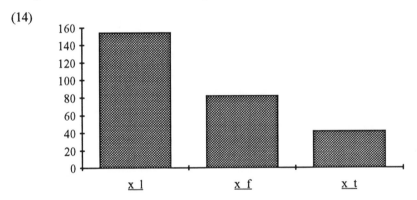

As the following illustration, which puts charts (9) and (14) together, makes obvious,

(15)

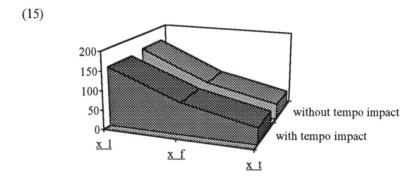

the two constraints on the lengthening process neither reverse nor distort each other's effect. If this is because they are not correlated with each other it can be shown that the effects of any one parameter will not be distorted by parameters that are correlated with each other either as long as none of them correlates with the parameter under consideration. To illustrate this I will bring in the third factor introduced above, namely speech register, and assume – for the sake of the argument – that formality and speech tempo are correlated. Let us say that formal speech incorporates fast, normal and slow speech not in a ratio of 1:1:1, but in a ratio of 1:2:4. For neutral speech let us assume a ratio of 2:3:2 and for casual speech a ratio of 4:2:1.

Four parts of formal speech will then also be slow. Therefore, they will not only double but actually quadruple an item's chance of being lengthened. Two parts of formal speech, i.e. the ones in normal tempo, will double it, and one part, namely the formal/fast part, will not alter it at all since the effects of formality and tempo cancel each other. Taking this correlation into account, we can then say that the factor by which formal speech increases the probability of lengthening will be the average of

(16) $$\bar{x} = \frac{4+4+4+4+2+2+1}{7} = 3$$

The factor by which neutral speech modifies the probability of vowel lengthening would analogically be the average of two parts neutral/slow speech (doubling the probability of lengthening), three parts neutral/normal speech (not influencing it) and two parts of neutral/fast speech (halving the probability of lengthening), i.e.

(17) $$\bar{x} = \frac{2+2+1+1+1+\frac{1}{2}+\frac{1}{2}}{7} = \frac{8}{7}$$

Finally, the factor by which casual speech modifies the probability of vowel lengthening would be the average of one part casual/slow speech (not influencing the probability of lengthening), two parts casual/normal speech (making the chance of lengthening half as likely as otherwise) and four parts of casual/fast speech (which makes lengthening four times as unlikely as otherwise), i.e.

(18)
$$\bar{x} = \frac{1 + \frac{1}{2} + \frac{1}{2} + \frac{1}{4} + \frac{1}{4} + \frac{1}{4} + \frac{1}{4}}{7} = \frac{3}{7}$$

Given that phonological environment is not correlated to either speech style or tempo, we can calculate the impact of combined speech style and tempo on the probability of lengthening in specific environments in the same way as we calculated the impact of speech tempo alone. We just have to replace the factors 2, 1 and 1/2 by 3, 8/7 and 3/7 respectively.

Thus, the average probability of an x l item to occur with a lengthened vowel will be equal to the average of a 3 times 4/5 (i.e. 12/13) chance, an 8/7 times 4/5 (i.e. 32/39) chance and a 3/7 times 4/5 (12/19) chance, i.e.

(19)
$$\bar{x} = \frac{\frac{12}{13} + \frac{32}{39} + \frac{12}{19}}{3} = 0.79$$

The chance of an x f item to get its vowel lengthened will accordingly be equal to the average of a 3 times 2/5 (i.e. 2/3) chance, an 8/7 times 2/5 (16/37) chance and a 3/7 times 2/5 (2/9) chance, i.e.

(20)
$$\bar{x} = \frac{\frac{2}{3} + \frac{16}{37} + \frac{2}{9}}{3} = 0.44$$

Finally, the chance of an x t item to have its vowel lengthened will be equal to the average of a 3 times 1/5 (i.e. 3/7) chance, an 8/7 times 1/5 (2/9) chance and a 3/7 times 1 to 4 (3:28) chance, i.e.

(21)
$$\bar{x} = \frac{\frac{3}{7} + \frac{2}{9} + \frac{3}{31}}{3} = 0.25$$

Among 200 occurrences of x l items we could thus expect to find 158 lengthened vowels, among the same number of x f items 88 lengthened vowels and among 200 x t items 50. Again, this can be illustrated in a chart showing the distribution of lengthened vowels with regard to the phonological environments in which they occur:

(22)

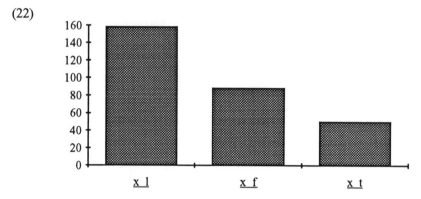

Comparing this chart with the other two shows that the impact of non-phonological factors does not make it any more difficult to reconstruct the influence of the phonological environment on lengthening from the distribution of lengthened tokens.

(23)

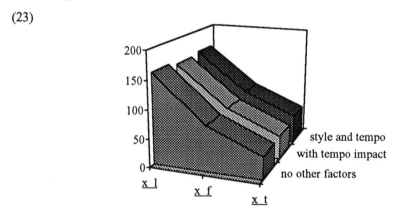

If it is assumed that the synchronic distribution of lengthened tokens correlates with the probability of an item's being lengthened diachronically through target re-interpretation, it follows that no individual parameter will obscure the diachronic effects of such constraints on lengthening that are not correlated with it either.

Once this is conceded, however, the relatively small importance of most conceivable cases of dialect mixture with regard to the diachronic implementation of a process follows automatically. After all, with regard to the distribution of lengthened vs. unlengthened occurrences of a vowel the mixture of regional dialects has no different status from the mixture of stylistic or tempo-related variants. Its effect will be equally quantitative and will not obscure the quantitative effects of other, uncorrelated factors.

Thus, if one dialect has a lengthening process constrained in the above manner, while another dialect has no lengthening at all, and if these two dialects get mixed in a ratio of, let us say, 1:1, the distribution of lengthened items in 200 occurrences of each item type will then be: 79 lengthened occurrences among x l items, 44 among x f items and 25 among x t items.

As illustrated below, the environmental constraint is still clearly recoverable, even if it might not be as drastically obvious as within the unmixed lengthening dialect.

(24)

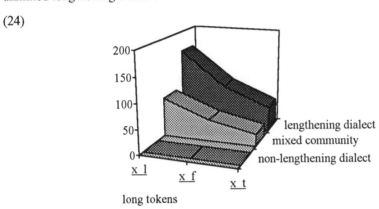

What all this amounts to, however, is that one may indeed take Modern English as evidence for the way in which the lengthening behind OSL was constrained. Any recoverable correlation between the distribution of lengthened items and such factors as the phonological environment of a vowel can fairly safely be assumed to reflect a genuine constraint on the original lengthening process, and there is little reason to believe that dialect mixture should have obscured the diachronic effects of phonological constraints on vowel lengthening.[28]

1.6   Sketching my approach

In my own investigation of Early Middle English quantity changes the following approach will therefore be taken:

First, I shall collect a sample of lexemes and wordforms from a hypothetical variety that might have been spoken before the relevant sound changes occurred (= *'pre-quantity-change English'*).[29] Then I will hold them against their counterparts in Modern English (which is taken as *post-quantity-change English* for the reasons outlined above and also because it is well attested, described in great detail and, contrary to any historical variety, still there to be examined). This comparison will show how many and which items have in fact implemented the processes under investigation.

From the distribution of 'changed' and 'unchanged' items, I will then try to reconstruct some of the constraints on the processes that were behind the changes. For practical reasons, these will primarily be structural-phonological constraints. Most non-structural constraints, such as speech style, register or the possible impact of dialect mixture, will be neglected, because lexical data from Modern Standard English are simply too difficult to classify with regard to the latter parameters. Thus, if one takes any Modern English dictionary entry one will have no practical, quick and reliable way of deciding whether its predecessor was, for instance, a typical formal speech item or a typical casual speech item, and the same argument holds true even more radically for an item's status with regard to typical speech tempo, of course.[30] As far as phonological structure – at least on the word level – is concerned, however, it is accessible in a straightforward manner, since it is unalienable from the item itself.

By this, I hope to gain what might be called profiles of the changes in question, and on the basis of these profiles I will re-address the question how the diachronic correspondences that have so far been described in terms of four independent sound changes can best be generalized. In particular, I will take up Luick's suggestion and deal with the question whether there might have been anything like a single motive behind the fact that during the Late Old English or Early Middle English periods processes altering the quantity of vowels came to be implemented diachronically.

Finally, a few remarks are due on the way in which sound correspondences between Early Middle and Modern English are to be described. While the standard descriptions employ rules that look like covering laws and consequently have difficulties with 'exceptions', I shall operate with the concept of **statistical laws** or **tendencies**. For my purposes, I will define a **tendency** as a rule of the format

(25) $p(Fx \rightarrow Gx) \leq 1$

> where p stands for 'probability', F for the conditions under which an item x will be affected by the tendency, and G for the characteristics attributed to that item x by the tendency. [A law in the traditional sense can be understood as the special case of a tendency applying with a probability of 1.]

Since Modern English is, as observed above, full of 'exceptions' to the changes under consideration, the decision to describe the changes in terms of tendencies instead of covering laws might seem like making a virtue out of mere necessity. However, the strategy has further advantages.

Thus, the traditional way of thinking of OSL in terms of an exceptionless sound law made the behaviour of high vowels problematic, because it appeared that hardly any word whose stressed vowel was /ɪ/ or /ʊ/ (in other words: a high vowel) had a POST-OSL counterpart with a long vowel, even though otherwise it might meet all the conditions which were thought to have 'triggered' the change. Since among high vowels the number of exceptions to OSL was in fact much greater than the number of items affected by the change, it was felt that they could not be simply attributed to dialect mixture. Rather, one went the opposite way and excluded high vowels from the range of OSL application altogether. Thus, it was assumed (see the descriptions of Jordan or Wright above, p. 5) that OSL affected only low vowels and should be described as

(26)
$$[-\text{long}] \rightarrow [+\text{long}]/\#X \begin{bmatrix} ----- \\ +V \\ +\text{STRESS} \\ -\text{HIGH} \end{bmatrix} \S\,\sigma\#$$

If the idea that sound changes ought to be described in terms of covering laws is discarded, on the other hand, the 'problem' of high vowels becomes just another aspect of the fact that there are exceptions to OSL altogether. This has the advantage of not forcing one to neglect those I/U words that do seem to reflect OSL altogether. After all, there are a few of them, such as

(27)   **OE**   **ModE**

> wiku   week
> yvel   evil
> duru   door

and their existence cannot be simply denied. So, if one takes the view – as I do – that OSL was never fully implemented even among words with non-high vowels, the difference between I/U words[31] on the one hand, and words with non-high vowels on the other, can be treated as a matter of degree rather than as one of essence: among both types of words there are such that do, and such that do not reflect OSL, only that the latter are much more frequent among I/U words than among words with non-high vowels.[32]

Minkova's (1982) finding that the process behind OSL led to a sound change in roughly 55 per cent of words with non-high vowels, and the fact that it did so in hardly any words with high vowels, would then be expressed in the following unified statistical version of OSL:

(28)
$$p([-\text{long}] \rightarrow [+\text{long}]/\#X \begin{bmatrix} \text{-----} \\ +\text{V} \\ +\text{STRESS} \end{bmatrix} \S \sigma\#) = x$$

where $0 < x < 0.55$

Informally, this rule would read: the probability that a short vowel in a Middle English word whose first syllable was open will come to have a long counterpart is somewhere between zero and 55 per cent.

Although such a statement has much less predictive power than the traditional version of OSL, it is more adequate and, crucially, more flexible and adjustable. Therefore, it will serve much better as a starting point for a fresh investigation than the standard description.[33]

The next sections can then be understood as an attempt to make rule (28) more descriptive. After all, it is disappointingly vague, for all its adequacy. This can be done in a straightforward manner. From what is already known about OSL, it would increase the descriptive power of (28) considerably, for instance, if it distinguished between high and non-high vowels. The implementation of OSL among non-high vowels could then be expressed in terms of a subrule such as

(29)
$$p([-\text{long}] \rightarrow [+\text{long}]/\#X \begin{bmatrix} \text{-----} \\ +\text{V} \\ +\text{STRESS} \\ -\text{HIGH} \end{bmatrix} \S \sigma\#) \approx 0.55$$

while the negligible number of lengthened reflexes of high vowels would be 'predicted' by a subrule such as

(30)

$$p([-\text{long}] \rightarrow [+\text{long}]/\#\,X \begin{bmatrix} ----- \\ +\text{V} \\ +\text{STRESS} \\ +\text{HIGH} \end{bmatrix} \S\,\sigma\#) \approx 0.1$$

Clearly, this way of splitting rule (28) in two subrules is just another way of expressing that vowel height was a significant constraint on the lengthening process behind OSL and influenced the probability of lengthening to result in diachronic change accordingly. Rephrasing what has been outlined above, the question pursued in the following sections will thus be the following: if OSL inputs are subcategorized with regard to other potentially constraining factors, will this uncover differences in the implementation of lengthening that are similarly significant as vowel height? All relevant findings will be put in terms of subrules to lengthening, and these will then be unified as far as possible, so that the broadest meaningful generalizations can be expressed.

2 Reconstructing OSL

The investigations are based on what could be called the 'Minkova corpus of potential OSL candidates' (see appendix I). Basically, it is a list of Early Middle English words whose stressed vowels were short and non-high, and which are attested in Modern English. The list was partly drawn up by Minkova herself (the words of Old English origin), and partly taken over from Bliss (1952/3) (Anglo-Norman loans). I have myself added a few random examples, which I happened to come across during my own studies. All in all, the corpus contains 428 items. Thus, although the corpus does not really exhaust the set of potential OSL candidates, it can probably be regarded as a representative sample, as it can be estimated to contain far more than 50 per cent of those OSL candidates with non-high vowels that are still attested in Modern English.

First, the items in the corpus were categorized with respect to the phonological parameters of **vowel quality**, the **consonant following the vowel** and the **syllable following the vowel**. Furthermore, the parameters **word class** and **etymological origin** were considered. I trusted that they included most of the qualities that might be relevant with regard to vowel lengthening. The phonological parameters include practically the complete environment of the vowels in question. Only word-initial consonants were not considered, and this was because even a first look at my data confirmed the well-established knowledge that syllable onsets do not systematically influence the length of following vowels. On the morpho-syntactic level a distinction between substantives, adjectives and verbs was made, and the etymological parameter divided the words into Old English, Scandinavian and Anglo-Norman items.

Then, in each of the subgroups gained through classification, the items whose Modern English counterparts have long vowels were counted and the numbers were translated into percentages. In accordance with the principles outlined in chapter 1, it was then concluded that the percentage of long items within a group reflected the degree to which Middle English vowel lengthening was constrained by the respective parameter. Thus, if a relatively large number of items within a given group had counterparts with long vowels in post-OSL English, it was concluded that the characteristic establishing the group favoured the lengthening leading to OSL, and the other way round.

The results are given in the following sections.

2.1   The impact of the second syllable

2.1.1   Stable vs. unstable final syllables

This parameter distinguishes between words that are still disyllabic in Modern English and words that have lost their final syllables due to such processes as schwa deletion. The assumption is that the syllables that were eventually lost, were probably already subject to optional deletion processes in Early Middle English.[1] Hence, such syllables are called 'unstable'.

Table 2.1

	Vowel in Modern English				
	Total	Long	%	Short	%
σ_2 unstable	205	190	94	15	6
σ_2 stable	223	41	18	182	82

Vowel lengthening was much more likely to be implemented in words with unstable final syllables than in words with stable ones.

2.1.2   The 'weight' of stable σ_2

2.1.2.1   Light vs. heavy σ_2

I shall deal with the suprasegmental aspects of OSL in much more detail in chapter 4. At this point, concepts relating to suprasegmental phonology will be given preliminary, non-technical definitions. Thus, I shall call such stable syllables that end in a short vowel light, all others heavy.

Table 2.2

	Vowel in Modern English				
	Total	Long	%	Short	%
σ_2 light	135	33	24	102	76
σ_2 heavy	88	7	8	81	92

Vowel lengthening was more likely in words with light final syllables than in words with heavy ones.

2.1.2.2 Heavy vs. very heavy σ_2

Non-light syllables whose rhyme consists of a short vowel plus a consonant are heavy, all others very heavy.

Table 2.3

	Vowel in Modern English				
	Total	Long	%	Short	%
σ_2 heavy	67	6	9	61	91
σ_2 very heavy	21	1	5	20	95

Although one might question the statistical significance of the distribution, it seems that vowel lengthening was a bit more likely in words with heavy final syllables than in words with very heavy ones.

2.1.3 Comment

The figures clearly show that the implementation of vowel lengthening depended on the structure of the second syllable. The Modern English counterparts of items whose second syllable was potentially deletable practically always have long vowels. Among items with stable second syllables, on the other hand, the lengthening process is only rarely reflected.

This observation was first made by Minkova (1982), who concluded from this that OSL 'affects the vowel in a much more restricted environment [and ...] is a much more context-sensitive change than has hitherto been admitted.' (Minkova 1982: 42) and should be reformulated in a way similar to

(1)

$$
[-\text{long}] \rightarrow [+\text{long}] \ / \ \#[X \begin{bmatrix} ----- \\ +\text{VOC} \\ +\text{STRESS} \\ -\text{HIGH} \end{bmatrix} [C]e]\#
$$

where *[ ]* stand for syllable boundaries, and where the *e* stands for the 'unstressed deletable /ə/ of Middle English' (Minkova 1982: 42).

Revolutionary as Minkova's findings were, however, there are reasons for which one might disagree with her conclusion: first, her reformulation of OSL involves the same type of hypothesizing about historical pronunciation as the Neogrammarian sound law: assuming that OSL applied only in words with deletable second syllables implies that words without such final syllables were never pronounced with long vowels. This assumption cannot be falsified any easier than Luick's assumption that at the end of the thirteenth century all vowels in open syllables of disyllabic words were pronounced in that way. That the approach I am taking in this study attributes no relevance to this essentially insoluble question, is one of the main reasons why I find it so appealing (see also Ritt 1988: 158ff.). Furthermore, Minkova's version of OSL does not account for those items that do have long vowels in their Modern English counterparts although their second syllables were stable. Even conceding that the number of those items is smaller than the number of items whose behaviour is described incorrectly by the traditional version of OSL, and that it might be better to leave something undescribed than to describe it incorrectly, it does strike one that the items Minkova's OSL does not cover seem to be too similar to those which her law handles for being shoved under the carpet altogether. In other words, although Minkova's finding was a true eye-opener, her reformulation of OSL was probably a bit too radical.

As regards this investigation, however, the strong impact of σ_2 raises quite a different problem: the potential deletability of the second syllable seems to be so powerful a factor with regard to OSL, that it might seriously blur the picture the statistics give of other potential constraints on lengthening, even if they are not correlated, strictly speaking, to σ_2 weight. It ought to be filtered out, because practically all items whose second syllables were deleted came to be lengthened and one cannot expect any other factor to leave any recognizable impact on such a group. And this holds for any group that contains a high proportion of items with unstable last syllables, of course. In order to get a clearer view of the impacts of other factors, then, one has to examine them separately for items with unstable final syllables on the one hand, and for items with stable ones on the other. If a clear picture is to emerge at all, of course, will do so within the latter group. Thus, the following analyses will not only show tables with the results of overall countings; additionally, they will contain tables in which the results for items with deletable second syllables and for items with stable second syllables are listed separately.

2.2 Vowel quality

2.2.1 ± low

Table 2.4

		Vowel in Modern English			
	Total	Long	%	Short	%
All σ_2 Types					
low	217	129	59	88	41
non-low	215	108	50	107	50
Unstable σ_2					
low	105	98	93	7	7
non-low	103	95	92	8	8
Stable σ_2					
low	112	31	28	81	73
non-low	112	13	12	99	88

As the last part of the table shows, low vowels were more likely to be lengthened than non-low vowels.

2.2.2 ± back

Table 2.5

		Vowel in Modern English			
	Total	Long	%	Short	%
All σ_2 Types					
back	89	50	56	39	44
front	126	58	47	68	53
Unstable σ_2					
back	45	42	93	3	7
front	58	53	91	5	9
Stable σ_2					
back	44	8	18	36	82
front	68	5	7	63	93

As evident from the last part of the table, back vowels were more likely to get lengthened than front vowels.

2.3   The consonant(s) at the end of the first syllable

2.3.1   Clusters vs. single consonants

Here I distinguish between vowels that are followed by single consonants and vowels followed by clusters. Note, however, that the classic description of OSL only covers such clusters that can be interpreted as onsets of the syllables to their right (see also p. 13 above). Hence, the clusters we are dealing with here are such clusters as the *st* in *haste* or *pr* in *April*, but not *nt* as in *plante* or *rt* as in *heart*.

Table 2.6

		Vowel in Modern English			
	Total	Long	%	Short	%
All σ_2 Types					
single C	408	232	57	176	43
cluster	24	4	17	20	83
Unstable σ_2					
single C	206	190	92	10	8
cluster	8	3	37	5	63
Stable σ_2					
single C	200	40	20	160	80
cluster	16	1	6	15	94

As the last part of the table shows, lengthening was more likely to be implemented before single consonants than before clusters.

2.3.2   Consonant sonority

Table 2.7

		Vowel in Modern English			
	Total	Long	%	Short	%
All σ_2 Types					
/r/	57	30	53	27	47
/l/	50	28	56	22	44
nasal	46	20	42	26	58
fricative	94	56	60	38	40
voiced stop	43	23	53	20	47
voiceless stop	116	73	63	43	37

Table 2.7 continued

Unstable σ_2					
/r/	28	28	100	0	0
/l/	30	30	100	0	0
nasal	19	19	100	0	0
fricative	37	37	100	0	0
voiced stop	17	15	88	2	12
voiceless stop	69	61	88	8	12
Stable σ_2					
/r/	22	0	0	22	100
/l/	27	0	0	27	100
nasal	27	1	4	26	96
fricative	48	20	42	38	58
voiced stop	26	8	31	18	69
voiceless stop	47	12	26	35	74

In a strange way, the impact of the following consonant on vowel lengthening seems to have depended on the stability of the second syllable. Consonant classes which favoured vowel lengthening in words with stable last syllables seem to have constrained the application of the process in words with unstable last syllables. Therefore, general statements about vowel lengthening and its relation to the quality of the consonants succeeding a vowel do not seem to make sense. I shall deal with this problem in greater detail below.

2.4 Syntactic category

As shown in table 2.8, lengthening seems to have been most likely among verbs, less likely among nouns and least likely among adjectives. However, as a comparison of the three parts of the table shows, syntactic category seems to be correlated to final syllable stability and therefore the picture conveyed by the first part cannot be taken at its face value. Rather, the fact that verbs have a greater percentage of counterparts with long vowels than nouns or adjectives, seems to be due mainly to the relatively great number of verbs with unstable last syllables. This factor being filtered out, then, the picture would seem to reverse itself, although the figures do not really speak a clear language. Thus, it appears that generalizations concerning the relevance of syntacic category for the probability of lengthening are very difficult to make.[2]

Table 2.8

	Vowel in Modern English				
	Total	Long	%	Short	%
All σ_2 Types					
nouns	290	142	49	148	51
adjectives	40	14	32	26	68
verbs	98	77	79	21	21
Unstable σ_2					
nouns	114	108	95	6	5
adjectives	8	8	100	0	0
verbs	85	76	89	9	11
Stable σ_2					
nouns	176	34	19	142	81
adjectives	32	6	19	26	81
verbs	13	1	8	12	92

2.5   Etymology

Table 2.9

	Vowel in Modern English				
	Total	Long	%	Short	%
All σ_2 Types					
Old English	258	169	66	89	34
Norman	137	42	31	95	69
Scandinavian	28	19	68	9	32
Unstable σ_2					
Old English	163	151	93	12	7
Norman	21	21	100	0	0
Scandinavian	20	17	85	3	15
Stable σ_2					
Old English	95	18	19	77	81
Norman	115	21	18	95	82
Scandinavian	8	2	25	6	75

As a comparison of the three parts of the table shows, etymology seems to be correlated to final syllable stability in a similar way to syntactic category. Consequently, the picture conveyed by the first part cannot be taken at its face value either. The fact that Germanic items have counterparts with long vowels more often than Romance words, seems to be due mainly to the great number of Germanic items with unstable last syllables. This factor being filtered out, the difference in behaviour between Romance and Germanic items turns out to be so small as to be negligible.

2.6   Conclusions

Even at first sight the figures suggest one thing very clearly: the class of potential OSL candidates is in fact very heterogeneous with regard to lengthening. At the same time, however, the way in which the items reflect OSL is not chaotic but corresponds rather straightforwardly to the way in which phonological factors constrained the lengthening process behind it. This becomes clear in the following summary of observations.

I   The potential deletability of the second syllable of a word seems to have greatly influenced the probability of lengthening: almost all of the words whose last syllables were unstable have lengthened reflexes, while words whose last syllables were stable mostly have short vowels in their Modern English counterparts.[3]

II   The chance that a vowel got lengthened was greater in words with light second syllables than in words with heavy second syllables.

III   Similarly, the chance that a vowel got lengthened was greater in words with heavy second syllables than in words with super-heavy second syllables.

IV   Low vowels seem to have been more likely to be lengthened than non-low vowels.

V   Back vowels seem to be more likely to be lengthened than non-back vowels.

VI   The chance for words in which the onsets of the second syllables were clusters to be lengthened was practically zero, while words with single consonants between the first and second syllables were rather likely to be lengthened.

VII   That verbs appear to have been affected more strongly by lengthening than nouns, will probably have to be regarded as a spin-off effect of the unequal distribution of stable and unstable final syllables among verbs and nouns respectively.

VIII In a similar way, the fact that words of Germanic origin reflect lengthening more often than verbs of Romance origin was probably due to the fact that a significantly smaller number of Romance items lost their final syllables.

Of course, observations I–III are related. Together, they suggest that the probability of a vowel's undergoing lengthening was inversely proportional to the weight of the last syllable, if the application of potential reduction processes is taken into account. As indicated above, this statement is made on the assumption that the shape which a final unstressed syllable has in Modern English reflects – roughly – the reductions and deletions to which the syllable was subject in Early Middle English. It does not mean that the Modern English form is identical with the most strongly backgrounded Early Middle English form. Rather, it means that there is a strong correlation between the two forms. Thus, I assume that Early Middle English final syllables not reflected in Modern English anymore – as for instance the final schwas of EME *cnave* (knave), *cele* (keel), *hope* (hope) – were reduced/deleted more often in fast or casual EME pronunciation than syllables that do have Modern English counterparts – such as *schadwe* (shadow), *heofen* (heaven), *comon* (common).

The relation between the weight of the final syllable and the probability of lengthening becomes very clear if illustrated in a chart:[4]

(2)

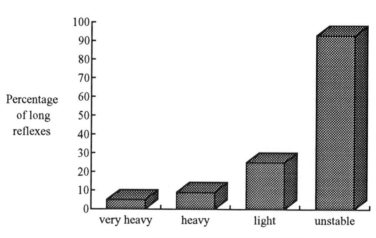

FINAL SYLLABLE WEIGHT

At the same time, the observation can be expressed in a formula of the type

(3) $p(V \rightarrow [+\text{long}]) \approx k/(\text{weight of } \sigma_2)$.

Thus, potential OSL candidates can be ordered on a scale of σ_2 weight, and their chance of being lengthened can be derived directly from their positions on that scale by means of the formula given above.

As observation **IV** shows, the chance that a vowel is lengthened seems to be inversely proportional to its height. There are clearly more long counterparts of /a/ than of /e/ and /o/. From that, then, the fact that there are hardly any long counterparts of /i/ or /u/ follows almost automatically. This view therefore does not force one to regard high vowels as exceptions to OSL. On the contrary, their behaviour with regard to that change is perfectly predictable. The relatively great height of /i/ and /u/ made the probability of their being lengthened relatively small. Chart (4) illustrates the underlying relation. (It is based on items with stable last syllables only, because the difference in behaviour between low and mid vowels before deletable last syllables is very small and does not yield sufficiently significant differences. Furthermore, it makes reference to items with high vowels although their behaviour has not been investigated statistically. It is well known, however, that they were practically never lengthened.)

(4)

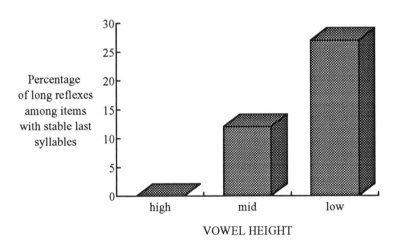

The rule behind this correlation could be formulated as:

(5) $p(V \rightarrow [+\text{long}]) \approx k/(\text{height of } V)$.

This means that vowel height, just like σ_2 weight, ordered items on a scale of lengthening probability rather than dividing them into mutually exclusive sets, one of which was lengthened and the other one not.

Combining the two rules would then yield

$$
(6) \qquad p(V \rightarrow [+\text{long}]) \approx \frac{k}{a(\text{height of V}) + b(\text{weight of } \sigma 2)}
$$

Another factor on which the probability of a vowel's being lengthened seems to have depended were the consonants following the vowel. This is expressed neither in the traditional version of OSL, nor in Minkova's reinterpretation. Both versions suggest that it does not make any difference what type of consonant or cluster follows the vowel, as long as it can be interpreted as the onset of the final syllable. As observed above, however, the figures suggest a different picture.

Thus, a vowel rarely came to have a long counterpart, if it was followed by more than one consonant – no matter which role a consonant cluster may have played within the final syllable. It seems, therefore, that the openness of a syllable, as it has traditionally been understood, is not quite suitable as a parameter in the description of OSL. This is another problem with which I shall deal in greater detail below.

Furthermore, not only the number of consonants that followed the vowel, but also the quality of those consonants seems to have been important with respect to OSL, albeit their influence does not appear to have been straight-forward. Particularly disturbing is the difference in behaviour between sonorant consonants (nasals and liquids) on the one hand, and obstruents on the other. Take items with sonorants first. All of the 87 words with unstable final syllables have long counterparts. Among the 76 items with stable final syllables, on the other hand, there is just a single word that has one. Thus, it seems that a sonorant had opposite effects on the probability of the preceding vowel's being lengthened, depending on whether the final syllable of a word was stable or unstable.[5]

Obstruents, on the other hand, behave less extravagantly. Their relative impact on vowel lengthening is roughly the same in items with stable last syllables as in items with unstable ones. Again the underlying relation becomes obvious in a chart:

(7)

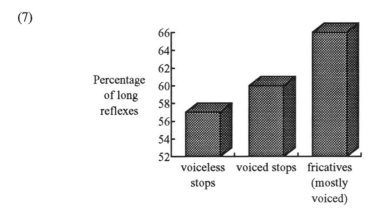

CODA CONSONANTS

In other words, the chance of a vowel to be lengthened before a single obstruent correlated with the relative sonority of that obstruent.[6] Integrating this with the observations made so far – and leaving the odd behaviour of sonorants aside for the moment – yields the following formula:

(8) $p(V \rightarrow [+long]/\_\_[+obstruent]) \approx k \dfrac{c(\text{sonority of obstruent})}{a(\text{height of V}) + b(\text{weight of } \sigma 2)}$

3   *Widening the meaning of OSL*

As I have already stated, Modern English data show that OSL did not affect the vowels of all its potential targets equally. Rather, some type of OSL targets were more likely to be changed by the process than others. This is, basically, what statements such as *Low vowels seem to have been more likely to be lengthened than non-low vowels* express.

What I would like to highlight here, then, is that these statements have so far been taken to be relevant *exclusively* with regard to potential OSL candidates. The corpus from which they were derived contained no other items. On second thoughts, however, hardly anything seems to speak against widening their potential applicability and interpreting them as general tendencies behind Early Middle English vowel lengthenings. This point is crucial and I would like to elaborate the argumentation on which it rests, although it might be viewed as rather pedestrian in essence.

Take, once more, the statement about vowel height and imagine, for a momentary excursion, that there were no other 'sound changes' apart from OSL, by which vowels were lengthened. This means that the probability of vowel lengthening would have been zero among all non-OSL candidates, no matter what the heights of their vowels were. Therefore, if OSL candidates and other words were combined into a single set, the relation between lengthened low vowels and lengthened high vowels would basically remain the same, although the difference will be relatively smaller. Thus, the statement that low vowels were more likely to be lengthened than high ones would still be true. Nothing would therefore speak against re-interpreting it as a general rule on the probability of Early Middle English vowels to be lengthened.

Although this is exactly what I would like to claim, I am aware that such a proposal must necessarily seem speculative at this point. The main argument that speaks against the generalization is, of course, the fact that OSL was not the only lengthening by which Early Middle English vowels are taken to have been affected, and any of the general statements about vowel quantity that I am proposing will have to be tested against all lengthenings that were not brought about by OSL before they can be taken as established. This will be done in a later chapter.

However, if it is assumed for the moment that the rules behind OSL could indeed be generalized to cover more than merely the set of OSL candidates, Early Middle English vowel lengthening could be understood as a change that reflected the combined impacts of the following general tendencies:

(1)

I **Phonological factors**

1 $$p(V \rightarrow [+\text{long}]) \approx \frac{k}{a(\text{weight of } \sigma 2)}$$

2 $$p(V \rightarrow [+\text{long}]) \approx \frac{k}{a(\text{height of } V)}$$

3 $$p(V \rightarrow [+\text{long}]) \approx \frac{k}{a(\text{frontness of } V)}$$

4 (a) $p(V \rightarrow [+\text{long}]/\_\_[-(\text{sonorant} + \text{stable } \sigma 2)]) \approx k(\text{sonority of C following V})$

(b) $p(V \rightarrow [+\text{long}]/\_\_[\text{sonorant} + \text{stable } \sigma 2]) \approx 0$

(c) $$p(V \rightarrow [+\text{long}]) \approx \frac{k}{a(\text{no. of C following V})}$$

II **Non-phonological factors**

1 $$p(V \rightarrow [+\text{long}]/\begin{bmatrix} ----- \\ +\text{GERMANIC} \end{bmatrix}) > p(V \rightarrow [+\text{long}]/\begin{bmatrix} ----- \\ +\text{ROMANCE} \end{bmatrix})$$

2 $$p(V \rightarrow [+\text{long}]/\begin{bmatrix} ----- \\ +\text{VERB} \end{bmatrix}) > p(V \rightarrow [+\text{long}]/\begin{bmatrix} ----- \\ +\text{NOUN} \end{bmatrix})$$

If the assumption that those rules could be generalized were indeed corroborated, however, they would not only be an alternative way of describing 'open syllable lengthenings'. Rather, they imply that the notion of open syllable lengthening could be regarded as a spurious generalization altogether, because the way in which vowels that belonged to the set of 'potential OSL candidates' were affected by lengthening was not essentially different from the way in which other vowels were affected. The difference is one of degree and does not justify the establishment of a special class. In other words, no set of OSL candidates could be defined that would admit of a rule such as

(2) $$p(V \rightarrow [+long] / \begin{bmatrix} ------------- \\ +\text{OSL CANDIDATE} \end{bmatrix}) = 1,$$

and that the complementary rule

(3) $$p(V \rightarrow [+long] / \begin{bmatrix} ------------- \\ -\text{OSL\_CANDIDATE} \end{bmatrix}) = 0$$

does not work either is equally well known. After all, vowels were also lengthened before homorganic groups and in other, 'isolated' (Luick's view) examples such as the Scandinavian loans *thar* or *whar* (showing up in ModE as *there* and *where*) (cf. Luick 1914/21:397).[1] All this means, however, that the concept of LENGTHENING IN OPEN SYLLABLES itself could be regarded as pointless in a description of the development of English.

If the rules in (1) were to take over the job of OSL, they would of course have to be complemented by the rules that are implicit in all traditional descriptions of OSL and that I have therefore not introduced as constraints on the change.

One of them is stress. Only stressed vowels were affected by the lengthenings, not unstressed ones. Although stress is quite a complex phenomenon and definitely not a property of items, I think that the correlation between stress and vowel lengthening could be handled by a rule such as

(4) $$p(V \rightarrow [+long]) = k(\text{STRESS})$$

even though it might represent an akward over-simplification.

On the other hand, there are 'syllable openness' and the fact that lengthening seems to have occurred only in penultimates.[2] These factors could be covered by rules such as

(5) $$p(V \rightarrow [+long] /\_\_\S) > p(V \rightarrow [+long] /\_\_(\neg\S)) \text{ and}$$
$$p(V \rightarrow [+long] / \begin{bmatrix} ------ \\ +\text{PENULT} \end{bmatrix}) > p(V \rightarrow [+long] / \begin{bmatrix} ------ \\ -\text{PENULT} \end{bmatrix})^3$$

If these tendency rules – i.e. the rules in (1) plus the ones in (4) and (5) – are valid for all Middle English vowel lengthenings, the overall probability of any individual vowel's being lengthened can be derived through the combined application of the rules on the respective item. Instead of saying that the vowel in a given word was a potential OSL candidate, one will then say that it combined many of the qualities that favoured vowel lengthening, and that it therefore was a prototypical lengthening candidate.[4]

The next thing to do now would be to put the proposed account on firmer grounds by testing it against independent evidence. In order to do so, chapter 6 will test the tendency rules that seem to have governed lengthening in Middle English words that happened to be thought of as OSL inputs against the evidence of items that have so far been viewed as having been lengthened through HOL. Before that, however, I would like to show that the rules in (1), (4) and (5) can be improved and streamlined, if descriptive devices of more recent, non-linear phonological theories are employed.

4 *A suprasegmental view of OSL*

So far, whenever I have wanted to express the fact that the 'POST-OSL' equivalents of words such as EME *maken* were words such as *maːke*, I have been talking in terms of 'vowels' and their counterparts, without giving due consideration to metalanguage. Of course, such terminological carelessness has its drawbacks.[1] Take, for instance, the very term *Open Syllable Lengthening* itself. Though basic to my considerations, it is not nearly as straightforward as it might seem. Thus, it can be read both as 'lengthening of something (in our case: vowels) in open syllables' or as 'lengthening of open syllables'. Now, this terminological ambivalence reflects that phenomena such as OSL might not only be conceived as lengthenings of vowel segments (implying that all the higher constituents in which a vowel figures get lengthened with it), but equally well as changes of syllable quantity that just happen to show in their nuclei, so that the vowel lengthenings could be regarded as sheer epiphenomena.[2] A further possibility of viewing OSL is suggested by Minkova, whose version of OSL clearly implies that the change might be understood as a foot restructuring in which a foot of two light syllables came to be replaced by a foot of one heavy syllable.[3] One aspect of these alternative interpretations is that both the syllable-based view of OSL and the foot-based one make sense only within a phonological theory that recognizes other descriptive levels than that of linear segmental organization. Since in the last decades a lot of research into the non-linear aspects of phonological organization has been done and has shed new light particularly on phenomena related to quantity,[4] I will try and re-approach OSL from various non-segmental angles to see whether thereby the changes can be described more meaningfully and/or elegantly.

47

4.1   The level of the syllable

Although contemporary phonological literature abounds with sometimes incompatible studies of the syllable[5] and, therefore, no undisputable definition
of the term can be provided, a few claims can be made with reasonable
safety. Thus, the term 'syllable' is generally used to refer to a 'unit of pronunciation typically larger than a single sound and smaller than a WORD'
(Crystal 1985: sv. *syllable*). Basically, syllable structure can be viewed as
reflecting the fact that human speech patterns into constantly alternating sequences of more sonorous ('vocalic') and less sonorous ('consonantal')
elements: the more sonorous a segment is, the more central will be its position within a syllable, and *vice versa* (less sonorous segments tend to be
found in the syllable margins).[6] In this respect, syllable structure is a highly
'natural' phenomenon (in the everyday meaning of the term), since it both
facilitates perception (by preventing sequences that are not sufficiently con-
trastive) and responds to the make-up of the human speech apparatus.[7]

A syllable, then, can be understood to consist of '(1) non-vocalic *onset*,
(2) *nucleus* or peak (most frequently a vowel), (3) non-vocalic offset or
coda, ... the nucleus [being] obligatory, the other two parts optional'
(Dressler 1985: 35, my emphases). The nucleus and the coda are subsumed
under a single constituent, namely the *rhyme*.[8] These aspects of syllable
theory are more or less undisputed. The basic model of syllable structure
that can be derived from them looks as in (1):

(1)[9]

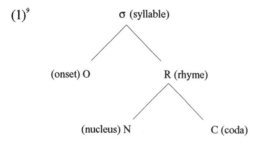

The fact that the roles of **O**, **N** and **C** may be filled by various types of
segments or segment clusters admits the distinction of various syllable
types. Of those, the following are of interest for my purposes: (1) syllables
without codas (**open** or **unchecked**) vs. syllables with codas (**closed** or
checked); (2) syllables whose rhyme consists of one short vowel only
(**light**) vs. syllables whose rhyme consists of more than that, i.e. at least a
long vowel, a diphthong, or a vowel plus a consonantal coda (**heavy**
syllables).[10]

Another view that is widely accepted among students of suprasegmental phonology and that I would like to adopt is that the relation between the segments of an utterance and its syllables is not straightforward. That is to say, segments do not simply fill slots in syllable structure, and syllable structure is not just the sum of the syllabic functions individual segments take. For example, stating that the /o/ was the nucleus of EME *sort*, the /s/ its onset, and the /rt/ cluster its coda is not a complete description of its syllable structure, because the units that figure in syllable structure are not identical with segments in the traditional sense of linear phonology. Rather, it seems that those aspects of segmental structure that have to do with the sonority of a segment are much more relevant to the role which a segment plays within a syllable than most of its other features.

The ways in which this can be expressed, however, are rather varied, and one's choice will probably depend on the theory and the notational system one prefers.[11] However, no matter which framework one prefers, there is one aspect which is common to most non-linear phonologies and which is highly relevant to this investigation. Any non-linear view of phonology relativizes the status of the concept 'phonological segment'. Among the parameters whose status has come to be questioned most radically, the parameter of 'length' is, of course, particularly important for the present purpose. Most non-linear approaches to phonology suggest that it should be represented as a suprasegmental phenomenon, rather than as a quality of individual segments.[12] Thus, within such frameworks as dependency or autosegmental phonology the length of a segment such as the /iː/ in ModE *sea* is represented by associating it with two positions in suprasegmental representations.

(2)

a.   Autosegmental phonology

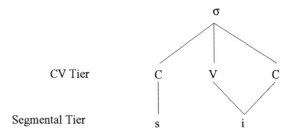

b.   Dependency phonology

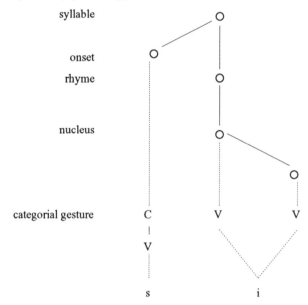

One of the greatest advantages of representing length in this way is that it allows the distinction between heavy and light syllables in purely suprasegmental terms: the former can be defined as having branching rhymes, the latter as having non-branching ones.[13] Therefore, the suggestion of non-linear phonology will be taken up and the description of the lengthening process behind OSL revised accordingly.[14]

Before that, however, another aspect of syllable structure needs to be mentioned that is generally considered to be problematic. It is the question of how syllable boundaries should be placed. Since it is of particular relevance for this study, I would like to discuss it at some length.

4.1.1   Approaches to syllable delimitation: onset maximal and/or general maximal?

The items we are dealing with are polysyllabic and the established view of OSL depends crucially on lengthened vowels to be immediately followed by syllable boundaries. Therefore, we cannot be careful enough where syllable delimitation is concerned. Take, for instance, ME *maken*, as a typical example of an 'OSL candidate'. In Luick's eyes, the first syllable was open and light, and it was natural for him to syllabify the word as *ma $ ken*. However, if one consults contemporary literature on the topic, one gets the impression that this kind of syllabification is *not* the only conceivable one. Rather, there seem to be different and apparently conflicting approaches to syllable delimitation, so that there is little reason to be certain that the *k* in EME *maken* really belonged to the second rather than to the first syllable.

Basically, most contemporary approaches to syllabification are based on either the so-called *onset maximal assumption* or the so-called *general maximal assumption*. As will be shown, however, the two are not quite as incompatible as they are often taken to be.

Both approaches begin syllabification by identifying syllable nuclei. This part is not yet very problematic, and can be performed in a relatively straightforward and objective manner. Syllable nuclei are at the same time sonority peaks and the relative sonorities of phonemes (or rather: phoneme classes) are among the less disputed aspects of suprasegmental phonology. Although there are disagreements about, for example, the relative sonority of /r/[15] as compared to that of glides, most of the generally accepted sonority scales resemble the following one, which is taken from Vennemann 1988 (p. 6):

(3)

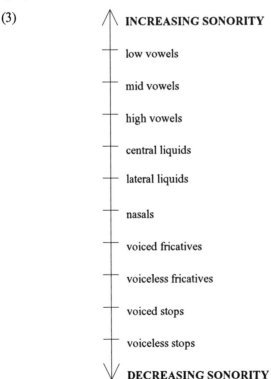

INCREASING SONORITY

low vowels

mid vowels

high vowels

central liquids

lateral liquids

nasals

voiced fricatives

voiceless fricatives

voiced stops

voiceless stops

DECREASING SONORITY

The nuclei of words such as EME *maken* (make), *wesle* (weasel) or *þrostel* (throstle) would thus be

(4)

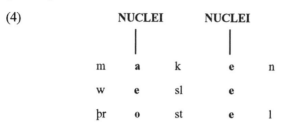

NUCLEI   NUCLEI

m   a   k   e   n

w   e   sl   e

þr   o   st   e   l

When it comes to the linking of consonants to nuclei, however, the general concensus ends. The argument revolves round the following issue. It is generally assumpted that all consonant clusters that occur at the beginning of words can be regarded as potential syllable onsets, while consonant clusters that occur at the end of words can be regarded as potential codas. Unfortunately, however, this allows more than one interpretation of intervocalic clusters, because there are many that occur *both* at the beginnings *and* at the ends of words. Thus, consonants such as the *k* in *maken* could theoretically be both the onset of the second syllable and the coda of the first one; and the same is true of clusters such as the *st*-cluster in *þrostel*, or the *sl*-cluster in *wesle*. In fact, things are even more complicated with the latter: the *sl* cluster as a whole occurs only at the beginning of Early Middle English words, while its first component, the *s*, can be found at the end of Early Middle English words as well. This means that the *sl*-cluster as a whole could be regarded as the onset of the second syllable, while the *s* could at the same time function as the coda of the first syllable, too.

The crucial question, then, is which of the roles that consonant clusters are theoretically capable of playing they should be assumed to actually play in concrete instances. The *general maximalist* position is to say that they actually play all of those roles at once, even though this means that some consonants must be regarded as *ambisyllabic* (belonging to two syllables at the same time; see Anderson 1985). The *onset maximalist* assumption, on the other hand, does not allow ambisyllabicity. To avoid it, it assigns prioity to the *onset* function, so that all consonant clusters between two syllables will be regarded as the onsets of the syllables to their right as long as they are possible in word-initial position. As far as my examples are concerned, a general maximal syllabification would yield

(5)[16]

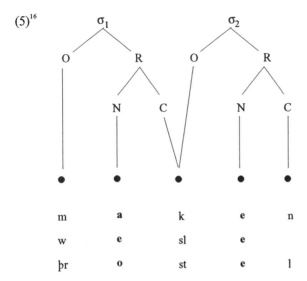

m	a	k	e	n
w	e	sl	e	
þr	o	st	e	l

The intermediate consonants or clusters *k*, *s* and *st* figure in both syllables and are therefore **ambisyllabic**.

The onset maximalist counterpart to this representation would be

(6)

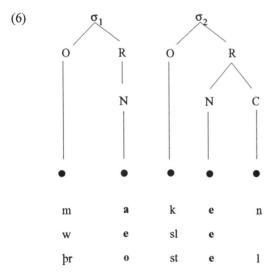

m	a	k	e	n
w	e	sl	e	
þr	o	st	e	l

While the final syllables have the same structure as within the *general maximal approach*, the structure of the first syllables is markedly different. Notably, it is only within the *onset maximal approach* that they could be regarded as open at all. If it could be shown that – at least for Early Middle English – the *general maximal approach* is more plausible, then this would be another argument for discarding the *open syllable* version of Early Middle English vowel lengthening. As I intend to argue in the next sections, this is indeed the case.

Generally speaking, the *onset maximal* approach, which was more or less taken for granted by Luick, also seems to be preferred in most contemporary studies that deal with syllable structure (e.g. Hogg and McCully 1987, or Vennemann 1988). Among the arguments normally proposed in its favour the following three are perhaps the most prominent ones.

First, the idea of ambisyllabic segments tends to make one feel slightly uncomfortable, because it destroys the concept of syllables as discrete units and therefore tends to be associated with inexactness and intuition. Second, CV syllables (syllables consisting of a consonantal onset plus a vocalic nucleus) occur much more often in the languages of the world than clear cases of CVC syllables, and there are no languages without CV syllables, while there are quite a few that have no CVC syllables. Furthermore, all languages with CVC syllables have CV syllables as well, but not *vice versa*. Therefore, it has been concluded that onsets were more essential to syllables than codas, and that a syllable that consisted of an onset plus a nucleus was more 'natural', or more ideal than a syllable that – additionally or alternatively – had a coda.

Furthermore, many syllables that seem to begin with vowels and, therefore, appear to be without onsets, are really pronounced with a glottal stop, so that phonetically speaking those syllables do have onsets after all. For syllables without codas a similar phenomenon is not observed.

Finally, the association of intermediate consonants with the following rather than the preceding nuclei seems to agree with most native speakers' intuitions about syllabification. This has become evident in tests and may also be concluded from word division rules both in German and in English (except where English word divison is morpheme based rather than syllable based, of course), and – for Old English – from medieval scribal practice.

As far as the arguments for a general maximal syllabification are concerned, they are normally of a less general character, and are often based on language-specific observations.

For most Modern English words, for example, syllable structure allows us to predict the location of primary stress, and the rules by which this is done work better on the basis of a general maximal syllabification (cf. Anderson, 1986: 88–90).

Also, there is phonetic evidence suggesting a general maximal, rather than an onset maximal syllabification. Thus, the intersyllabic consonants in words such as

(7)   happy, accolade, beaker, goiter, wacky, attitude

are often pronounced unaspirated, which is atypical of onset position (compare p^h*ort*, k^h*eep*, t^h*ower*, for instance) (cf. Selkirk 1982: 366).

As these arguments, which are normally used to support either of two approaches to syllabification, show, and as has already been indicated above, the disagreement between the two theories is not really insurmountable. The arguments for the two theories belong to two different theoretical levels, and therefore they cannot, strictly speaking, contradict each other. In fact, such observations as that onsets seem to be generally more essential to syllabification than codas are easy to reconcile with language-specific arguments. It is argued, for example, that general maximal syllabification and ambisyllabic consonants are typical of stress-timed and fusional languages, such as German and English, while generally – and therefore in most other languages – onset maximal syllabification is to be assumed. (cf. Dressler 1985: 37). Alternatively, one could assume a resyllabification in stressed syllables by which they would come to incorporate consonants to their right. Underlying syllable divisions could so be regarded as onset maximal (which would reflect the more basic status of this kind of division), and, at the same time, the phonetic evidence from languages such as English could be accounted for.[17]

As a matter of fact, the only argument that seems to prevent a reconciliation of the two approaches, because it speaks strongly against maximal general syllabifications even in stress-timed languages such as English, is based on native speaker intuitions. It was probably also the argument which induced Karl Luick to consider any syllabification that was not onset maximal as completely out of the question. When asked to divide words such as *boundary*, *coda* or *open* into syllables, it happens that native speakers will more often go for *boun $ da $ ry*, *co $ da* and *o $ pen*, rather than *bound $ da $ ry*, *cod $ da* or *op $ pen* , or even *bound $ ar $ y*, *cod $ a* or *op $ en*. It appears to me, however, that the validity of this argument is highly questionable. In order to see this, one only has to reflect on what a native speaker actually does when asked to divide a word into syllables. It is as good as certain that one will pronounce the word (either loudly or silently by oneself) slowly and with clear pauses where one thinks that the syllable boundaries are. In this process, however, the syllables of the words will practically be raised to the status of autonomous words[18] themselves, and –

crucially – all of them will get more or less the same stress. It is on the basis of this type of fully stressed monosyllables that native speakers decide where the syllable boundaries in polysyllabic words are. Obviously, such judgements are inherently irrelevant for the purposes of syllable delimitation in natural speech, for – as appears self-evident to me – the type of monosyllabic pseudo-words on which they rest have little to do with the words from which they were derived, and do not reflect the way in which these words are syllabified in natural speech. After all, it is one of the essential aspects of syllables that they are organized into more complex structures and change their shapes in this process. In this respect, syllables do not differ from segments, and certainly nobody would argue that the final /t/ in *ballot* was aspirated because a native speaker produced an aspirated /tʰ/ when asked to pronounce the word 'a sound at a time'. Yet, as far as syllable boundaries are concerned those kinds of native speaker intuitions are still widely accepted (cases in point are the paper Ann Cutler delivered at the fourth international phonology meeting at Krems/Austria or Lutz 1986, where word division by Anglo-Saxon scribes is taken as evidence for the position of syllable boundaries in Old English.)

For the purposes of this study, all this means that there is no reason to assume that fully stressed syllables were not general maximal. After all, Middle English was probably similarly stress-timed as Modern English, and the specific phonetic evidence provided by the latter outweighs – in my view – the more theoretical and general arguments.

Apart from this basic decision, then, there remain a couple of questions that are tricky to resolve. Thus, it is difficult to decide whether to assume general maximal syllabification in *all* syllables or only in stressed ones; nor is it known whether general maximal syllabification should be regarded as underlying or whether it should be derived by some resyllabification rule. Both questions are closely related to the status of stress placement. Thus, the assumption that stressed syllables are general maximal due to resyllabification rules crucially depends on prior stress assignment. On the other hand, the strongest argument for assuming general maximal syllabification in *all* syllables is that all other syllabifications make wrong predictions about stress placement, which clearly implies that stress must *not* be assigned before syllabification (cf. Anderson 1986: 86ff.).

In Early Middle English, stress placement was largely dependent on morphological information. The rule was that a lexical item would have primary stress on the leftmost syllable of its stem (including prefixes in the case of nouns, excluding them in the case of certain verbs; cf. Kastovsky

1989: 290). Contrary to many Romance suffixes that entered the English language during the Middle English period, Germanic suffixes (both inflectional and derivational) were generally stress neutral, so that there were hardly any stress alternations – with the exception of those that were brought about by the fact that many Germanic prefixes were stressed in nouns, but not in verbs. For instance, OE *æt+spyrning* (N) 'offence' vs. OE *os+spúrnan* (V) 'stumble', OE *bí+genga* (N) 'inhabitant' vs. *be+gán* (V) 'occupy'. However, the relatedness of such pairs was probably not fully transparent anymore even in Old English, and would have been less so in Middle English. Furthermore, they are of little relevance with regard to the data that are investigated in this study and can therefore be more or less neglected.

Generally speaking, then, all the information necessary to determine which of the syllables of a possible wordform would get primary stress was already contained in the form of the lexical item as such. Principally, all forms of a lexeme would be stressed on the same syllable, no matter which suffixes they incorporated, if any at all. It need therefore not be assumed that Early Middle English post-lexical phonology incorporated any stress-shifting rules.

Since Middle English did not have such stress alternations as Modern English, then, there is no reason to assume that there were any alternations of syllable structure either: the syllables that were stressed would always be general maximal as well.

Furthermore, since stress placement did not depend on the syllabic structure of a word, but could be predicted exclusively on morphological grounds, we need *not* assume any special type of underlying syllabification from which to predict stress placement. Therefore, the assumption of post-stress resyllabification rules can be dismissed, for it presupposes the assumption of a level on which syllable structure is not specified – and, as has been shown, such an assumption would be unnecessary and redundant. I shall therefore assume that, on all levels of phonological representation, Early Middle English stressed syllables were general maximal, while all others may have been onset maximal.

Clearly, these arguments are of a rather general character and also somewhat hypothetical, so that it would be rash if I took general maximal syllabification in Early Middle English for granted. Therefore, the next sections serve a double function. On the one hand, they describe OSL from a syllabic point of view and are designed to throw more light on the process. On the other hand, however, they serve to test the model of Early Middle

English syllable structure which we have just sketched. If it should turn out that the OSL facts cannot be described as well with a general maximal syllabification as with an onset maximal syllabification, I shall regard this as counterevidence to my assumption. If the opposite should be the case, I shall consider it to be corroborated.

4.1.2   A syllable-based interpretation of OSL implementation

As mentioned above, general maximal syllabification would attribute the following structure to the syllables that were supposed to get their nuclei lengthened through OSL (my examples are again *maken*, *þrostel* and *wesle*.)

(8)

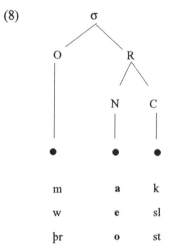

m	a	k
w	e	sl
þr	o	st

Contrary to the traditional analysis, they do not qualify as 'open'. As I have said, this renders meaningless both Luick's version of OSL and any statement to the effect that vowels in open syllables were more likely to be lengthened than vowels in closed syllables. Since the openness of syllables does seem to have had an effect on the probability of nucleus lengthening, this seems to speak against the general maximal assumption. I will show, however, that the opposition described by the traditional distinction of open vs. closed syllables can also be expressed within a general maximal framework. In fact, there are even some aspects of OSL that either can be described more elegantly if a general maximal syllabification is assumed or cannot be reasonably expressed at all within an onset maximal framework.

First, take words such as *maken* on the one hand, and words such as *resten* on the other. As can be seen from table 2.6 on page 34, they differ significantly with regard to lengthening, in that words of the *maken* type are much more likely to be lengthened than words of the *resten* type. An onset maximal syllabification (on the basis of which the first syllables of both *maken* and *resten* would be decribed as open and light) makes it difficult to categorize Early Middle English syllables in a way that would reflect this difference. On the basis of a general maximal syllabification, on the other hand, *maken* could be analysed as

(9)

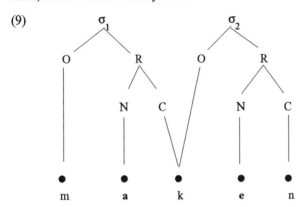

while *resten* could be viewed as

(10)[19]

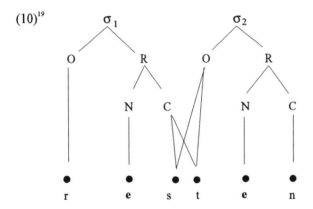

On the basis of such an analysis, the first syllable in *maken* has a simple coda, while the first syllable in *resten* has a complex (or: branching) one. This distinction is similar to that between heavy and light syllables (see above, p. 50), and is closely related to the concept of 'syllable weight'.

Normally, syllable weight is measured in moras (or: morae) and there is much literature on that unit.[20] Within this study, however, a comparatively unsophisticated approach is taken. It is based on Vennemann's (1988: 6) simple proposal that 'the number of moras of a syllable is simply the cardinality of its rhyme'. Whenever I use the term 'mora' in the rest of this study, I will do so mainly to avoid the use of more clumsy phrasings. I do not claim any theoretical significance for my over-simple definition of the term. To calculate the weight of a syllable I will simply count the number of elements in its rhyme.[21]

Of course, the status of ambisyllabic segments is a little tricky in this connection. Sticking to my reasoning, however, I will simply assume that half of their weight goes to the rhymes of the syllables to their left, while the other half is swallowed by the onsets of the syllables to their right (which means that it is lost, for onsets do not count in the determination of syllable weight).

According to this assumption, the first syllables of words of the *maken* type would weigh 1½ moras, while the weight of the first syllables in words of the *resten* type would be 2 moras. Re-interpreting in this spirit the observation that the probability of vowel lengthening in open syllables was inversely correlated with the number of consonants following the vowels, one can therefore say – on the syllabic level – that

(11)   A syllable that weighed 1½ moras was more likely to have its nucleus lengthened than a syllable that weighed 2 moras.

Of course, it is also possible to express this relation on the basis of an on-set maximal syllabification, although no onset maximalist version of OSL has ever attributed much attention to it at all. It could be said, for example, that

(12)   A syllable was more likely to have its nucleus lengthened if the onset of the syllable to its right was complex, than if it was simple.

While such a statement is less elegant than one based on syllable weight alone, for which reason alone the solution based on general maximal syllabification might be preferred, aesthetic arguments of this kind cannot really be considered as compelling. A slightly stronger point that could be made against the onset maximalist version of the rule is that interdependencies of this kind are considered to be more likely between tautosyllabic than between heterosyllabic segments (see e.g. Kahn 1976, or Nespor and Vogel 1986).

Next, take the observation that has been central to all orthodox versions of Early Middle English vowel lengthening, namely that open syllables were more likely to be lengthened than closed ones. Since it does not make sense within a general maximal framework, it has to be reformulated. This can be done in one of the following ways.

The more obvious one would be to simply redefine the category of open syllables as the class of syllables whose codas are fully ambisyllabic. This criterion would distinguish words of the types [ma[k]en] and [re[st]en] on the one hand from words of the type [plan[t]e] on the other, in a way that is fully equivalent to the traditional distinction of open vs. closed syllables. One could then say that

(13)   Syllables whose codas were fully ambisyllabic were more likely to have their nuclei lengthened than syllables whose codas were not.

The other possibility would be to operate with syllable weight again: within the simple framework proposed above, the first syllables of words of the type [plan[t]e] would weigh 2½ moras, while the first syllables of words of the types [ma[k]en] and [re[st]en] would weigh 1½ and 2 moras respectively. Because of this difference, one could express the openness criterion in a statement such as

(14)   Syllables that weighed 2 or less moras were less likely to have their nuclei lengthened than syllables that weighed 2½ moras.

Although it is not quite as faithful an image of the traditional open vs. closed syllable distinction, the latter possibility has two compelling advantages over the former: first, it can be combined with statement (11), which is also based on syllable weight, so that both are included in a generalization such as

(15)   The probability of a syllable's having its nucleus lengthened was inversely proportional to its weight.[22]

On the basis of an open vs. closed syllable distinction, this is impossible. Furthermore, a weight-based approach is preferable because it does not group words of the types [ma[k]en] and [re[st]en] together on any level. Thus, it is more adequate than both the traditional open vs. closed syllable distinction and its general maximal equivalent, since the behaviour of words of the type [re[st]en] is indeed at least as similar to words of the type [plan[t]e] as to words of the type [ma[k]en].

4.1.2.1 Conclusions
Since the first syllables of both [ma[k]en] and [re[st]en] would equally count one mora within an onset maximal analysis, there is no onset maximal equivalent to statement (11). Therefore, if syllable weight is calculated on the basis of an onset maximal syllabification, the special status of words of the [re[st]en] type cannot be expressed. Statement (15)

would thus only handle the traditional open vs. closed syllable distinction, but not the distinction between clusters and single consonants. Thereby, a significant generalization would be missed.

On the principle that of two otherwise equal descriptions the one that yields more significant generalizations is to be preferred, a general maximal syllabification of Early Middle English stressed syllables is to be preferred to an onset maximal syllabification. Its superiority with regard to the description of lengthening has thus confirmed the original assumption that Early Middle English syllables ought to be regarded as general maximal.

At the same time, we have gained new insights into Early Middle English vowel lengthening itself. The openness of syllables seems to have played not as crucial a role for the probability of lengthening as has traditionally been assumed. The probability of a word's showing vowel lengthening did not crucially depend on whether or not it had an open first syllable. Rather, it seems to have depended on the position of a word on what might be called 'a scale of syllable weight'. Since the difference between words of the [re[st]en] type and words of the [ma[k]ken] type can also be expressed by reference to such a weight scale, replacing rule (1. 4(c)) on page 44 through

(16) $$p(V \rightarrow [+\text{long}]) \approx \frac{k}{(\text{weight of } \sigma)}$$

makes rule (5) on page 45 redundant as well.

4.1.3   Vowel lengthening as nucleus branching

Since I have taken the point of view that vowel quantity itself ought to be regarded as a suprasegmental, rather than as a segmental phenomenon, it follows that concepts such as 'vowel lengthening' should be given a non-linear reading as well. Thus, the process underlying OSL can be conceived as a nucleus branching process that might be represented as

(17)

Although it might seem that it does not make a difference whether one speaks of vowel lengthening or of nucleus branching, I will show that the way in which one thinks of 'vowel lengthening' can influence one's description of Middle English vowel lengthening. Interestingly, the arguments

are related to a problem which – at first sight – does not seem to be immediately related to matters of phonological organization at all.

4.1.4   The syllabic status of sonorants

As has been observed above (see page 40), the influence of sonorants on the probability of nucleus branching seems to have been rather erratic. The influence of obstruents, on the other hand, could be viewed as a straightforward reflection of their positions on the sonority scale. In fact, if it were not for the sonorants we could replace (1. 4(a) and (b)) on page 44 by a simple formula of the type

(18) $p([\bullet]_N \rightarrow [\bullet\bullet]_N) \approx k(\text{SONC})$

This could then be easily combined with formula (1. 4(c)) so that the influence of the coda of a syllable on the probability of nucleus lengthening could be summed up as

(19) $p([\bullet]_N \rightarrow [\bullet\bullet]_N) \approx k\dfrac{(\text{SONC})}{(\text{WEIGHTC})}$

Therefore it is a pity that sonorants fail to behave 'regularly' in words with stable final syllables. In order to save (19), which seems to work otherwise, one would be forced to mark words with stable final syllables and sonorants between σ_1 and σ_2 as exceptions. Of course, such a solution is deplorably *ad hoc*. Although the failure of disyllabic items with sonorant codas to follow (19) can be expressed in phonological terms, there seems to be no good reason why words containing an ambisyllabic sonorant[23] should behave as idiosyncratically as they seem to have done in the case of Middle English vowel lengthening.[24]

I will try to show, however, that there might indeed be a deeper cause for the strange behaviour of sonorants in words with stable final syllables. I will argue that it is an effect of the exceptional behaviour of sonorants within syllable structure altogether. Although the idea might appear strange at first sight, I think that vowel or nucleus lengthening failed to take place in the presence of ambisyllabic sonorants, because – in a sense – these nuclei were already long. They incorporated the postvocalic sonorants. At the same time the further vocalization of those nucleus nodes was impeded through the concomitant role sonorants had to play as onsets of the syllables to their right. Of course my suggestion is highly hypothetical and works only if one allows syllable nuclei to comprise other than purely vocalic segments, if one admits the boundary between nucleus and coda to be fuzzy rather than clear cut, and if, at the same time, one describes vowel length(ening) as a phenomenon that essentially involves both the segmental and the suprasegmental levels. In spite of all this, I hope to show that there is some plausibility to my view.

First take a closer look at rhyme structure. According to the model of syllable structure used so far, the only difference between words like

(20)   *alum* 'alum', *anet* 'anet' *anis* 'anise', *baron* 'baron', *baril* 'barrel', *barrat*
        'barrat', *barren* 'barren', *baru(h)* 'barrow', *beli* 'belly', *berie* 'berry',
        beril 'beryl', *bonnet* 'bonnet'

on the one hand, and words like

(21)   *ale* 'ale', *bale* 'bale', *bane* 'bane', *barin* 'bare', *bere* 'bear', *beren* 'bear'
        bleren 'blear', *bole* 'bole', *borin* 'bore', *care* 'care', *col* 'coal', *crane*
        'crane', *dale* 'dale', *darin* 'dare', *dene* 'dean' *derien* 'dere', *dore* 'dor',
        erien 'ear', *faren* 'fare', *fole* 'foal', *game* 'game', *geare* 'gear'

on the other, would be that in the former the codas of the first syllables were ambisyllabic (see (22a)), while in the latter they ceased to be so when the syllables were deleted (see (22b)). After that, the consonants belonged fully to the syllables to their left.

(22)   a.   b.

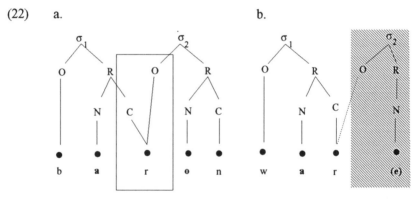

The Modern English counterparts of words of the *ware* type do not only reflect nucleus lengthening, but exhibit /r/-deletion at the same time (at least in the non-rhotic dialects). In a similar manner, the final /l/ in words such as *full* may come to be assimilated to the preceding vowel even to the point of being fully vocalized. And although a similar deletion of word-final nasals is not very common in Modern English, the process does occur in other Germanic languages (for instance in Viennese German, where you get /wãː/ for *wann*, or /schẽː/ for *schön*). Of course, these vocalizations are not contingent on the diachronic lengthenings that I am dealing with. The reason why they are brought in is that they might reveal something on the syllabic processes typical of the items in which they occur. Knowing more about these, then, might shed new light on the role which sonorants played in the syllables that showed Early Middle English nucleus lengthening.

As far as syllable structure is concerned the difference between ME *ware* and ModE *ware*, /ful/ and /fuː/, or Viennese /wãː/ and German /wan/ is that the rhymes of the words with surfacing consonants branch into nucleus and coda, while the rhymes of the words with vocalized consonants have no codas at all, but branching nuclei instead (see below).

(23)   a.   b.

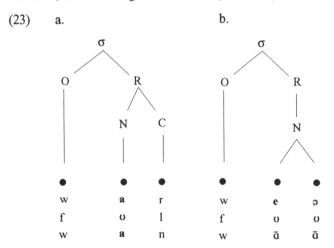

Of course, such restructurings can be regarded as secondary expressions of essentially segmental processes. The sonorants are vocalized, and since vowels cannot be codas, they are attached to nuclei instead. However, it seems to me that this view degrades syllable structure to a mere method of parsing segment strings. Therefore, I prefer to regard these restructurings as an interplay between the attraction that holds between nuclei and sonorous elements on the one hand, and the tendency of nuclei to increase the vocalicness of elements that are attached to them.

The assumption of such tendencies can be motivated both on theoretical and on empirical grounds. First, both tendencies reflect the fundamental principle of syllable organization that the centrality of a segment within a syllable is – generally speaking – a function of its sonority, and *vice versa*. In other words, the relative vocalicness or consonantality of a segment correlates to the role it plays within the syllable. A massive amount of evidence for this principle, which can be regarded as widely acknowledged, has been collected and interpreted in Vennemann 1988. The same principle is appealed to by Lass and Anderson 1975 (cf. pp. 5–9), who argue that in Old English the surface analyis of underlying /i/ and /u/ as either glides or vowels was fully dependent on syllable structure.[25]

Furthermore, examples of sonorants actually figuring as syllable nuclei are legion. Take, for example, ModE *battle*, or *bacon*, whose final consonants are syllablic. Finally, in Indo-European verbal *Ablaut*, the third class, i.e. roots with the rhyme structures VOWEL+LIQUID+CONSONANT or VOWEL+NASAL+CONSONANT, behaved in the same way as the first two classes, whose bases had DIPHTHONG (i.e.: VOWEL+VOWEL) +CONSONANT rhymes.

All this suggests that syllables of the type [Onset+V+{N/L}(+C)] might tend to be analysed as (24a) rather than as (24b)

(24)   a.   b.

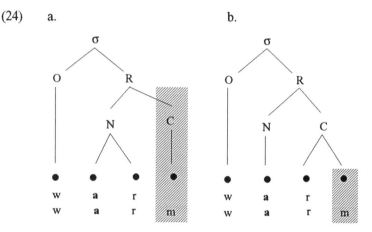

or, if one wants to express the ambivalence of the sonorant between nucleus and coda function, as

c.

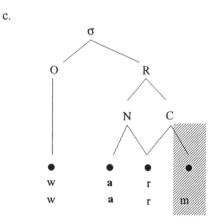

On the basis of such an analysis, then, the further vocalization of the so-norants could be understood as an adaptation of segments to the function they play within the syllable.[26] A similar principle is addressed by Ven-nemann (1988: 27),[27] and, as a matter of fact, syllabifications that are quite similar to the ones suggested above have been proposed by Anderson (1986: 75f., 100), although rather tentatively. As far as I am concerned, I can think of no better way of expressing the fact that sonorants sometimes behave more like vowels and sometimes more like consonants.

What implications does all this have for Middle English vowel lengthening, then? First, the view that vowel lengthening is the same as nucleus branching has to be modified if VOWEL+SONORANT sequences may also be represented as branched nuclei. Only those branched nuclei can be regarded as long vowels, then, that have both nodes attached to fully vocalic segments, and the process behind 'vowel lengthening' is to be viewed as

(25)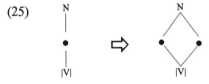

Branched nuclei involving a vocalic and a sonorant node might then be regarded as an intermediary step on one of the possible ways that may lead to vowel lengthenings. This view makes it easy to account for the fact that the presence of postvocalic sonorants in words such as the ones in (22b) in-creased the probability of vowel lengthening considerably, because the nuclei were already half-way there, so to speak.[28] The process of vocalization might then have been completed along the following lines. First, the vocalicness of the sonorant increased. This resulted in a configuration that could impressionistically and very informally be described as a long vowel with the trace of something consonantal at the end. Graphically, it might be represented as:

(26)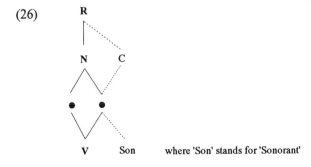

where 'Son' stands for 'Sonorant'

Such an ambiguous configuration may then be resolved in one of the following ways. Either the consonantal element gets lost altogether. Its colour may be reflected in the vowel which comes to be re-interpreted:

(27)   long monophthongs: diphthongs:

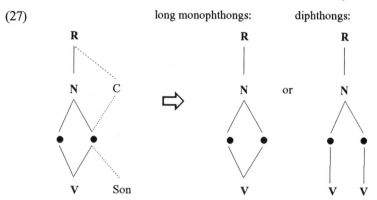

Such cases represent classical compensatory lengthenings or straight-forward vocalizations as illustrated in the Viennese examples given above, i.e. /wɑ̄ː/ for *wann*, and /schēː/ for *schön* or in /fɔɪ/ for *Fall*.

Alternatively, however, the consonantal trace may be reconstituted as a segment in its own right, detaching itself from the branched nucleus and leaving a long vowel in it.

(28)

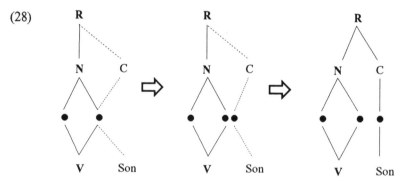

As can be seen from the OSL data, Middle English vowel lengthening has resulted in structures of the latter type.[29]

Consider then words such as EME *peril*. If they are analysed along the principles outlined for words such as ME *ware*, the postvocalic sonorants in them are not only attached to nucleus and coda nodes, but also to the onset nodes of the following syllables. Graphically, such words could be represented as in,

(29)

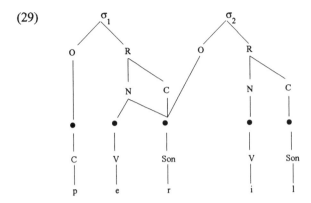

Having to fulfil a prototypically consonantal function in a stable syllable, the sonorants are not allowed to increase their inherent vocalicness at the cost of their consonantal qualities.[30] Thus, the second nucleus node cannot be attached to a fully vocalic gesture. At the same time, however, the fact that it *is* also a nucleus node prevents the nucleus from branching further, because this would create ternary branching nuclei and such structures seem to be impossible or at least strongly avoided (see Hogg and McCully 1987).

Informally speaking, one could therefore say that the sonorants resisted vocalization because they were needed as onsets. At the same time they were vocalic enough to satisfy the nucleus's desire for a second node. Thus, they prevented it from creating an epenthetic vowel, i.e. from lengthening.

4.2   The level of the foot

Syllables are not the last word in suprasegmental phonology. They are organized into higher phonological constituents, i.e. feet. A foot is normally defined as a string of one relatively strong and any number of relatively weak syllables. The syllable that is relatively strong is called the **head**. For languages such as English, 'relatively strong' means '(relatively) stressed', acoustically relatively prominent and therefore relatively easy to perceive, while 'relatively weak' means 'unstressed' and of relatively little prominence. Thus, it can be said that a foot comprises 'the space in time from the incidence of one stress-pulse up to, but not including, the next stress-pulse' (Abercrombie 1964: 11). A further property of feet in languages such as English, 'in which the *stressed* syllables occur at regular intervals' (Couper-Kuhlen 1986: 53) is that, in any given utterance, they tend to last about equally long. Thus, feet are basic units of speech rhythm.

Since, by definition, it is the leftmost syllable in a foot that is strong, while all others are weak, the structure of a foot is normally represented as

(30)[31]

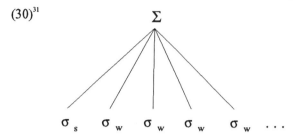

A full representation of the suprasegmental structure of a sentence such as *This is the house that Jack built* would therefore be

(31)

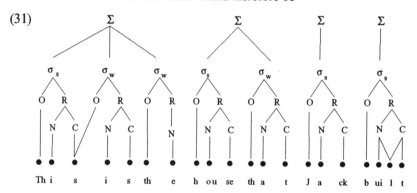

A question that is of some importance for the present study concerns the relation between feet and (morphological) wordforms, because wordforms are the data under investigation. Words and feet belong to different domains. It is both possible – as illustrated in (31) – that a foot may comprise more than one wordform, and that words (namely those with so-called secondary stress) may consist of more than one foot: cf. Hogg and McCully (1987: 85), who analyse *emigration* as in

(32)

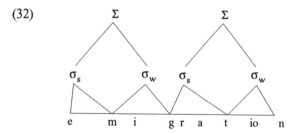

The problem of secondary stress can of course be neglected for the present purposes, because OSL candidates generally do not contain any, or at least it is agreed that if they do (such as *'nightingale*), then this is of no relevance to the quantity changes under investigation. The point that may *not* be neglected, however, is that feet are neither isomorphous nor necessarily fully contained in morphological word(form)s. Thus, Vennemann (1986) proposes that the category of the foot is completely irrelevant to word phonology and that for the analysis of (morphological) words it is enough to mark which syllable is a potential carrier of stress. This would mean that the foot is irrelevant for the purposes of this study as well. I will try to show that this argument is not waterproof.

Vennemann's observation that feet and morphological words are not im-mediately related is undeniably right in principle. One cannot object to it. For many practical purposes, however, and in particular for this study, it is almost as negligible as the theory of relativity for the description of most phenomena of everyday life. Ignore, for the sake of the argument, the fact that such words as articles, prepositions, conjunctions or *have* as a marker of the perfect aspect are significantly less likely than others to occur in stressed position. This problem aside, it can be maintained that the structure of morphological words contains ample information about the structures of the feet in which they may occur. This is particularly true of Early Middle English, where stress, and thus the position of the foot head, was dependent on the morphological structure of a word (see above, p. 56).

Consider, for example, a typical OSL candidate such as *maken* or any of its inflected forms, let us say *make*. Since the leftmost syllable in the stem is the one that will come to be stressed, the minimal foot in which *make* may figure will have the structure

(33)

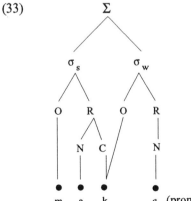

e (pronunciation of the final schwa is assumed)

Since all Early Middle English words could potentially come to figure as feet by themselves, all language-specific constraints on the structure of the smallest possible foot will have been reflected in the structure of word(form)s. Furthermore, the number of weak syllables potentially following *make* in an actual context will have been limited (cf. Anderson 1986: 110f.), so that the possible foot structures of *make* will have been

(34) $[\sigma_s\sigma_{w1}(\sigma_{w1+1})(\sigma_{w1+2})(\sigma_{w1+3})...(\sigma_{1+n})]_\Sigma$

> Where optional syllables are parenthesized and **n** stands for the greatest number of weak syllables following a word.

For words with different syllable structures the following foot structures can be assumed:

(35)   a. monosyllabics (e.g.: *child*): $[\sigma_s(\sigma_{w1})(\sigma_{w2})(\sigma_3)...(\sigma_{wn})]_\Sigma$

   b. trisyllabics (e.g.: *superne*): $[\sigma_s\sigma_{w1}\sigma_{w2}(\sigma_{w2+1})(\sigma_{w2+2})(\sigma_{w2+3})...(\sigma_{2+n})]_\Sigma$

It can be assumed that *n* will tend to be the same for most words. Therefore, when comparing words to one another, optional syllables may be neglected. Since this study *is* primarily concerned with comparisons, namely a comparison of the behaviour of different words with regard to the implementation of nucleus lengthening, the present investigations can safely be based on the minimal feet in which our items may figure. For clarity's sake, then, the data of this study will be dealt with as if they constituted integral feet in their own right.

4.2.1   The foot and vowel lengthening

I will now return to vowel lengthening. It has been known since the days of Karl Luick that the change was rather unlikely in words that tended to occur significantly more often in unstressed than in stressed positions. As Luick observed, lengthening occurred only in fully stressed, syllables, in weaker syllables shortness was preserved.[32]

In terms of foot structure this observation can be expressed as

(36)   Nucleus lengthening is more or less restricted to foot heads.

Another observation that can be expressed with reference to foot structure is that nuclei were more likely to lengthen in penultimate syllables than in antepenultimate syllables:

(37)   Nucleus lengthing was more likely in disyllabic feet than in larger feet.

This statement can in turn be extended to cover the fact that lengthening was more likely before unstable than before stable syllables, because the feet which resulted from the deletion of the final syllables were monosyllabic:

(38)   The probability of nucleus lengthing was inversely proportional to the number of weak syllables in a foot.

Furthermore, if the weak sections of feet are counted in moras (i.e. number of segments in the rhymes), rather than syllables, this statement can be further generalized to cover the relation between lengthening and the weight of final syllables as well. It can simply relate the probability of lengthening to the overall weight of the weak foot constituents:

(39)   The probability of nucleus lengthening was inversely proportional to the overall weight of the weak syllables in a foot.[33]

or

$$p([\bullet]_N \to [\bullet\bullet]_N) \approx \frac{k}{\text{WEIGHT}\,(\sigma_{w1-wn})}$$

Since the probability of lengthening depended in a similar way on the weight of the foot head itself, it might even be tempting to propose as an even more general rule that vowel lengthening was simply negatively correlated to foot weight, such as in

(40) $$p([\bullet]_N \to [\bullet\bullet]_N) \approx \frac{k}{(\text{WEIGHT})\Sigma}$$

Unfortunately, however, such a rule would be too blunt. The influence of the weight of the foot head seems to have been greater than that of the weight of the final syllable Words of the *plante* type were less likely to lengthen than words of the type *bever*, although – given the deletion of the final syllable in *plante* and my, admittedly primitive way of counting weight – both would weigh 2½ moras. Therefore, if rule (16), i.e.

$$p(V \to [+\text{long}]) \approx \frac{k}{(\text{weight of } \sigma)}$$

and (39) are to be combined, then it will have to be in a statement such as

(41) $$p([\bullet]_N \to [\bullet\bullet]_N) \approx \frac{k}{x(\text{WEIGHT } \sigma_s) + y(\text{WEIGHT}\sigma_{w1-wn})}$$

where $x > y$

5   *Summary: OSL refined*

As the previous chapter has shown, practically all of the factors governing the implementation of Middle English vowel lengthening can be thought of in scalar rather than digital terms. Their combined influence can be expressed mathematically, and the relatively complex statement of OSL as proposed in (1) and (5) in chapter 3, can be unified and rewritten as a comprehensive formula in the following way:

(1)
$$p([\bullet]_N \rightarrow [\bullet\bullet]_N) \approx k \cdot \frac{t(s\sigma) + u(\text{sonc}) + v(b_N)}{x(w\sigma s) + y(w\sigma wl \cdot wn) + z(h_N)}$$

The probability of vowel lengthening was *proportional* to
a. the (degree of) stress on it
b. its backness
c. coda sonority

and *inversely proportional* to
a. its height
b. syllable weight
c. the overall weight of the weak syllables in the foot

In this formula **t, u, v, x, y** and **z** are constants. Their values could be provided by the theoretical framework and/or by induction (= trying the formula out on actual data).[1] Obviously, this solution would be circular and can therefore not be regarded as satisfactory). However, within this study this task cannot be accomplished, and it will have to be enough for the moment to have narrowed the description of OSL down to constants at all. That their values are as yet unknown is unfortunate but cannot be helped for the time being.

s_σ is short for a syllable's status within foot structure, or, in other words, for the stress of the syllable in question. I assume that its values can be either 1 or 0, depending on whether a syllable is a foot head or not. Stress, or headship, appears to be the only quasi-digital parameter governing Middle English vowel lengthening.[2]

sonc stands for coda sonority. As was shown above, the fact that liquids and nasals practically block nucleus lengthening is not directly related to coda sonority, but is a disturbing side effect of their special status in syllable structure.

$w(\sigma_s)$ stands for the weight of the strong syllable, and

$w(\{\sigma_{w1\text{-}wn}\})$ for the combined weight of all weak syllables in the foot.

h_N and b_N stand for the height and the backness of the nucleus respectively. In fact, it may be possible to subsume the two under a single factor, since the allophones of front vowels have always had a greater tendency towards height than their back counterparts (take, for instance, the asymmetry of the Great Vowel Shift, or the position of ModE short /o/ as against that of short /e/). It is difficult to say, however, what this common factor should be. Both sonority and vowel height (governing 'inherent vowel length') suggest themselves, and without phonetic data it is probably impossible to make a reasonable decision. Therefore, within this study, the two parameters will be treated as separate.

5.1   Qualitative side effects of Middle English vowel lengthening

Quantity changes are the main concern here. However, one cannot avoid dealing with vowel quality as well, if a change of quantity causes, goes hand in hand with, or, generally speaking, is closely related to a quality change. Middle English (Open) Syllable Lengthening seems to have been a case in point. As Rochelle Lieber (1979: 7) puts it, 'Short, high vowels in open syllables merged with original long midvowels; short midvowels in open syllables, with original long, low vowels. Short, low vowels in open syllables merely lengthened.' 'Merging', in this statement, means that articulatory targets became identical. Thus, before the change in question, the pronunciations of the vowels in words such as OE *guma* 'man' and OE *dōm* 'judgement' would differ not only in relative timing, but also with regard to the intended tongue position (it would be distinctively lower for *do:m* than for *guma*). After the change (which we have called 'lengthening'), however, both the timing difference *and* the difference in intended tongue position would be removed, so that the targets underlying the pronunciations of the vowels *gome* and *dome* would be identical.[3] It is in this sense that OE /u/ in open syllables **merged** with OE long /oː/.

Since a similar thing happened to the other vowels as well, one might argue that Middle English Open Syllable Lengthening was a complex sound shift that changed both the length and the height of vowels, rather than a mere lengthening. The only exception was /a/, which could not be lowered for the simple reason that it was already maximally low. A picture of the correspondences is given in the following diagram:

(2)

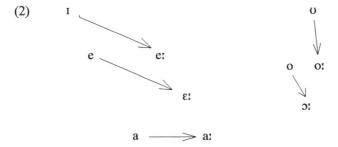

Of course, instead of assuming a single process affecting both the length and the articulatory gesture of vowels in open syllables, one can say that vowels in open syllables were lengthened *and* lowered. In that case one would have to deal with the question which of the two processes occurred first and whether there were items that were affected just by one but not by the other. (This is what we would have to expect, actually, since we have seen that processes do not affect all words equally in all intralinguistic and extralinguistic contexts.)

However, the mergers referred to by Lieber might also be accounted for without assuming a lowering process at all. Thus, if one prefers the idea that Middle English Vowel Lengthening was a pure lengthening, one can argue that the long vowels were simultaneously undergoing a raising. This would mean that the tongue height of the vowels with which the products of Middle English Open Syllable Lengthening merged was the same as that of the short vowels that were lengthened. Although the original long vowels might have been lower at some earlier stage, they had been raised one level by the time the mergers took place. This interpretation is illustrated in the diagram in (3):

(3)   lengthening

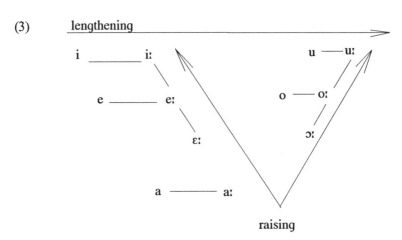

raising

One argument that speaks for this interpretation (proposed by Stockwell (1985) in a slightly different form) is that English long vowels have indeed been showing a tendency towards raising ever since the Middle English period, as it witnessed by the processes known as the 'Great Vowel Shift'. However, the same argument can also be turned against this interpretation, because there is no general agreement at all that the processes eventually leading to the Great Vowel Shift had already started at the time when Middle English vowel lengthening was being implemented.

Within the scope of this study I will not be able to express any definite views on that controversy. As Lieber states

there is absolutely nothing in the synchronic facts of thirteenth-century Middle English to choose between [the two types of analysis]. Each ... is based on an interpretation of the ... facts that is equally consistent with all the evidence about Lengthening in Open Syllables we have. (1979: 22)

What I have found out about Middle English vowel lengthening so far, however, suggests that it was very strongly determined by suprasegmental phenomena such as syllable weight, foot weight and isochrony. It could even be argued that these factors, in a certain way, 'explain' Middle English vowel lengthening. The same factors could not account for a change of quality, however. This suggests that a potential lowering process might not have been as closely related to the lengthening process as an analysis along the lines of diagram (2) implies.

Furthermore, if one interprets language change as a complex event in which both production and reception play a role, an explanation of the mergers offers itself that depends neither on the assumption that the Great

Vowel Shift started 250 years earlier than has ever before been assumed nor on the rather *ad hoc* introduction of a lowering process. One view of the development of English vowels is that by the end of the twelfth century a tense-lax distinction had come to be introduced into the phonology of Middle English in such a way that all short vowels were systematically laxer than their long counterparts and long vowels tenser than their lax counterparts. One way of describing this would be to say that Middle English contained a rule by which all long vowels were made tense.[4] A tense vowel is *eo ipso* more peripheral than a corresponding lax vowel. Thus, in order to pronounce a tense /e/, for example, one tends to raise one's tongue higher and to push it further forward than when one pronounces a lax /e/. And the same is true of all other vowels except maybe /a/ – of which it is not clear whether it admits of a tense-lax opposition at all.[5]

Now, it can be assumed that Middle English vowel lengthening started as a postlexical phonological process, responding to (if not triggered by) the suprasegmental factors discussed above. Thus, its outputs will not have been affected by the tensing rule, because the latter would be thought of as a prelexical rule expressing a phonotactic well-formedness condition. However, the tensing rule being part of prelexical phonology, the outputs of Middle English vowel lengthening may have been interpreted as being affected by it as well. Therefore, a long /ɪː/, for example, may easily have been interpreted as going back to a long vowel that was tensed rather than a short vowel that was lengthened. The long vowel that could have been the input of a tensing rule whose output was /ɪː/ was a close /eː/. And this is exactly what lengthened /ɪ/ came to be re-interpreted as. In the same manner, all the outputs of Middle English vowel lengthening could easily be ('wrongly') interpreted as the outputs of a tensing rule applying on a less peripheral (i.e. lower) underlying vowel: thus, /eː/ came to be re-interpreted as a tensed /ɛː/, /oː/ as a tensed /ɔː/, and /ʊː/ as a tensed /oː/. Only /aː/ was not re-interpreted in this manner, because /aː/ could not be derived through tensing.

Although I lack positive evidence in much the same way as all other linguists who have dealt with the apparent lowering that accompanied Middle English vowel lengthening, it seems to me that this is by far the most economic explanation of the notorious mergers. That it has not become the standard view is strange since it was first publicly proposed by Robert Stockwell as early as 1961. Actually, neglecting minor differences in the interpretation of phonetic detail, the only essential difference between his account and the one given here is that Stockwell does not make the distinction between synchronic processes and their historical implementations in the way I do. Otherwise, my interpretation is very much in line with Stockwell's. Anyway, as far as this study is concerned, I shall continue to regard Middle English vowel lengthening as a simple lengthening process and assume that it was not accompanied by any quality changes at all.

6 Homorganic Lengthening

6.1 Introduction

As follows from what has been said so far, this chapter will not simply describe the diachronic correspondences normally referred to as lengthening of vowels before homorganic consonant clusters. Rather, it will focus on their relation to the lengthenings discussed in chapter 1, and pursue the question whether HOL and OSL can be regarded as one great quantity change or whether they represented essentially different phenomena. If the data normally accounted for through HOL turn out to be compatible with the generalizations inherent to formula (1) of chapter 5, this will be taken to mean that there was indeed only one change. Should they turn out incompatible, however, it will have to be accepted that OSL and HOL were separate sound changes in their own right and that no unified account is possible. The hypothesis that formula (1) of chapter 5 'predicts' all Early Middle English quantity changes will then be regarded as falsified.

The description of HOL will be carried out along the same lines as that of OSL. With the help of the *Oxford Etymological Dictionary* a list of more than 200 potential inputs that have survived into Modern English has been drawn up.[1] It gives a representative view of the long-term implementation (that is to say, the constraints) of the process in question (see appendix II). The list has then been subjected to a similar kind of analysis as the Minkova corpus.

In its widest interpretation, Homorganic Lengthening was a process by which short vowels were lengthened, if they were followed by clusters of two consonants. The first of these consonants had to be a sonorant (that is to say, a liquid or a nasal: /r/, /l/, /n/, /m/, /ŋ/), and the second a voiced stop. The stop had to be articulated at roughly the same place as the preceding sonorant. If the sonorant was /r/, the second cluster element could also be a voiced fricative or a nasal (see Luick 1914/21: 242; Campbell 1968; Pilch 1970; Beade 1975, Anderson and Jones 1977; Phillips 1981; Hubmayer

81

1986). The process is assumed to have been responsible for correspondences such as the ones between the items in the left- and the right-hand columns in the following table

(1) **Pre-HOL** **Post-HOL**

	Pre-HOL	Post-HOL
ld:	cild	cīld
	feld	fēld
	gold	gōld
	geldan	gēldan
rd:	word	wōrd
	sword	swōrd
mb:	climban	clīmban
	cemban	cēmban
	dumb	dūmb
nd:	behindan	behīndan
	ende	ēnde
	hund	hūnd
ng:	singan	sīngan
	lang	lāng
	tunge	tūnge
rl:	eorl	ēorl
rn:	stiorne	stīorne
	georn	gēorn
	korn	kōrn
	murnan	mūrnan
rð:	eorðe	ēorðe
	weorðe	wēorðe
	wyrðe	wȳrðe
	furðor	fūrðor
rs:	earsas	ēarsas

It is assumed that the process affected the English language about 400 years before Middle English Open Syllable Lengthening. The main reason for this is the fact that in certain Anglo-Saxon manuscripts from that period the vowels in question were marked with diacritic signs that normally indicated length (see e.g. Jones 1989: 30). Other arguments for this dating are based on the relation of Homorganic Lengthening to other changes such as the 'lowerings' that are assumed to have occurred in connection with Middle English Open Syllable Lengthening. (Vowels lengthened by Homorganic Lengthening did not undergo any such 'lowering', which can be taken to mean that they were already long when the 'lowering' took place.)

I shall not go into the problem of absolute chronology, because within an investigation of the long-term effects of sound changes, as carried out here, it does not play a significant role. Since it cannot be completely ignored, because it seems to represent a strong argument against the assumption that HOL and OSL were one and the same change, I shall show below that the traditionally assumed chronologies are not at all waterproof. For the present, I shall give a time-neutral description of HOL and its relation to OSL.

6.2   The format of the process

The nuclei that resulted from HOL and OSL were fully vocalic and branching in both cases. As to the input to the change, the vowels of HOL candidates were by definition followed by sonorants. Sticking to my analysis of such configurations (see above p. 66), the nuclei of HOL inputs are to be conceived as branching, with vowels as first and sonorants as second nodes.

(2)

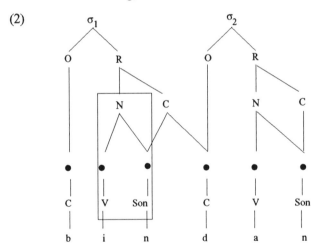

Since this type of nucleus is also found among OSL inputs (cf. above, (24) and (29) of chapter 4), it does not constitute an essential difference between HOL and OSL.

6.3   The constraints on the process

6.3.1   Foot structure
HOL was restricted to foot heads in the same way as OSL, so that the prediction

(3) $p([\bullet]_N \to [\bullet\bullet]_N) \approx k(s\sigma)$

is borne out by the HOL data.

One of the most powerful factors in the implementation of OSL was the stability of the final syllable. Also – as table 6.1 shows – the long-term implementation of HOL reflects similar constraints. The traditional description of HOL differs from that of OSL, of course, in so far as HOL does admit monosyllabic inputs. Since these merge eventually with disyllables with unstable final syllables, I have decided not to keep the two apart but to subsume them in a common category of items that are monosyllabic in Modern English.

Table 6.1 *HOL and foot structure*

	Vowel in Modern English				
	Total	**Long**	**%**	**Short**	**%**
all	218	107	49	111	51
Σ:[σ]	176	93	53	83	47
Σ:[σσ(σ)]	42	14	33	28	67

Also in this respect, then, HOL can be regarded as equal to OSL, since the prediction

(4) $p([\bullet]_N \to [\bullet\bullet]_N) \approx \dfrac{k}{(w\sigma wl - wn)}$

is as valid for the implementation of HOL as for that of OSL.

6.3.2   The weight of the strong syllable
At first sight it would seem that the role which syllable weight played in the implementation of HOL differed considerably from the one that it played in connection with OSL. There, syllables that contained more than one ambisyllabic consonant in their codas were extremely unlikely to be lengthened, even if – as in the case of words of the type [re[st]en] – whole coda clusters were ambisyllabic. The syllable structure of a typical HOL candidate, such as OE *bindan*, would have been [bin[d]an]. Its first syllable would thus weigh 2½ moras – and for syllables of that weight the rules

derived from OSL predict lengthening to be as good as impossible. This seems indeed to imply a crucial difference between the two sound changes. It contradicts the hypothesis that HOL and OSL were one change and is in line with the traditional analysis, where syllables lengthened by OSL were regarded as open and syllables lengthened by HOL as essentially closed.

However, it was suspected by Karl Luick himself that the behaviour of the rhyme structures of HOL candidates was peculiar with regard to such matters as syllable weight, or timing. Recently Luick's suspicion came to be corroborated by – basically – phonetic evidence. Such was found, for instance, in a study (by Herbert) of the origin of prenasalized stops in certain African and Austronesian languages. There, tautosyllabic clusters containing a sonorant and a voiced stop have a strong tendency to simplification, i.e. they become prenasalized stops. As Herbert (1986: 61) shows, this is due to the fact that homorganic clusters tend not to consume more time in articulation than single consonants do. Although it would of course be absurd to argue that Old English should have had prenasalized consonant phonemes, it is not at all implausible to assume that phonetically the same shortenings (which, as Herbert notes, are based on the way articulatory hardware works and can thus be assumed to apply rather generally) happened. If syllable weight is regarded as a matter of timing, the special status of homorganic clusters with respect to timing might be mirrored in their suprasegmental representation, for example, by letting those clusters share a single mora. Such a weight reduction rule could be represented as:

(5)

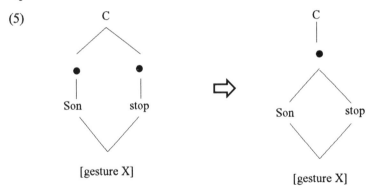

It would reduce the syllable weight of words of the *bindan* type by one mora to 1½ moras. Of such syllables rule (1) of chapter 5 says that they were relatively likely to be lengthened, of course.[2] At the same time the suprasegmental structure of the rhymes that are generated by this process of 'coda reduction' is identical to that of the rhymes for which traditionally OSL has been assumed, and which favour lengthening. This demonstrates that syllable structure is not necessarily an argument for keeping HOL apart from OSL. Rather, it can be argued that the weight-based constraints that governed the implementation of lengthening were the same in both cases.

Given the analysis just suggested, HOL could be considered to comply with

(6) $$p([\bullet]_N \to [\bullet\bullet]_N) \approx \frac{k}{(w\sigma s)}$$

6.3.3   Coda sonority

The codas of typical HOL inputs were by definition highly sonorous. That they should have favoured vowel lengthening is therefore correctly predicted by rule (1) of chapter 5. As far as sonority differences between the eight cluster types are concerned, the data do not really allow any conclusions on whether or not they had any influence. As table 6.2 shows, the picture is rather confusing, and the various cluster types seem to have influenced the implementation of lengthening in what looks like an unpredictable manner:

Table 6.2 *HOL and cluster type*

	mb	nd	ng	ld	rd	rz	rð	rn	rl
a	0/1[a]	0/12	0/11	8/9	8/8	NA[b]	NA	2/2	3/3
e	0/1	0/6	0/8	5/11	6/6	NA	1/1	10/10	3/3
o	2/2	0/2	0/16	4/4	6/6	NA	2/2	4/4	NA
i	1/2	11/15	0/16	3/8	6/6	NA	NA	2/2	NA
u	1/3	10/16	0/14	1/2	3/3	3/3	1/1	6/6	1/1

Notes: [a] read: zero out of one. [b] NA= not attested

Still, if one wishes to see things that way, the prediction that (1) in chapter 5 makes on the impact of coda sonority seems to be borne out by the HOL data. On a sonority scale the clusters would be ordered as in

(7)   ŋg
                   nd   rd   rz
                   mb   ld   rð   rn   rl

      + $\longleftarrow$ |――――|――――|――――|――――| $\longrightarrow$ _

Table 6.2 shows that of the items with nasal + stop clusters 25 per cent are lengthened in Modern English, while items with /ld/ clusters show up with long vowels in 60 per cent of all cases, and items with clusters that contained /r/ all have branching nuclei today.

Of course, it would be holistic to the extent of over-simplicity to claim that the implementation of HOL was a straightforward reflection of coda sonority. In particular, the fact that vowels before what once were clusters beginning with /r/ are long in Modern Standard English is generally regarded as having been brought about by an Early Modern English process of /r/-vocalization, which obscured the implementation of HOL to such a considerable extent that in this special case Modern English data shed as good as no light on the implementation of earlier lengthening processes.

Nevertheless, it can be maintained that the way in which coda sonority influenced the implementation of HOL is not in contradiction to its effects on the other Early Middle English lengthenings.

6.3.4 Vowel quality

Table 6.3 *HOL and vowel quality*

	mb	nd	ng	ld	rd	rz	rð	rn	rl
a	0/1[a]	0/10	0/8	7/7	8/8	NA[b]	NA	2/2	2/2
e	NA	0/6	0/6	5/9	6/6	NA	1/1	9/9	2/2
o	2/2	0/2	0/8	4/4	5/5	NA	1/1	4/4	NA
i	1/1	11/12	0/14	3/6	4/4	NA	NA	1/1	NA
u	1/2	9/9	0/13	0/2	1/1	3/3	NA	6/6	NA

Notes: [a] read: zero out of one. [b] NA= not attested

As table 6.3 – which includes only items with stable second syllables – indicates, the influence of vowel quality on the implementation of Homorganic Lengthening seems to have been as complex as the influence of coda sonority. More disturbingly, a generalized view of the influence of vowel quality seems even to be at odds with (rather than supportive of) the predictions inherent in formula (1) of chapter 5.

Table 6.4 *Cluster type and vowel height*

	Long in Modern English			
	mb(%)	nd(%)	ld(%)	Total(%)
high	50	95	44	53
mid	100	0	69	60
low	0	0	100	47

The influence of vowel quality on the implementation of HOL seems to have depended strongly on what type of cluster followed the vowel. Nasal clusters seem to have favoured lengthening of high vowels and disfavoured that of low vowels, while /ld/ clusters seem to have behaved exactly the other way round. This type of interrelation is a problem with which I shall deal in greater detail. Before that, however, a first summary of the observations made so far is in order.

6.3.5   A first summary

Vowel quality aside, the implementations of HOL and OSL show that the two appear indeed to have been brought about by the same type of process and constrained by the same factors. This, in turn, strongly suggests that the two sound changes might be regarded as a single one. It might simply be called Middle English vowel lengthening.

However, there are a few problems with this view. For instance, the fact that vowel quality does not seem to have influenced the implementation of HOL as (1) in chapter 5 would predict needs to be explained. Similarly, one would need an explanation for the fact that there are such apparently unsystematic differences in the ways in which Homorganic Lengthening was inplemented before the different cluster types. On more basic levels, finally, one will have to explain why the long vowel phonemes produced by HOL did not merge with the same phonemes with which the outputs of OSL merged and why HOL was reflected in writing 400 years earlier than Middle English Open Syllable Lengthening was assumed to have taken place.

6.4   Problems for a unified view of HOL and OSL

6.4.1   Idiosyncrasies in the influence of cluster types on the implementation of vowel lengthening.

If the fact is left aside that /r/ vocalization produced long nuclei in all words that once had /rC/ clusters, tables 6.2 and 6.4 reveal that HOL seems to have been implemented to very different degrees even among the rest of po-tential inputs. The differences seem to be related to the specific nature of the clusters. Thus, HOL was practically not implemented at all before /ng/ clusters, rarely before /mb/ clusters, but rather frequently before clusters having /d/ as their final components.

If one wants to explain these differences, it should first be recalled that lengthening in HOL items involved two types of rhyme restructuring: on the one hand, HOL created branching nuclei that were fully vocalic – this constituted the 'lengthening' proper; on the other hand, however, HOL also involved – at some level – a reduction of the coda to a single mora. Thus, it may have generated structures representing something that could be described as 'a long vocalic nucleus plus a short (i.e. monomoric) consonantal offset, which contained a nasal and a plosive component'. (See diagram (8) below.) Those structures could, theoretically, have been resolved in more than one way. First, the coda could be interpreted as containing a (pre-)nasalized stop. Obviously, this possibility must be ruled out for English.

(8)

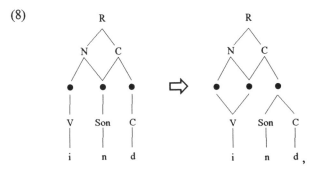

Second, 'epenthetic lengthening' could have taken place. The process is illustrated in

(9)

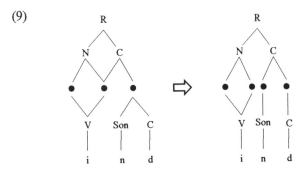

Informally speaking, it creates a new mora to replace the one that has been robbed by the nucleus. Nasality and stop occupy a mora each, so that, from the point of view of the coda, the original situation is restored. The third possibility, then, would have been 'compensatory lengthening'. In this process, the mora that the coda has lost to the nucleus is not replaced. Since the coda remains monomoraic and prenasalized stops are ruled out, either the sonorant or the stop gesture are deleted. This is illustrated in (10):

(10)

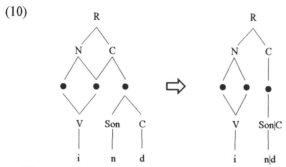

What seems to have happened in the case of HOL was epenthesis. Crucially, however, the outputs of this epenthesis were in conflict with certain tendencies that had come to determine the shape of English syllables. As Hogg and McCully (1987: 47) show, rhymes that contain four elements are not generally possible in Modern English. Rather, they are only allowed if the final position is 'filled by a [+coronal] obstruent'. Although Hogg and McCully concede that before the time of Chaucer other types of sound might have occurred in that position as well, it is plausible to assume that processes deleting all but coronal elements in that context already operated in Middle English. The reason why coronal obstruents were not deleted there was probably that the 'analogy with inflected forms such as *weaned*' (Hogg and McCully 1987: 47).

As I would like to argue, this explains part of the apparently unsystematic relation between HOL implementation and cluster type. Structures produced by (9) coincided with a well-established syllable structure only if the final position was taken by a coronal obstruent, as in /ld/ and /nd/ clusters. Clusters that ended in other sounds had become very infrequent and were on the way to dying out. It is hardly surprising, therefore, that /nd/ and /ld/ clusters favoured the implementation of lengthening to a greater degree than other clusters.

It is easy to conclude, then, that lengthening before /mb/ clusters would have been implemented only rarely. It is equally clear why it was accompanied or followed by a deletion of the final /b/. What still remains to be explained, however, is why no lengthened nuclei at all have survived before /ng/ clusters, because the observations just made imply that they ought to have behaved in a similar way as /mb/ clusters. There is a factor, though, which made the implementation of lengthening before /g/ clusters particularly improbable. It was the fact that Middle English did not have /ŋ/ as a(n underlying) phoneme. Therefore, underlying /ng/ clusters would always be recoverable, if – in actual pronunciation – they came to be simplified to velar nasals. Crucially, the same would not have been the case with simplified /mb/ or /nd/ clusters. These would simply merge with /n/ and /m/. A rhyme that was realized in such a way that it could be interpreted as deriving from either underlying VVC or VCC would therefore always have been interpreted as the latter if its consonantal part was /ŋ/. In other words, all /Vŋ/ sequences that were too long for being just two segments were analysed as /Vng/ rather than /VVŋ/ This explains why lengthening before /ng/ clusters was ruled out altogether.

Thus, the strange behaviour of the different cluster types with regard to vowel lengthening did not have anything to do with the lengthening process as such. Rather, it had independent reasons and does not, in my view, provide good grounds for separating lengthenings through HOL from lengthenings through OSL.

6.4.2   Vowel height

As shown in table 6.4, the lengthening of high vowels occurred much more often than (1) of chapter 5 predicts. This represents another aspect in which the HOL data are at odds with the generalized Vowel Lengthening Rule I am proposing. If the latter is to be saved, this behaviour of (some) inputs to HOL also has to be explained in a way which is independent of the lengthening process behind it.

Above, I have proposed that the lengthening of vowels before homorganic clusters can be understood as the establishment of a connection between a vocalic articulatory gesture and a suprasegmental node originally attached to a nasal/liquid gesture.

(11)

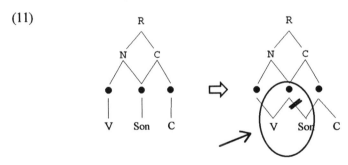

In a way, this process can be compared to monophthogization, and thus to assimilation. It is a general principle, however, that the tendency towards assimilation between segments is the stronger, the greater the similarity between the involved segments. Since the point at which the clusters /mb/

and /nd/ are articulated is closer to the points at which high vowels are articulated, this principle explains why nasal clusters should have favoured branching of /i/ and /u/ more than that of /a/. Therefore, the fact that there is a surprisingly great proportion /i/s and /u/s that show up as long before nasal clusters is not necessarily an argument against regarding HOL and OSL as one and the same sound change either.

6.4.3   Why /i/ and /u/ did not lower when lengthened before homorganic clusters

The final phonological argument for keeping HOL and OSL apart is that vowels that were lengthened before homorganic clusters did not merge with the same vowels as the outputs of OSL did. Again, it can be shown, however, that the factors which might have caused this discrepancy were principally independent of the vowel lengthening itself. First, nasals have always had a tendency to raise preceding vowels. Thus, a nasal raising rule accounts for the root vowel in class IIIa strong verbs, such as OE *bindan* as against class IV verbs such as OE *beran* (see e.g. Jones 1972: 80). Furthermore, the immediate neighbourhood of grave (or in terms of dependency phonology: *u*-coloured) elements makes palatal elements increase their *i*-colour (e>e, e>ɪ, ɪ>i,...) (cf. Donegan 1979: 91ff.). Since the mergers of lengthening products with underlyingly 'lower' phonemes might have been due to a rule tensing (and thus peripheralizing) the latter but not the former, such mergers must clearly have been prevented by processes peripheralizing the former as well. There is good reason to assume that HOL inputs were indeed affected by processes that peripheralized them, and therefore the absence of the mergers that are so typical of OSL is no argument against keeping the two lengthenings apart.

6.4.4   Chronology

The last argument for treating HOL and OSL separately is absolute chronology. It is, of course, of minor importance given the approach that I have taken, but – as observed above – one cannot completely dismiss it. Recall, however, that the chronology of sound changes is notoriously uncertain, especially when vowel quantity is concerned. It seems to be generally advisable, therefore, to treat with caution the datings that have been passed down from the Neogrammarians. For instance, a typical argument normally given for dating OSL 400 years after HOL is that in Old English manuscripts of the ninth century length markers (similar to acute accents) occasionally appeared on vowels before homorganic clusters – while such markers were absent in open syllables. However, this fact can also be explained on the assumption that HOL and OSL took place at roughly the same time. If vowels tended to be pronounced longer in open syllables, scribes and readers could assume by default that a vowel that had only one consonant (or perhaps, *st*) after it, would be pronounced long. Therefore, its length did not have to be marked graphically. Crucially, however, homorganic clusters would not serve as indicators of vowel length in the same way, because they were written as two consonant symbols. If, as I am assuming, they counted as single segments for purposes of timing and rhythm, homorganic clusters would be exceptions to the general assumption mentioned above, and therefore their length would need to be graphically marked. It might therefore be argued that the accents which can be found in Late Old English manuscripts point to the simultaneity of OSL and HOL rather than to the opposite. At least, it seems justified to argue that the appearance of diacritic markers cannot be accepted as conclusive evidence for assuming HOL to have occurred 400 years before OSL.

6.5   Conclusion

It appears, therefore, that formula (1) of chapter 5 can indeed be taken to cover both HOL and OSL data. All lengthenings of Middle English vowels can be regarded as instances of one and the same process of Middle English Vowel Lengthening.

7 Shortenings

7.1 Introduction

Like the chapter on HOL, this chapter has a double purpose. First, it describes two sets of diachronic correspondences between vowels that have traditionally been regarded as separate sound changes in their own right, namely **Trisyllabic Shortening** and **Shortening before Consonant Clusters**. Second, and more importantly, their relatedness to the changes just discussed will be investigated. What will be shown is that both Middle English Vowel Lengthening and the two shortenings can be understood as instances of a single tendency, which might most appropriately be called **Early Middle English Quantity Adjustment**.

The process behind vowel shortenings can be thought of as symmetrical with the one behind lengthenings. In a comparison of the two process types one can assume that the effect which a constraint had on one will be inverse to that which it had on the other. In other words, what favours lengthening can be assumed to disfavour shortening and *vice versa*.

For the present purposes this means that if the two shortenings with which this chapter deals should turn out to mirror Middle English Vowel Lengthening both with regard to the underlying process types and with regard to the constraints on their implementations, we shall say that all changes in question – lengthenings as well as shortenings – deserve to be subsumed under a single label. I shall therefore try to show whether a reversed version of formula (1) of chapter 5, i.e.

(1)
$$p([\bullet\bullet]_N \to [\bullet]_N) \approx k\,\frac{x(W\sigma_s) + y(W\sigma_{wl \cdot wm}) + z(h_N)}{t(s\sigma) + u(\text{sonc}) + v(b_N)}$$

The probability of vowel shortening was **proportional** to
a. its height
b. syllable weight
c. the overall weight of the weak syllables in the foot

95

and **inversely proportional** to
a. the (degree of) stress on it
b. its backness
c. coda sonority

makes correct predictions with regard to the implemenations of SHOCC and TRISH.

As mentioned above (see pp. 1ff.), the idea that the Early Middle English vowel shortenings and contemporary lengthenings were related has a long history. It might therefore be in order to highlight a few of the differences between traditional views of this relation and my own approach.

First, I do not merely assume that diachronic implementations of lengthening on the one hand and shortening on the other may have conspired on some level to make vowel length fully dependent on the phonological environment. Rather, I want to go as far as to say that – for the purpose of diachrony – all lengthenings and shortenings may indeed be regarded as one single change, which might be called Middle English Quantity Adjustment[1] and could be formalized as in

(2)
$$p([\bullet\bullet]_N \to [\bullet]_N) \approx \frac{k}{p([\bullet]_N \to [\bullet\bullet]_N)} \approx l\frac{x(w\sigma_s) + y(w\sigma_{wl \cdot wn}) + z(hN)}{t(s\sigma) + u(\text{sonc}) + v(bN)}$$

The other point follows from the assumption that an environment that favours lengthening will constrain shortening – and *vice versa*, of course. Thus, if a large number of syllables in a foot make it unlikely that the head of such a foot gets lengthened if short, then it must be expected that they will increase the probability of a long foot head's being shortened. Many cases will be more complicated than that, of course, because there are more than one parameter on which the probability of lengthening (and thus shortening) in Early Middle English seems to have depended. Thus, it is perfectly conceivable that foot heads should occur in environments that favour foot head length in some respects and disfavour it in others. This would have been the case if, for example, a foot head was a high vowel (which disfavoured lengthening), but occurred before an unstable syllable (which favoured lengthening). Another such situation would occur, for example, if a nucleus was followed by a coda that consisted of just one ambisyllabic consonant (which would favour lengthening), but the next syllable was very heavy (which would favour shortening).

Many contemporary theories of language change operate with the concept of phonological environments triggering language changes. Language change is then described by rules of the type

(3) $X \rightarrow Y/\_\_Z$

so that an environment can either trigger a change or not. Apart from the fact that such models have great problems when it comes to 'exceptions' (see above pp. 13ff.), the possibility that in (practically) identical environments both (diachronic) lengthenings and shortenings of vowels should occur would be difficult to accommodate. Within the approach taken in this study, on the other hand, phonological environments are not regarded as triggers of phonological processes. Rather, they may favour the implementation of processes to a greater or lesser extent, while being principally independent of them.[2] Thus, formulas such as (2) make it possible to order items on scales according to the extent to which they favour/disfavour the implementation of a process. On the asssumption that symmetrical processes such as vowel lengthening and vowel shortening will be constrained by environmental factors in exactly reverse ways, the respective scales can be collapsed into a single one, as shown in the following diagram.

(4)

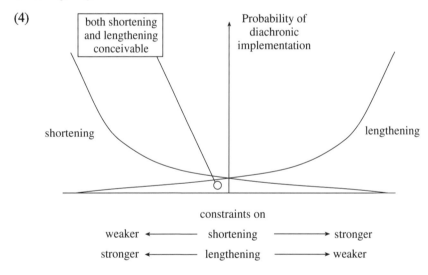

Thus, it is perfectly conceivable within my approach that there should be environments in which – diachronically speaking – both lengthenings and shortenings came to be implemented, although such cases will be relatively rare. It will be shown below, however, that such environments seem to have existed and that a probabilistic approach such as the one taken here can handle them better than a non-probabilistic one.

7.2   The standard accounts

The acknowledged view is that Trisyllabic Shortening affected long vowels if they were in antepenultimate syllables of wordforms, while Shortening before Consonant Clusters shortened vowels if they were followed by clusters of more than one consonant (homorganic clusters and such clusters as could function as syllable onsets being excepted).

Luick (1914/21) describes the changes in the following way.

[Es] trat Verkürzung in allen Fällen ein, in denen ein Vokal vor zwei oder mehr Konsonanten stand. (p. 324)

[Es] wurden nun lange Vokale vor einfachen Konsonanten und den Konsonanten-verbindungen, die sonst Länge begünstigten, in Dreisilbern gekürzt. (p. 392)

He gives the following examples:

(5)   **Shortening before Consonant Clusters** (cf. pp. 324ff. and 392)

kepte	'kept'
læfde	'let'
brohte	'brought'
sohte	'sought'
þuhte	'thought'
demde	'deemed'
cyþde	'announced'
mette	'met'
hatte	'called' (Gmn *heißen*)
lædde	'led'
sprædde	'spread (past)'
bledde	'bled'
fedde	'fed'
hydde	'hid'
softe	'soft'
fifta	'fifth'
leoht	'light'
hihþu	'height'
æht	'property'
dust	'dust'
jrist	'corn'
blæst	'blast'
breost	'breast'
fyst	'fist'

mist	'mist'
druhþ	'drought'
clænsian	'cleanse'
halja	'holy (man), saint'
mædd	'mad'
fætt	'fat'
wræþþo	'wrath'
cyþþo	'kin'
feoll	'fell'
fifti3	'fifty'
twenti3	'twenty'
bledsian	'bless'
wisdom	'wisdom'
wifman	'woman'
hlæfdi3e	'lady'
3osling	'gosling'
ceapman	'chapman'
ceapfaru	'trade'
nehhebur	'neighbour'
siknesse	'sickness'

Trisyllabic Shortening (cf. Luick 1914/21: 328f. and 392f.)

heafodu PL	'head'
hryþeru PL	'cattle'
cicenu PL	'chicken'
linenes GEN	'linen'
wiþi3as PL	'willow'
æni3e PL	'any'
ærende	'errand'
æmette	'ant'
suþerne	'southern'
westenne DAT	'waste (desert)'
deorlingas PL	'darling'
feorþin3as PL	'farthing'
feowerti3	'forty'
freondscipe	'friendship'
hali3da3	'holiday'
alderman	'alderman'
heringes PL	'herring'
stiropes PL	'stirrup'
Monendai	'Monday'
Thuresday	'Thursday'
seliness	'silliness'
redili	'readily'

bretheren PL	'brethren'
evere	'ever'
othere ACC	'other'
redeles PL	'riddle'
boseme ACC	'bosom'
wepenes PL	'weapon'

The changes traditionally thought to account for the correspondences can be represented as

(6)   **Shortening before Consonant Clusters**
$$V \rightarrow [-\text{long}]/\_\_\text{CCX},$$
where CC is not a homorganic cluster

Trisyllablic Shortening
$$V \rightarrow [+\text{long}]/\_\_\_\text{C(C)}\sigma\sigma$$

7.3   TRISH, SHOCC and the constraints on vowel quantity adjustments

It follows from the very definitions of TRISH and SHOCC that the correspondences for which they stand are in keeping with the predictions that can be derived from (2).[3] Therefore, their relatedness to OSL has hardly ever been disputed. I will support this point in detail in the following sections.

7.3.1   Weight-based constraints

The prediction that vowels would be shortened in antepenultimate syllables of words is handled by the statement that the probability of a nucleus's being shortened is proportional to the overall weight of the weak syllables in a foot. Similarly, the statement that the probability of nucleus shortening is proportional to the weight of the affected syllable predicts that vowels would tend to be shortened before consonant clusters.

As far as SHOCC is concerned, it furthermore seems that the final syllable behaved exactly as one would predict from the role it played with regard to Middle English Vowel Lengthening. Thus, the percentage of items reflecting SHOCC is higher among polysyllabic items than among monosyllabic ones. A counting of wordforms from *The Owl and the Nightingale* shows that about 20 per cent of monosyllabic wordforms (tokens) seem to reflect shortening in their Modern English counterparts, while 60 per cent of polysyllabic items do so (see appendix III). Of course, these figures can probably not be taken at face value, since the small amount of data available cannot really be viewed as representative. Also, the results might be badly distorted by factors such as morphology or the impact of later sound changes. In any case, the prediction that the probability of shortening will be proportional to the weight of the weak syllables of the foot is definitely not falsified by the data that are normally explained by means of SHOCC.

Furthermore, it is generally acknowledged that long nuclei before consonant clusters had already been shortened in Old English if they were in antepenultimate syllables (thus, OE *sāmcucu* 'half-dead', *sāmsoden* 'half-cooked' *sāmboren* 'born too early' and *twēntiʒes* 'twenty' probably already had short vowels in Early Middle English; cf. Luick 1914/21: 187f.). Thus, it can be taken for granted that the overall weight of the weak syllables was as relevant for SHOCC as it was for all the other quantity changes we have discussed so far.

7.3.1.1 The special status of /st/ clusters

A point with regard to which my approach differs from the traditional ones is connected to the status of /st/ clusters with regard to SHOCC. As I will show, my Vowel Quantity Rule can account for it more elegantly, because it refers to the weight of the foot-head instead of the mere number of consonants following the vowel.

Thus, a closer look at the traditional description of SHOCC reveals that it seems to be at odds with the classical version of OSL. SHOCC is taken to account for the shortenings in such words as EME *dust*, *fyst* and *mist*, while in words of the type *haste*, *chaste* and *taste*, the cluster – which was analysed as the onset of the final syllable – is regarded as the 'trigger'[4] of OSL. It has traditionally been assumed that the former items were monosyllabic in the nominative while the latter consisted of two syllables, so that only *haste*, *chaste* and *taste* would have had open syllables, whereas in *dust*, *fyst* and *mist* the /st/ cluster would belong fully to the rhymes of the stressed syllables. However, it is dubious whether this can be regarded as a good solution to the problem. First of all, *dust*, *fyst* and *mist* would be as bisyllabic in many of their inflected forms as *haste*, *chaste* and *taste*.[5] Second, it has been shown that in Early Middle English words of the latter type had probably lost their underlying schwas too. An optional rule of schwa insertion, which had been introduced into the language, would then equally affect words of the type *dust*, *fyst* and *mist*. (cf. Minkova 1991).

Therefore, the fact that /st/ seems to have caused both lengthenings and shortenings remains to be explained.

Contrary to the traditional analyses, the approach taken here can provide such an explanation quite easily. At the same time, it does not have to disregard the fact that forms such as *duste*, *fyste* and *miste* were probably as common as monosyllabic *dust*, *fyst* and *mist*, and that *haste*, *chaste* and *taste* were probably pronounced without the final schwa as often as not.

First of all, Middle English stressed syllables were almost certainly general maximal. /st/ clusters were therefore fully ambisyllabic. Furthermore, the 'openness' of syllables was probably irrelevant to the quantity of the preceding vowel. What counted instead was the weight of the coda. On the simple assumption that ambisyllabic segments weigh half as much as segments that fully belong to the rhyme of a syllable, it turns out that codas consisting of ambisyllabic /st/ clusters weigh less than codas consisting of such clusters in which only the final element is ambisyllabic (e.g. /ft/, /kt/, /mp/, etc.), but more than codas that consist only of single ambisyllabic consonants. This explains why OSL was rarely implemented before /st/ clusters, items such as *taste* or *haste* being the exception. By the same token, it can explain why /st/ clusters might have sometimes led to shortenings, as in *dust* or *fist*. As a matter of fact, the analysis developed in this study predicts exactly what seems to have been the case, namely that /st/ clusters were in fact rather ambivalent with regard to the quantity of the preceding vowel, and that whether or not shortening or lengthening came to be implemented probably depended on other factors. In the case of the examples just given, it even seems obvious what those decisive factors might have been, namely vowel height. Most of the examples in which /st/ seems to have led to shortening had high vowels, while those words in which OSL was implemented had low vowels, so that once again the predictions of (2) are borne out.

7.3.2 Other constraints

Apart from showing the relevance of vowel height to SHOCC, there is little that the data tell about the general influence of vowel height on the implementation of the shortenings in question. And unfortunately, the same is true of the influence of coda sonority. However, from all that can be told, the way in which the two parameters may have influenced the implementation of Early Middle English Shortening was not at odds with the predictions of formula (2).

7.4   Conclusion

It may indeed be claimed therefore that the single rule of Quantity Adjustment proposed above can describe all Early Middle English changes of vowel quantity in a unified and comprehensive way. Luick's intuition about the relatedness of Early Middle English quantity changes has thus been corroborated.

7.5   Afterthoughts on TRISH and SHOCC

Apart from the fact that there is no need to assume separate rules for either TRISH or SHOCC, there are reasons to suspect that the shortenings were probably not primarily due at all to the factors which the traditional rules foreground. For example, reconsider the examples which Luick presents to illustrate TRISH. With the exception of *ærende*, *æmette* and *evere* (3 out of 28, i.e. hardly more than 10 per cent) all of them are morphologically complex. Luick quotes plural forms, datives, genitives, accusatives, compounds and derivatives. This practice is strangely in contrast with Luick's treatment of OSL data, for example, and is difficult to justify. After all, there will hardly have been an Early Middle English stem or base form that never appeared in a wordform where its stressed syllable happened to be penultimate. If it were possible to relate Modern English base forms to either inflected or derived or even compounded Early Middle English wordforms, then anything could be 'explained', and an explanation that explains everything is of course as good as one that explains nothing. It may therefore be claimed that the evidence which Luick presented to illustrate TRISH was rather ill-chosen.

The main reason why Luick gave such inappropriate examples was probably that there were no others. Thus, a search for potential inputs to the change in *The Owl and the Nightingale* yielded rather straightforward results. As chart (7) shows,

(7)

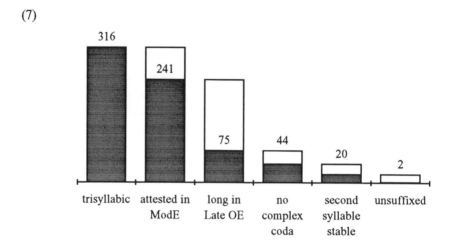

there were only few among more than 300 trisyllabic wordforms in the text
which had a long vowel in the first place. Fewer still had a simple coda, so
that a potential shortening could not have been due to syllable weight. Of
the items that were left many had rival forms in which the second syllable
was deleted consonant clusters were created. Of the few remaining items,
practically none were morphologically simple. This more or less means that
TRISH was a sound change without inputs. This is a further reason for
giving it up and for letting the few examples that it could account for be
handled by Middle English Quantity Adjustment.

Why, one might ask, was Luick so keen on establishing TRISH as an
Early Middle English sound change, if it was difficult for him to find even a
small number of convincing examples? What I suspect is that he needed the
sound change as a cleverly disguised *deus ex machina* that helped him to
deal with data that would otherwise emerge as uncomfortable exceptions to
other nicely devised sound laws. Thus, the phonological structures of *linen,
hryþer, cicen* and *seli* would, according to Luick's version of OSL normally
cause vowels to be lengthened, while *deorling, feorþinȝ, freond* and *alder*
would constitute inputs to HOL if their vowels had been short in Old English. Since it would have overturned the principles of the Neogrammarian
theory of language change, which was crucially based on the concept of exceptionless sound laws, Luick simply could not recognize that one and the
same environment might cause lengthening in some cases and shortening in
others. TRISH was his 'solution' to the problem. In combination with the
concept of analogical levelling, TRISH made it possible to account for the
(reflexes of) short vowels in Modern English words such as *chicken, linen,*

silly, darling, farthing or *friend*, while adhering to the idea that both 'open syllables' and 'homorganic clusters' were lengthening environments.

Interestingly, SHOCC seems to have played a similar role at times; e.g. when Luick accounts for the short vowel in ModE *sick* by means of SHOCC in ME *siknesse* and subsequent analogical levelling.

Within my approach, Luick's problem never poses itself, since my theory actually predicts that in certain environments both lengthenings and shortenings can occur. In addition, however, my theory actually suggests that words such as *linen, hryðer, cicen, æniʒ, bosom, other, riddle* and *seli* might be possible candidates for shortening, because all of them exhibit a combination of at least two factors that favour shortening and disfavour lengthening: stable final syllables and high vowels. The latter is also true of *sick*, which Luick derives from *sickness*. In addition to this the consonant in its coda belongs to the class of the least sonorant consonants, and such a coda favours shortness of the preceding vowel as well. Finally, *linen* and *seli* have ambisyllabic sonorants, and as has been shown above, such structures tended to block the implementation of OSL. That they should have led to occasional shortenings therefore comes as no surprise.[6]

8 *Epilogue: explaining Middle English Quantity Adjustment*

This section pursues the question if and how it is possible to explain Middle English Quantity Adjustment, the constraints on it and its place in language history.

For this purpose 'explanation' will be defined as any answer that can be given to a why-question. It consists of the **explanandum** (the facts to be explained) and the **explanans** (the explanation proper). In the explanans both a **law** and the **conditions** for the law to apply need to be stated. As stated above, a law is taken to be a function of the general structure

(1) $p(Fx \rightarrow Gx) = y$, where $0 \leq y \leq 1$.

p stands for the probability of the law's actual application, and in all cases where **y** does not equal **1** or **0** one can speak of statistical laws or 'tendencies'.

On the basis of this definition, the laws summarized in formula (2) of chapter 7 and the fact that words such as EME *maken, bindan, kepte* and *erende* satisfied the conditions for these laws to apply can be said to explain why short vowels came to play the roles of original long vowels in *kepte* and *erende*, and why long vowels played the roles of short ones in *maken* and *bindan*.

However, while laws such as (2) of chapter 7 can be taken to explain the correspondences between Late Old English or Early Middle English *maken, bindan, kepte* and *erende*, on the one hand, and Modern English *make, bind, kept* and *errand* on the other, the explanation lacks depth, so that more questions seem to be raised than are answered: in particular, the questions of why the application of law (2) of chapter 7 depended on such factors as the ones it makes reference to, and why it applied only during a particular period and only in a particular language community. Since the latter questions are in fact more interesting or relevant than the questions that laws such as (2) of chapter 7 do answer, it might even be argued that no 'sound laws' – regardless of whether they are of the Neogrammarian type or of my format – have any explanatory value with regard to 'sound changes' at all. What they provide would then be regarded as a mere description. Given the definition of 'sound change' as on p. 7, and 'explanation' as above, however, such a restrictive view is out of place, of course. Still, it has to be admitted that the explanations provided by laws such as (2) of chapter 7 are rather shallow. I shall therefore try to increase the depth of my explanations and deal with the questions raised by that law.

8.1   Explaining the constraints on Quantity Adjustment

Why was the adjustment of nucleus length in Early Middle English con-strained by the factors contained in law (2) of chapter 7? The method by which these factors were derived was basically inductive. What was investigated was the implementation of nucleus lengthening in a section of the English vocabulary that was traditionally handled by the sound law of OSL. This implementation turned out to have been systematic and certain patterns could be observed. It was shown that these patterns reflected a couple of parameters characterizing the phonological environments of the nuclei in question. It was tentatively assumed, then, that those parameters could be taken as explanations of the implementation of nucleus lengthening in Middle English. This hypothesis was confirmed when it was tested against the data traditionally accounted for by HOL. When it was not falsified either, when compared to the correspondences usually accounted for by TRISH and SHOCC, this was accepted as an indication that it might actually deserve the title 'theory'. Thus, the method has been strictly empirical.

When confronted with the question *why* it was the particular parameters contained in law (2) of chapter 7 that constrained Quantity Adjustment in the way they did, one might feel tempted to answer that they simply must have done so, because if they had not they would not have made the right predictions with regard to the data. Obviously, however, such an 'explanation' would be circular. If one explains correspondences with the influence of certain parameters, one cannot explain the influence of these parameters with the correspondences. Therefore, explanations of the constraints on Quantity Adjustment ought to be independent of the data which they are themselves supposed to explain.

Fields from which proper explanations of the constraints on Quantity Adjustment could be derived are research into linguistic universals, (articulatory and auditory) physiology, neuro-psychology and – perhaps[1] – acoustics. In the next sections we shall therefore briefly discuss whether these fields might provide independent evidence for the constraints contained in formula (2) of chapter 7.

8.1.1 Weight-based constraints

Both the influence of syllable weight and that of the overall weight of the weak syllables of a foot could be explained by the principle of isochrony, i.e. the tendency of '*stressed* syllables [to] occur at regular intervals' (Couper-Kuhlen 1986: 53). Assume that the time between two prominence peaks tended to be as constant in Early Middle English utterances as in Modern English, regardless of the number of syllables or segments that had to be accommodated between those peaks. Since stress peaks (that is to say, the peaks of measurable intensity) are actually located at the transition between the onset and the nucleus of stressed syllables, nuclei of stressed syllables are therefore not stress peaks themselves, but are, phonetically speaking at least, between two such peaks. If the time interval between such stress peaks is constant, it follows that the speed with which elements between peaks are pronounced will be proportional to the number of those elements, and this includes the nuclei of the peak syllables. By the same token, the time attributed to the pronunciation of each element between stress peaks will be inversely proportional to the number of such elements. The more elements there are between the stress peak of a word and the next word boundary, the more elements there will be between this stress peak and the next (other things being equal, of course). There are two consequences which follow from this: first, stressed nuclei (of foot heads) will tend to be pronounced more rapidly (and therefore be pronounced shorter, and be shortened by a shortening process) in words with a greater number of weak syllables than in words with a smaller number of weak syllables (where they will be pronounced longer and tend to be lengthened by lengthening processes); second, the nuclei of foot heads will tend to be pronounced more rapidly (and therefore be pronounced shorter, and be shortened by a shortening process) in words with longer rhymes than in words with shorter rhymes (where they will tend to be pronounced longer and tend to be lengthened by lengthening processes) (cf. Dressler 1985: 44).

Since there is a likely correlation between the probability of a vowel's being analysed as underlyingly short or long and the average duration of the articulation of that vowel in utterances, it follows that both syllable weight and the weight of the weak syllables in a foot will influence the implementation of lengthening and shortening processes in the way in which they did in Early Middle English.

8.1.2   Vowel height

There seems to be a general tendency for low vowels to lengthen more easily than high vowels, while high vowels shorten more easily than long vowels.[2] At least two explanations can be proposed for this. First, there is the fact that low vowels are more sonorous than high vowels. Their greater sonority makes them louder and more easily perceived, and this relative prominence might be re-interpreted as relative length. This would explain why low vowels are more easily re-interpreted as long vowels than high ones.

Second, it is well known that vowels differ from each other with regard to what has been called their 'internal duration'. In particular, the pronunciation of low vowels tends to last longer than the articulation of high vowels. Lehiste (1970) has argued that this is due to the fact that the articulation of low vowels involves jaw lowering and therefore takes longer than the articulation of high vowels, for which the jaw does not have to be moved as far from its resting position. Although Catford (1982) contends that this is really the reason for the differences in 'internal vowel duration', one may claim that – whatever motivates the phenomenon – it provides a good explanation for the way in which vowel height seems to have constrained the implementation of Quantity Adjustment processes in Early Middle English.

8.1.3   Backness–frontness

As has been pointed out above, the influence of backness on the implementation of Early Middle English Quantity Adjustment is not as obvious as that of the other factors. Since it can be observed only among mid vowels, this parameter seems to be the weakest part of law (2) of chapter 7. It might even be assumed that the differences between the implementations of /o/-lengthening and /e/-lengthening were just side effects of the influence of vowel height, since English /o/-allophones seem to have tended towards lowness, while /e/-allophones appear to have tended towards height.[3] However, given the assumption that the back–front opposition did play an independent role in the implementation of Quantity Adjustment, one has to see whether an explanation can be found. And, at least as far as the influence of backness on the quantity of vowels of middle height (viz. /o/ and /e/ phonemes) is concerned, this seems to be possible on acoustic/auditory grounds. As Fry (1979: 127) states, the relative intensity (= loudness) of /o/ (28db) is much greater than that of /e/ (23db). From this it follows that /o/-allophones will tend to be perceived as relatively more prominent than /e/-allophones, and will therefore be more easily re-interpreted as long.

8.1.4 Coda sonority

It seems to be a linguistic universal that duration of vowels depends on the sonority of the subsequent consonants. The effects of this tendency can be observed quite clearly in Modern English, but it also seems to hold[4] – albeit not quite as obviously – for German (cf. Meyer 1903), Spanish (cf. Zimmermann and Sapon 1958), Norwegian (cf. Fintoft 1961), French, Russian or Korean (for all three cf. Chen 1970), to name just a few languages that have been investigated in this respect.

As far as the phonetic background of the phenomenon is concerned, Hubmayer (1986) provides a summary of potential explanations (unfortunately, most phonetic investigations have restricted themselves to the voiced–voiceless opposition, and, as will become obvious, the results of these studies cannot always be generalized to serve as explanations for the influence of sonority in general).

Studies of articulatory processes have shown that in the transition between a vowel and a voiceless obstruent the closure can be achieved more rapidly than in the transition between a vowel and a voiced obstruent, which might be due to the fact that 'The necessary wide separation of the vocal cords [needed for voiceless consonants] can be achieved more rapidly than the more finely adjusted smaller separation of a voiced consonant' (Halle and Stevens 1967, as quoted in Mohr 1971: 81). Alternatively, it has been shown (cf. Javkin 1978: 90–114) that listeners perceive vowels to last longer before voiced consonants than before voiceless consonant. This may be due, Javkin argues, to 'the continuation of voicing into the consonant' (1978: 103).

Although I am in no position to check the relative plausibilities of the two explanations, the parameters investigated by Javkin are more similar to the ones with which I have been operating in this study, while I am not certain that the approach taken by Halle and Stevens (1967) can be generalized to explain the influence of different degrees of coda sonority on nucleus length.

8.1.5   Summary

As I hope to have shown, it was probably not just a historical coincidence that the parameters contained in (2) of chapter 7 influenced the implementation of lengthening/shortening the way they did. All constraints can be explained through articulation and/or perception and might therefore be taken as quasi-universal.[5]

Although the depth of my explanation of Early Middle English quantity changes has now been increased by one level, so to speak, and although it has been shown that there are independent reasons why the parameters of law (2) of chapter 7 should have influenced these quantity changes the way I assume they did, a question remains that has been puzzling linguists almost since historical linguistics was invented and has been dismissed by many as unanswerable. If the constraints on lengthening and shortening are universal in time and space, why have the language changes they brought about been so sporadic. In other words, why did the sound changes that I have called quantity adjustments occur particularly in the transitional period between Old and Middle English?

8.2   Explaining the temporal restrictedness of Quantity Adjustment through the development of English morphology

As I have argued, the constraints on quantity adjustments are, theoretically, universal since they follow from ultimately physiological regularities. (They are not linguistic universals in the sense that they would be relevant in all languages, of course, because such constraints as those based on foot iso-chrony, for example, can only occur in languages that have feet.) Similarly, the quantity adjustments themselves are universal, since, by definition, the fact that something is a nucleus admits the application of law (2) of chapter 7.[6] What needs to be explained, then, is why **Quantity Adjustment** had not led to a complementary distribution of vowel quantity (with the exception of those cases that are ambivalent in the sense of diagram (4) in chapter 7 long before the Early Middle English period and why it ceased to apply during the Middle English period.[7]

As Dressler (cf. 1985: 260ff.) has pointed out, most arguments high-lighting this problem do not take the factor of 'goal conflict' into account.

Thus, speech sounds are not only subject to laws relating to their pronounceability or to the ease of their reception; they also figure, for example, as distinguishers of meaning and as building blocks of which morphemes consist. In this respect they will be subject to regularities that may easily counteract phonetico-phonological tendencies. For example, from the point of view of morphonological transparency it would be 'undesirable' if in inflectional paradigms such as Austrian German

(2)   **Sg.**   **Pl.**
     1   geh'   geh'n
     2   gehst   geht
     3   geht   gehn

the underlying /eː/ of the second person singular were re-interpreted as underlying /e/, although the /st/ cluster might suggest such a change. Therefore, although the /eː/ in *gehst* might synchronically (and thus theoretically also diachronically) be more likely to be shortened than the /eː/s in the other persons, the implementation of this tendency is counteracted by morphological factors. This means that laws such as (2) in chapter 7 are in fact incomplete. In order to 'predict' the actual occurrence of diachronic quantity changes, they would have to incorporate information about morphological factors, as well as about possible other ones which might either increase or decrease the probability of their application.

The way in which various components of language interact to generate language change has long been of interest to linguists, but the results that have so far been produced are of a rather general and very often also speculative kind (see Kastovsky 1988; Stampe and Donegan 1983). When, in the following sections, I deal with the possible ways in which morphological factors might have first favoured and then blocked the diachronic implementation of Quantity Adjustment, I would like to stress that the proposed solutions will necessarily be tentative. I want them to be understood as a contribution to the question how such problems can at all be approached.

8.2.1   Early Middle English morphology

As Kastovsky (1984, 1988, 1989 and 1990) has pointed out, the morphology of Late Old or Early Middle English represented the final stage in a metamorphosis that had probably already started in Old English.

Originally, i.e. in Pre Old English, both nominal and verbal inflection and derivation had been stem-based. Most wordforms occurring in actual texts (e.g. *cyme* 'coming', nom./acc. sg.) consisted of a (complex) stem (*kum+i*) plus an inflectional ending (∅). The stems themselves did not appear as actual wordforms in actual texts. In this system, the abstract representations of the underlying stems differed considerably from the actual shapes they would assume in actual wordforms, because the latter depended on the suffixes that were attached to the stems. However, they were derived by a set of relatively straightforward phonological rules. Thus, an underlying representation such as

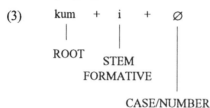

(3)   kum   +   i   +   ∅

          ROOT   STEM
          FORMATIVE

          CASE/NUMBER

would undergo the following phonological rules: the /u/ of the stem would have been *i*-umlauted to /y/ and the stem formative /i/ might have been optionally reduced to a central vowel. Both would have been transparent, though. The advantage of such a system was that the relatedness of *cyme* 'coming' to words such as the verb *cuman* 'to come' was still recoverable via the common underlying root morpheme {kum}. Its greatest disadvantage, on the other hand, was that surface wordforms were formally very different from the underlying morphemes from which they were derived.

Already in the Old English period, then, a set of sound changes had made the phonological relationship between underlying stems and surface wordforms increasingly opaque, and the original morphonological system came to be superseded by one in which (phonological) differences between lexical representations of words and actual wordforms came to be minimized.

Thus, the /i/ which used to underlie the final vowel in *cyme*, for example, and which probably surfaced as some sort of schwa, ceased to be recoverable, and the final schwa was maybe interpreted as the default realization of an unspecified V-segment. Whatever the details of this change may have been, it resulted in the loss of the underlying /i/, which had originally constituted the environment that triggered the (synchronic) rules by which surface *cyme* was derived from underlying *kum* (in this case *i*-umlaut). As a consequence, the *i*-umlaut rule relating underlying *kum* to surface *cyme* 'denaturalized' and became an allomorphy rule.

Phonologically, the underlying representation of *cyme* would then have been

(4)   kym + e
         | |
        STEM |
             CASE/NUMBER

As this representation shows, the +*e*, which originated in the stem formative +*i*+, also came to be re-interpreted morphologically as an inflectional ending. This reflects that reduction (and consequent merging) had deprived stem formatives such as +*i*+, +*a*+, or +*u*+ of their stem-differentiating function.

In a next step, then, endings such as the +*e* in the nom./acc. sg. of *cyme* came to be re-interpreted as part of the stem. Thus, *cyme* came to be analysed as shown in representation

(5)   kyme + ∅
         | |
        STEM |
             CASE/NUMBER

As Kastovsky states, this was probably due to the analogy of such inflectional paradigms in which overt nom./acc. sg. markers had already been lost before the Old English period (viz. the Old English *a*-stems, cf.

(6)   **Sg.**   **Pl.**
    NA   #cyning#   #cyning+as#
    G   #cyning+es#   #cyning+a#
    D   #cyning+e#   #cyning+um#)

It did not take long for this type of analysis to oust that of (5), and it was probably fully generalized by the end of the Old English, or the beginning of the Middle English period. At this stage, the relation between related words such as *cyme* and *cuman* was of course no longer transparent,[8] because they had no common underlying forms anymore. On the other hand, it had become rather common that underlying stems and certain surface wordforms were formally identical[9] (words of the *cyme* type had joined ranks with words of the *cyning* type). That meant that stems could actually figure as surface wordforms themselves. They no longer needed the support of additional morphemes, nor did they undergo any morphonological transformations. Although such surfacing stems first appeared in the nominal system, they were rather common in the verbal system as well at the end of the Old English period. This means, however, that English morphology had ceased to be based on abstract stems and that much more surface-oriented 'base forms', or 'words', took their place.

8.2.2   Consequences for phonology: rule loss and target re-interpretation

As has already been pointed out above, one of the greatest differences between a morphology that is based on abstract stems and one that operates with surfacing base forms, is that the former is often characterized by morphonological alternations among related surface wordforms while the latter is not. Also, in a stem-based morphology, the derivational distance between surface representations and underlying stem will tend to be equal for all related wordforms (see (7a)) none of them having any priority. In a morphology that is built around surfacing base forms, on the other hand, one wordform is *by definition* more basic than all others, which are derived from that 'base form' (see (7b)).

(7)   a.

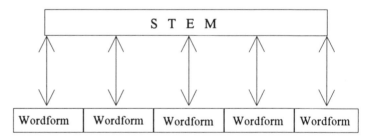

b.

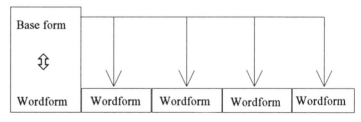

In such a system, the derivational distance between the underlying and the surface representations of that base form will tend to be minimalized (ideally, they will be separated only by phonetic realization rules). This reflects the principle of iconicity, as outlined in Dressler (1982: 104ff.), for example. Thus, in a morphology that is built around surfacing base forms the number of phonological rules that apply to base forms will be relatively small, while in a morphology that is based on stems, underlying phonological representations will be rather abstract, and a relatively large set of phonological rules will guarantee that the relatedness of all wordforms based on a common stem remains transparent.

If a morphology changes from a stem system to a base-form system, we must therefore expect corresponding changes in the phonology as well. Typically, they will involve the loss of phonological rules and the re-interpretation of surface forms as underlying targets rather than as the outputs of rules that have ceased to be transparent anyway and that have lost their morphological relevance as well. This, of course, is exactly what seems to have happened in the case of Early Middle English Quantity Adjustment. The next section will clarify the point.

8.2.3 Quantity Adjustment and target re-interpretation

Recall, first of all, that probably no aspect of Quantity Adjustment was ever really implemented into English as a phonological rule of any generality. This is to say, there was probably no stage in which rules of the type

(8) $\quad V \rightarrow [-\text{long}]/\_\_CC$

$\quad V \rightarrow [-\text{long}]/\_\_\sigma\sigma$

or

$\quad V \rightarrow [+\text{long}]/\_\_\S$

would have yielded correct results for every part of the lexicon. As argued above, what seems to have happened in the case of Early Middle English Quantity Adjustment, is that the outputs of optional low-level processes affecting phonetic realization were re-interpreted as underlying targets. As Dressler (1982) has shown, such developments are not uncommon and seem to be the typical way in which foregrounding processes such as lengthening tend to denaturalize.

To obtain a more concrete picture of what is likely to have happened, take the example of EME *maken*. The forms that are attested in *The Owl and the Nightingale* are

(9)   1544:   þa heo hine   **makie**   kukeweld

       354:    7 ouerfulle   **makeþ**   wlatie
       638:    þat node   **makeþ**   old wif urne
       650:    an after þan we   **makeþ**   ure
       1390:   for flesches lustes hi **makeþ**   slide
       1444:   þat of so wilde   **makeþ**   tome
       1648:   an summe of the schawles **makeþ**

       339:    7   **makest**   þine song so unwurþ

Given that a synchronic version of law (2) of chapter 7 operated on these wordforms, we may assume that a long vowel will have been pronounced most often in realizations of *makie* (the ⟨i⟩ spelling being ignored), less often in *makeþ*, and least often in *makest*. Generally speaking, we may therefore assume that there will have been a more or less systematic variation between [maːk] pronunciations and [mak] pronunciations. The underlying representation of all surface forms will probably have been /mak/ and the long vowel in forms such as [maːkə] will have been derived by an optional rule of allophonic variation, producing, in this case, the allophone [aː]. As has been argued above, however, /make/, which was most often realized as [maːk(ə)], came to be thought of as the base form of the paradigm, so that all other forms such as *make+st* and *make+þ* were secondarily derived from that base form. Since the base form had priority over all other tauto-paradigmatic wordforms, the principle of iconicity required that the differences between its phonetic realization and its underlying representation be minimalized, even if this would increase the differences between the underlying representations and surface realizations of other wordforms. So, instead of deriving the [aː] in the realizations of the base form from an underlying /a/, the [aː]s were taken to be realizations of underlying /aː/s, and the shorter pronunciations of the vowels in *make+st* and *make+þ* would then be re-interpreted as optional phonetic shortenings along the lines of law (2) of chapter 7. A schematic representation of the states before and after the re-interpretation is given in (10) (where all other sound changes, such as the re-interpretation of optional schwa loss as optional schwa insertion, are disregarded).

(10)

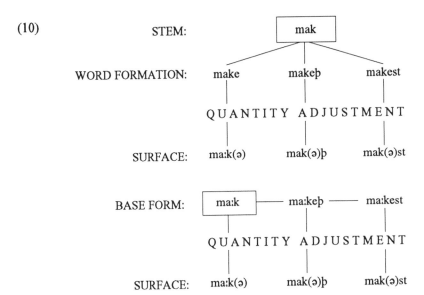

Since the transformation of English morphology from a stem-based to a word-based system was well under way, if not more or less completed, at the beginning of the Middle English period (approximately up to and during the thirteenth century),[10] it is not at all surprising that Quantity Adjustment was implemented through target re-interpretation during the same period as well. QED.

Implicitly, the claim that the realizations of (uninflected) base forms came to be re-interpreted as underlying during the implementation of Quantity Adjustment, more or less rules out the possibility that the quantity of inflected forms would survive in base forms through analogy. There are two points which indicate that this seems to have been the case. First, I have demonstrated that most of the examples in which the quantity of an inflected form is assumed to have survived (see Luick's examples of TRISH above), can also be explained on the basis of the structures of the base forms alone. Also, the fact that the relative stability of the final syllables seems to have been such an important factor for the implementation of vowel lengthening supports this view as well. In particular the Quantity Adjustment Rule makes correct predictions only if it operates on base forms rather than on the infinitive or any other inflected form. Had I based my investigations on forms such as *maken*, *makeþ* or *makest*, for example, rather than on *make*, which was to become the base form, I could not have characterized their second syllables as unstable and would therefore have wrongly predicted that words of the type *maken* were unlikely to be lengthened.[11]

Another way in which the restructuring of English morphology might have been linked to the implementation of Quantity Adjustment is the following. When final schwas lost their morphological function and were reanalysed as part of the stem/base form (#*make*# as opposed to #*mak+e*#) the number of disyllabic and simultaneously monomorphemic wordform types increased disproportionally. As (11a and b)[12] show, this development ran counter to a general trend of English monomorphemic wordforms to be monosyllabic.

(11)   The relation between prosodic and morphological constituents: the number of syllables in monomorphemic wordforms (*types*):

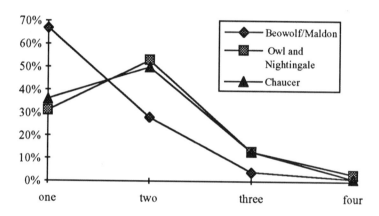

(12)   The relation between prosodic and morphological constituents: number of syllables of monomorphemic wordforms (*tokens*):

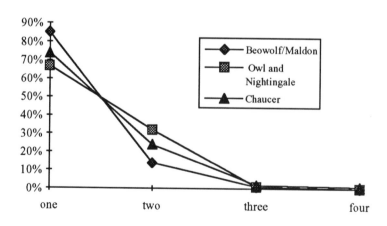

Having been stripped of their morphological functions, the final syllables were an easy prey for reduction processes: the effort spent on their pronunciation ceased to be worthwhile from the morphological point of view. They represented those unstable final syllables, then, that played such an important role in Quantity Adjustment. It can therefore be argued that morphology, through the re-interpretation of inflectional endings, contributed to the implementation of Quantity Adjustment in yet another way.

Summing up, it would seem that the restructuring of the morphological system can indeed explain why Quantity Adjustment came to be implemented in English at the time it was. The question why Quantity Adjustment ceased to be productive during the Middle English period, however, has yet to be dealt with.

8.3.4 The interface between morphology and prosodic phonology

Although this question is probably even more difficult to answer than the first, there is an explanation that seems to offer itself. One of the most powerful factors in Quantity Adjustment was foot weight. Thus, if Quantity Adjustment was implemented through the phonological restructuring of base forms, one can regard the change as an interplay of the prosodic and the morpho-lexical components of grammar. It can be argued that English morphology and prosody were closely related during the Old English and at the beginning of the Middle English period but that they drifted apart during the latter. It might therefore be suggested that this dissociation of the two components blocked the further transfer of prosodic processes into morpho-lexical representations.

As has been observed above, following Vennemann (1986), the hierarchies of prosody and morphology are not necessarily isomorphous. Syllables cannot be equated to morphemes and, most importantly, feet cannot be equated to words. However, a morpheme *can* coincide with a syllable, and a word *can* happen to be identical with a foot if it happens to be stressed on the leftmost syllable and if the following word starts the next foot. While it is easy to see why the tendency of morphemes to be monosyllabic should be rather widespread (the minimal linguistic sign coincides with the minimal unit that can be pronounced), the probability that feet should coincide with wordforms will not be equal for all languages at all times. Thus, if a language has free stress, such as French has to a certain degree, it is not very likely, because in such a language foot structure will not respect word boundaries at all. Similarly, if a language consists mostly of monosyllabic words, it is not very likely either, because feet tend to consist of stressed *and* unstressed syllables, and therefore it is as likely as not that a word will stand in the position of a foot head, depending on sentence rhythm. If, however, a language has fixed stress on the leftmost syllable of the stem morpheme and if its wordforms normally consist of at least two syllables, the probability that word boundaries and foot boundaries coincide is relatively great.

It seems that English changed from a language in which isomorphy between feet and wordforms was relatively common into one in which it was the exception rather than the rule. As has already been stated above, Old English word stress fell, as a rule, on the leftmost syllable of the stem. Furthermore, Old English wordforms tended to consist of a stem plus inflectional endings, so that Old English wordforms would typically consist of one stressed and one or more unstressed syllables. Since this type of structure is practically identical with the optimal foot structure,[13] it is easy to see why Old English wordforms very often tended to coincide with feet. It can be assumed that this tendency of feet and wordforms to coincide remained unchanged until well into the Middle English period. Then, however, the relationship became unbalanced due to two factors. First, the number of monosyllabic words, which was already high in Old English, increased steadily until monosyllabism became typical of English wordforms. A comparison of Old English texts (*Beowulf* and *The Battle of Maldon*) and Middle English ones (*The Owl and the Nightingale* and Chaucer's *Canterbury Tales*) shows that in Old English less than half of all wordforms used were monosyllabic, while in Middle English roughly two-thirds were. Second, a large number of French loan words were integrated into the English lexicon, and many of them were stressed on their final syllables. It is easy to see that the combination of these two factors must have decreased the probability of feet to coincide with wordforms considerably.

When Quantity Adjustment started to be implemented, the principle that feet and wordforms were isomorphous was probably still intact, so that in the beginning foot-based constraints on Quantity Adjustment were easily incorporated into wordform representations, and it might even be assumed that the principle of isochrony might have been generally transferred from the foot domain to the domain of wordforms. Once foot structure came to be dissociated from wordforms, however, wordforms ceased to be a domain for the prosody-based constraints on Quantity Adjustment as well. Since Quantity Adjustment was primarily a prosodically conditioned change, it is easy to see why it ceased to be implemented in the phonological representations of wordforms almost simultaneously. This might explain why Quantity Adjustment stopped being productive during the Middle English period.

ModE	ME	long	σ2	V	ə	W	C	S	E
ache	aken	•	-	a*	•	-	1	V	O
acorn	akern	•	•	a	•	3	1	N	O
acre	aker	•	•	a	•	1	1	N	O
addle	adlen	-	•	a	•	1	C6	V	O
alder	aler	-	•	a	•	1	6	N	O
ale	ale	•	-	a	•	-	6	N	O
alum	alum	-	•	a	•	2	6	N	N
anet	anet	-	•	a	•	2	5	N	N
anise	anis	-	•	a	-	2	5	N	N
ape	ape	•	-	a	•	-	1	N	O
aspen	aspen	-	•	a	•	1	C1	A	O
azure	azur	-	•	a	-	1	2	A	N
azure	azur**	•	•	a	-	1	2	A	N

* The analysis on which this as well as the following lists are based distinguishes only five articulatory positions: low /a/, mid front /e/, mid back /o/, high front /i/ and high back /u/.

** Items such as *azure*, for which Modern Standard English admits pronunciations with both long and short stressed vowels, have received two entries.

Abbreviations and symbols:
long = long V in ModE; **V** = vowel in σ₁; σ2 = stable second syllable; ə = schwa as nucleus of σ2; **W** = weight of the final syllable; **C** = type of intersyllabic consonant (cluster)s: 1 = voiceless plosive, 2 = voiced plosive, 3 = voiceless fricative, 4 = voiced fricative, 5 = nasal, 6 = lateral liquid (/l/), 7 = central liquid (/r/), C1 = /s/ + voiceless plosive, C2 - C7 = other cluster types; **S** = syntactic category; **E** = etymology: O = Old English, N = Anglo Norman, S = Scandinavian, L = Latin

ModE	ME	long	σ2	V	ə	W	C	S	E
bacon	bacon	•	•	a	•	1	1	N	N
bake	baken	•	-	a	•	-	1	V	O
bale	bale	•	-	a	•	-	6	N	O
bane	bane	•	-	a	•	-	5	N	O
bare	barin	•	-	a	-	-	7	V	O
baron	baron	-	•	a	-	2	7	N	N
barrat	barrat	-	•	a	•	2	7	N	N
barrel	baril	-	•	a	-	2	7	N	N
barren	barren	-	•	a	•	2	7	A	N
barrow	baru(h)	-	•	a	-	2	7	N	O
basin	basin	•	•	a	-	1	3	N	N
basket	basket	-	•	a	•	2	C1	N	O
bastard	bastard	-	•	a	-	3	C1	N	N
bathe	baþien	•	-	a	•	-	2	V	O
batten	battin	-	•	a	•	1	1	V	S
queath	cweþen	•	-	e	•	-	4	V	O
bead	bede	•	-	e	•	-	2	N	O
bear	bere	•	-	e	•	-	7	N	O
bear	beren	•	-	e	•	-	7	V	O
beath	beþjen	•	-	e	•	-	2	V	O
beaver	bever	•	•	e	•	1	2	N	O
beck	bek(e)	-	-	e	•	-	1	N	S
behave	(be)habben	•	-	a	•	-	2	V	O
belly	beli	-	•	e	-	1	6	N	O
beneath	(bi)neoþen	•	-	e	•	-	2	P	O
berry	berie	-	•	e	-	1	7	N	O
beryl	beril	-	•	e	-	2	7	N	N
besom	besme	-	•	e	•	1	C5	N	O
besom	besme	•	•	e	•	1	C5	N	O
better	bet(e)r(e)	-	•	e	•	1	1	A	O

ModE	ME	long	σ2	V	ə	W	C	S	E
bezant	besant	-	•	e	•	3	4	N	N
blade	blad(e)	•	-	a	•	-	2	N	O
blather	blather	-	•	a	•	1	4	V	S
blaze	blasen	•	-	a	•	-	4	V	O
blazon	blason	•	•	a	-	1	4	N	N
blear	bleren	•	-	e	•	-	7	V	O
bode	bodien	•	-	o	•	-	2	V	O
body	bodig	-	•	o	-	1	2	N	O
bole	bole	•	-	o	•	-	6	N	S
bonnet	bonnet	-	•	o	•	2	5	N	N
bore	borin	•	-	o	-	-	7	V	O
bottom	boþem	-	•	o	•	1	4	N	O
bracken	braken	-	•	a	•	1	1	N	S
brake	brake	•	-	a	•	-	1	N	O
braze	brasen	•	-	a	•	-	4	A	O
break	breken	•	-	e	•	-	1	V	O
brevet	brevet	-	•	e	•	2	4	N	N
broke	broke	•	-	o	•	-	1	V	O
brothel	broþel	-	•	o	•	1	3	N	O
cackle	cacel	-	•	a	•	1	1	A	?
cake	cake	•	-	a	•	-	1	N	S
callow	calu	-	•	a	-	2	6	A	?
camel	camel	-	•	a	•	1	5	N	O
canon	canon	-	•	a	-	2	5	N	O
capon	capon	•	•	a	-	2	1	N	N
care	care	•	-	a	•	-	7	N	O
cast	kasta	-	-	a	•	-	C1	N	S
castle	castel	-	•	a	•	1	C1	N	N
cattle	catel	-	•	a	•	1	1	N	N
cellar	celer	-	•	e	•	1	6	N	N

ModE	ME	long	σ2	V	ə	W	C	S	E
chafer	ceafer	•	•	a	•	1	3	N	O
chalice	chalis	-	•	a	-	2	6	N	N
channel	chanel	-	•	a	•	1	5	N	N
chaste	chaste	•	-	a	•	-	C1	A	N
chattel	chatel	-	•	a	•	1	1	N	N
choke	cheoke	•	-	o	•	-	1	V	O
clamour	clamor	-	•	a	-	1	5	N	N
claret	claret	-	•	a	•	2	7	N	N
clatter	clater	-	•	a	•	1	1	N	O
cloak	cloke	•	-	o	•	-	1	N	N
closet	closet	-	•	o	•	2	4	N	N
clove	clove	•	-	o	•	-	4	N	O
coal	col(e)	•	-	o	•	-	6	N	O
cocker	koker	-	•	o	•	1	1	N	O
cockle	cokel	-	•	o	•	1	1	N	N
coffin	cofin	-	•	o	-	2	3	N	N
collar	colar	-	•	o	•	1	6	N	N
collop	colop	-	•	o	-	2	6	N	S
common	comon	-	•	o	•	2	5	A	N
copper	coper	-	•	o	•	1	1	N	O
coral	coral	-	•	o	•	2	7	N	N
cote	cote	•	-	o	•	-	1	N	O
cothe	coþe	•	-	o	•	-	4	N	O
cove	caf(e)	•	-	o	•	-	4	N	O
crack	crack(e)	-	-	a	•	-	1	N	O
cradle	cradel	•	•	a	•	1	2	N	O
crake	crack(e)	•	-	a	ə	-	1	N	S
crane	crane	•	-	a	•	-	5	N	O
crave	craven	•	-	a	•	-	4	V	O
craze	crasen	•	-	a	•	-	4	V	S

ModE	ME	long	σ2	V	ə	W	C	S	E
creddle	cradel	-	•	a	•	1	2	N	O
crotchet	crochet	-	•	o	•	2	C3	N	N
dale	dale	•	-	a	•	-	6	N	O
damask	damask	-	•	a	•	3	5	N	?
dare	darin	•	-	a	-	-	7	V	O
dean	dene	•	-	e	•	-	5	N	N
deavour	devor	-	•	e	-	1	4	X	N
dere	derien	•	-	e	•	-	7	V	O
desert	desert	-	•	e	•	2	4	N	N
dor	dore	•	-	o	•	-	7	N	O
dote	dotien	•	-	o	•	-	1	V	O
dragon	dragon	-	•	a	-	1	2	N	N
drake	drake	•	-	a	•	-	1	N	O
drepe	drepen	•	-	e	•	-	1	V	O
drop	drope	-	-	o	•	-	1	N	O
ear	erien	•	-	e	•	-	7	V	O
eat	eten	•	-	e	•	-	1	V	O
eaves	eves(e)	•	-	e	•	-	4	N	O
edder	ether	-	•	e	•	1	4	V	O
eddish	edisch	-	•	e	-	2	2	N	O
even	efen	•	•	e	•	1	4	A	O
fade	faden	•	-	a	•	-	2	V	N
faggot	fagot	-	•	a	-	2	2	N	N
fallow	falu	-	•	a	-	2	6	A	O
fare	faren	•	-	a	•	-	7	V	O
fast	fasten	-	-	a	•	-	C1	V	O
father	fader	-	•	a	ə	1	2	N	O
favour	favor	•	•	a	-	1	4	N	N
feather	feþer	-	•	e	•	1	4	N	O
feaze	fasel	•	-	a	•	-	4	N	N

ModE	ME	long	σ2	V	ə	W	C	S	E
felon	felon	-	•	e	-	2	6	N	N
fennel	fenel	-	•	e	•	1	5	N	O
ferry	ferien	-	•	e	•	1	7	V	S
fester	fester	-	•	e	•	1	C1	N	N
fetter	feter	-	•	e	•	1	1	N	O
fettle	fetlen	-	•	e	•	1	C2	V	O
flake	flake	•	-	a	•	-	1	N	S
flatter	flator	-	•	a	•	1	1	V	N
flavour	flavor	•	•	a	-	1	4	N	N
float	flotien	•	-	o	•	-	1	V	O
florin	florin	-	•	o	-	2	7	N	N
foal	fole	•	-	o	•	-	6	N	O
foreign	forain	-	•	o	-	2	7	A	N
forest	forest	-	•	o	•	3	7	N	N
fret	freten	-	-	e	•	-	1	V	O
gable	gable	•	•	a	•	1	C6	N	S
gallon	galon	-	•	a	-	2	6	N	N
game	game	•	-	a	•	-	5	N	O
gammon	gamen	-	•	a	•	2	5	N	O
gannet	ganet	-	•	a	•	2	5	N	O
gape	gapin	•	-	a	-	-	1	V	S
gate	gate	•	-	a	•	-	1	N	O
gather	gadrian	-	•	a	•	1	C7	V	O
gave	gav(e)	•	-	a	•	-	4	V	O
gavel	gavel	-	•	a	•	1	4	N	O
gaze	gasen	•	-	a	•	-	4	V	?
gear	geare	•	-	e	•	-	7	N	S
get	geten	-	-	e	•	-	1	V	S
grave	grafe	•	-	a	•	-	4	N	O
gravel	gravel	-	•	a	•	1	4	N	N

ModE	ME	long	σ2	V	ə	W	C	S	E
graze	grasen	•	-	a	•	-	4	V	O
groat	grot	•	-	o	•	-	1	N	?
groom	grom(e)	•	-	o	•	-	5	N	?
habit	habit	-	•	a	-	2	2	N	N
haddock	hadok	-	•	a	-	2	2	N	N
hake	hake	•	-	a	•	-	1	N	S
hame	hame	•	-	a	•	-	5	N	O
hammer	hamer	-	•	a	•	1	5	N	O
hare	hare	•	-	a	•	-	7	N	O
harry	hergien	-	•	e	•	1	7	V	O
hasp	haspe	-	-	a	•	-	C1	N	O
haste	haste	•	-	a	•	-	C1	N	N
hatchel	hechil	-	•	e	-	1	C3	N	O
hate	hatien	•	-	a	•	-	1	V	O
haven	haven(e)	•	•	a	•	1	4	N	S
hazard	hasard	-	•	a	•	2	4	N	N
hazel	hasel	•	-	a	•	1	4	N	O
heaven	heofen	-	•	e	•	1	4	N	O
heavy	hefi	-	•	e	-	1	4	A	O
herald	heraud	-	•	e	•	3	7	N	N
hole	hol(e)	•	-	o	•	-	6	N	O
holly	holi	-	•	o	-	1	6	A	O
honour	honor	-	•	o	-	1	5	N	N
hope	hope	•	-	o	•	-	1	N	O
hope	hopien	•	-	o	•	-	1	V	O
hose	hose	•	-	o	•	-	4	N	O
hovel	hovel	-	•	o	•	1	4	N	?
hover	hove(n)	-	•	o	•	1	4	V	?
jaspis	jaspis	-	•	a	-	2	C1	N	O
jealous	jelos	-	•	e	-	2	6	A	N

ModE	ME	long	σ2	V	ə	W	C	S	E
jolly	joli	-	•	o	-	1	6	A	N
keel	kele	•	-	e	•	-	6	N	S
keel	kele	•	-	e	•	-	6	V	S
kennel	kenel	-	•	e	•	1	5	N	N
kettle	chetel	-	•	e	•	1	1	N	S
knave	cnave	•	-	a	•	-	4	N	O
knead	cneden	•	-	e	•	-	2	V	O
knock	cnoka	-	-	o	•	-	1	V	O
label	label	•	•	a	•	1	2	N	N
labour	labor	•	•	a	-	1	2	N	N
lade	(h)laden	•	-	a	•	-	2	V	O
ladle	(h)ladel	•	•	a	•	1	2	N	O
lake	lac(e)	•	-	a	•	-	1	N	N
lame	lame	•	-	a	•	-	5	A	O
lane	lane	•	-	a	•	-	5	N	O
lap	lapen	-	-	a	•	-	1	V	O
latchet	lachet	-	•	a	•	2	C3	N	N
late	late	•	-	a	•	-	1	A	O
latin	laten	-	•	a	•	1	1	N	N
latten	laton	-	•	a	-	1	1	N	N
latter	later	-	•	a	•	1	1	A	O
lave	laven	•	-	a	•	-	4	V	N
leak	leken	•	-	e	•	-	1	V	O
lean	leonien	•	-	e	•	-	5	V	O
lease	lesen	•	-	e	•	-	4	V	O
leather	leþer	-	•	e	•	1	4	N	O
lecher	lechor	-	•	e	-	1	C3	N	N
legate	legat	-	•	e	•	2	2	N	N
lesson	lesson	-	•	e	-	1	3	N	N
loak	loce	•	-	o	•	-	1	N	O

ModE	ME	long	σ2	V	ə	W	C	S	E
make	make	•	-	a	•	-	1	N	O
make	makien	•	-	a	•	-	1	V	O
mane	mane	•	-	a	•	-	5	N	O
manor	manor	-	•	a	-	1	5	N	N
many	manig	-	•	a	-	1	5	A	O
maple	mapel	•	•	a	•	1	1	N	O
marish	mareis	-	•	a	-	2	7	N	N
maslin	maslin	-	•	a	-	2	C4	N	O
mason	mason	•	•	a	-	1	3	N	N
mast	mast(e)	-	-	a	•	-	C1	N	O
mate	mate	•	-	a	•	-	1	N	?
maze	mase	•	-	a	•	-	4	N	O
mead	mede	•	-	e	•	-	2	N	O
meal	mele	•	-	e	•	-	6	N	O
meat	mete	•	-	e	•	-	1	N	O
mellow	melu	-	•	e	-	2	6	A	O
mere	mere	•	-	e	•	-	7	N	O
metal	metal	-	•	e	•	1	1	N	N
mete	meten	•	-	e	•	-	1	V	O
moat	mote	•	-	o	•	-	1	N	N
moment	moment	•	•	o	•	3	5	N	N
moral	moral	-	•	o	•	2	7	N	N
mote	mote	•	-	o	•	-	1	N	O
naked	nake	•	-	a	•	2	1	A	O
name	name	•	•	a	•	-	5	N	O
narrow	naru	-	•	a	-	2	7	A	O
nave	nave	•	-	a	•	-	4	N	N
navel	navel	•	•	a	•	1	4	N	O
nephew	neve	-	•	e	•	2	4	N	N
nether	neþer	-	•	e	•	1	4	A	O

ModE	ME	long	σ2	V	ə	W	C	S	E
nettle	netel	-	•	e	•	1	1	N	O
gale	gale	•	-	a	•	-	6	N	O
nose	nose	•	-	o	•	-	4	N	O
odour	odor	•	•	o	-	1	2	N	N
ope	ope	•	-	o	•	-	1	V	O
open	open	•	•	o	•	1	1	A	O
otter	oter	-	•	o	•	1	1	N	O
oven	oven	-	•	o	•	1	4	N	O
over	ofer	•	•	o	•	1	4	P	O
palace	palace	-	•	a	•	2	6	N	N
palate	palat	-	•	a	•	2	6	N	N
panel	panel	-	•	a	•	1	5	N	N
paper	paper	•	•	a	•	1	1	N	N
patient	patient	•	•	a	•	2	1	A	N
pea(s)	pese	•	-	e	•	-	4	N	L
pear	pere	•	-	e	•	-	7	N	L
peat	pete	•	-	e	•	-	1	N	L
pebble	pible	-	•	i	•	1	1	N	O
pennon	penon	-	•	e	-	2	5	N	N
penny	pening	-	•	e	-	1	5	N	O
pepper	peper	-	•	e	•	1	1	N	O
peril	peril	-	•	e	-	2	7	N	N
place	place	•	-	a	•	-	3	N	N
planet	planet	-	•	a	•	2	5	N	N
plate	platen	•	-	a	•	-	1	V	N
poke	poken	•	-	o	•	-	1	V	N
poppy	popi	-	•	o	-	1	1	N	O
pose	pose	•	-	o	•	-	4	N	N
pote	poten	•	-	o	•	-	1	V	N
pottle	potel	-	•	o	•	1	1	N	N

ModE	ME	long	σ2	V	ə	W	C	S	E
prelate	prelat	-	•	e	•	2	6	N	N
present	present	-	•	e	•	2	4	A	N
process	proces	•	•	o	•	2	3	N	N
profit	profit	-	•	o	-	2	3	N	N
provost	provost	-	•	o	•	3	4	N	N
quake	cwakien	•	-	a	•	-	1	V	O
quean	cwene	•	-	e	•	-	5	N	O
radish	redic	-	•	e	-	2	2	N	O
rake	rakien	•	-	a	•	-	1	V	O
rate	raten	•	-	a	•	-	1	V	N
rathe	raþ	•	-	a	•	-	4	A	O
rather	raþur	-	•	a	-	1	4	A	O
raven	(h)raven	•	•	a	•	2	4	N	O
razor	rasor	•	•	a	-	1	4	N	N
ready	readi	-	•	e	-	1	2	A	O
reap	repen	•	-	e	•	-	1	V	O
reckon	recen	-	•	e	•	1	1	A	O
record	record	-	•	e	-	3	1	N	N
relic	relik	-	•	e	-	2	6	N	N
repple	repel	-	•	e	•	1	1	N	O
rest	resten	-	-	e	•	-	C1	V	O
revel	revel	-	•	e	•	1	4	V	N
rochet	rochet	-	•	o	•	2	C3	N	N
rot	rotien	-	-	o	•	-	1	V	O
saddle	sadel	-	•	a	•	1	2	N	O
sake	sake	•	-	a	•	-	1	N	O
sale	sale	•	-	a	•	-	6	N	O
sallow	salou	-	•	a	-	2	6	A	O
same	same	•	-	a	•	-	5	A	S
satchel	sachel	-	•	a	•	1	C3	N	N

ModE	ME	long	σ2	V	ə	W	C	S	E
satin	satin	-	•	a	-	1	1	N	N
savour	savor	•	•	a	-	1	4	N	N
scale	scale	•	-	a	•	-	6	N	N
scathe	scaþin	•	-	a	-	-	4	V	S
scrape	schrapien	•	-	a	•	-	1	V	S
seal	sele	•	-	e	•	-	6	N	N
second	second	-	•	e	-	2	1	N	N
senate	senat	-	•	e	•	2	5	N	N
seven	seofon	-	•	e	•	1	4	A	O
shackle	scakel	-	•	a	•	1	1	N	O
shade	schade	•	-	a	•	-	2	N	O
shadow	schadwe	-	•	a	-	2	2	N	O
shake	schaken	•	-	a	•	-	1	V	O
shale	scale	•	-	a	•	-	6	N	O
shamble	schamel	-	•	a	•	1	5	N	O
shame	schame	•	-	a	•	-	5	N	O
share	schar(e)	•	-	a	•	-	7	N	O
share	scharen	•	-	a	•	-	7	V	O
shave	schaven	•	-	a	•	-	4	V	O
shoal	schole	•	-	o	•	-	6	N	O
shote	schote	•	-	o	•	-	1	N	O
shovel	scofle	-	•	o	•	1	4	N	O
skate	scate	•	-	a	•	-	1	N	S
slade	slæd	•	-	a	•	-	2	N	O
slake	slakien	•	-	a	•	-	1	V	O
smear	smere	•	-	e	•	-	7	N	O
smoke	smoke	•	-	o	•	-	1	N	O
smother	smoren	-	•	o	•	1	7	V	O
snake	snake	•	-	a	•	-	1	N	O
snare	snare	•	-	a	•	-	7	N	O

ModE	ME	long	σ2	V	ə	W	C	S	E
soak	sokin	•	-	o	-	-	1	V	O
socket	soket	-	•	o	•	2	1	N	N
solace	solaz	-	•	o	•	2	6	N	N
sole	sole	•	-	o	•	-	6	N	O
sollar	soler	-	•	o	•	1	6	N	N
spade	spade	•	-	a	•	-	2	N	O
spare	sparien	•	-	a	•	-	7	V	O
speak	speken	•	-	e	•	-	1	V	O
spear	spere	•	-	e	•	-	7	N	O
spele	spelien	•	-	e	•	-	6	V	O
spake	spak(e)	•	-	a	•	-	1	V	O
stake	stake	•	-	a	•	-	1	N	O
stale	stale	•	-	a	•	-	6	N	N
staple	stapel	•	•	a	•	1	1	N	N
stare	starin	•	-	a	-	-	7	V	O
statute	statute	-	•	a	-	3	1	N	N*
stave	staf(e)	•	-	a	•	-	4	N	O
steady	stedi	-	•	e	-	1	2	A	O
steal	stelen	•	-	e	•	-	6	V	O
steed	stede	•	-	e	•	-	2	N	O
-stoke	-stoc	•	-	o	•	-	1	N	O
stole	stole	•	-	o	•	-	6	N	O
stove	stove	•	-	o	•	-	4	N	O
swaddle	swaþel	-	•	a	•	1	4	N	O
swathe	swaþe	•	-	e	•	-	4	V	O
swear	swerien	•	-	e	•	-	7	V	O
tabard	tabard	-	•	a	•	2	2	N	N
tabor	tabor	•	•	a	-	1	2	N	N
take	taken	•	-	a	•	-	1	V	S
tale	tale	•	-	a	•	-	6	N	O

ModE	ME	long	σ2	V	ə	W	C	S	E
talent	talent	-	•	a	•	3	6	N	N
talon	talon	-	•	a	-	2	6	N	N
tame	tame	•	-	a	•	-	5	A	O
taper	taper	•	•	a	•	1	1	N	O
tar	tere	•	-	e	•	-	7	N	O
tarry	tary	-	•	a	-	1	7	V	O
tassel	tasel	-	•	a	•	1	3	N	N
taste	taste	•	-	a	•	-	C1	N	N
tear	teren	•	-	e	•	-	7	V	O
tenant	tenant	-	•	e	•	3	5	N	N
tenor	tenor	-	•	e	-	1	5	N	N
tetter	teter	-	•	e	•	1	1	N	O
thead	thede	•	-	e	•	-	2	N	S
theal	thele	•	-	e	•	-	6	N	O
theve	þefe	•	-	e	•	-	4	N	O
thode	thode	•	-	o	•	-	2	N	O
thole	thole	•	-	o	•	-	6	N	O
thole	tholien	•	-	o	•	-	6	V	O
thrave	þrave	•	-	a	•	-	4	N	O
throat	þrote	•	-	o	•	-	1	N	O
throne	trone	•	-	o	•	-	5	N	N
throstle	þrostel	-	•	o	•	1	C1	N	O
throttle	throtel	-	•	o	•	1	1	N	O
travel	travel	-	•	a	•	1	4	N	N
tread	treden	-	-	e	•	-	2	V	O
treadle	tredel	•	•	e	•	1	2	N	O
trivet	trevet	-	•	e	•	2	4	N	N
uvver	ofer	-	•	o	•	1	4	P	O
vacant	vacant	•	•	a	•	3	1	A	N
valour	valor	-	•	a	-	1	6	N	N

ModE	ME	long	σ2	V	ə	W	C	S	E
vane	fane	•	-	a	•	-	5	A	O
vapour	vapor	•	•	a	-	1	1	N	N
vassal	vasal	-	•	a	•	1	3	N	N
venom	venom	-	•	e	-	2	5	N	N
volume	volüm	-	•	o	-	3	6	N	N
wade	waden	•	-	a	•	-	2	V	O
wag	wage	-	-	a	•	-	2	V	O
wake	waken	•	-	a	•	-	1	V	O
wale	wale	•	-	a	•	-	6	N	O
wane	wanien	•	-	a	•	-	5	V	O
ware	war	•	-	a	•	-	6	N	O
warrant	warant	-	•	a	•	3	7	N	N
water	water	-	•	a	•	1	1	N	O
wattle	watel	-	•	a	•	1	1	N	O
wave	waven	•	-	a	•	-	4	V	O
weal	wele	•	-	e	•	-	6	N	O
wean	wenen	•	-	e	•	-	5	V	O
wear	werien	•	-	e	•	-	7	V	O
weasel	wesle	•	•	e	•	1	4	N	O
weather	weder	-	•	e	•	1	2	N	O
weave	weven	•	-	e	•	-	4	V	O
weir	wer(e)	•	-	e	•	-	7	N	O
wether	weþer	-	•	e	•	1	4	N	O
whale	whal	•	-	a	•	-	6	N	O
wheal	welen	•	-	e	•	-	6	V	O
whether	weþer	-	•	e	•	1	4	C	O
wreak	wreken	•	-	e	•	-	1	V	O
yare	geare	•	-	e	•	-	7	A	O
yellow	gelu	-	•	e	-	2	6	A	O

ModE	OE	ME	L	H	O	σ2	V	W	C	S
accurse	accursian	acursien	•	-	-	-	u	-	6	V
alderman	aldor-mon	alderman	-	-	S	•	a	-	4	N
among	ȝemang	imang	-	-	L	-	o	-	3	P
and	and	and	-	-	S	-	a	-	1	C
angle	angel	angel	-	-	-	•	a	1	3	N
bairn	bearn	bern	•	•	-	-	e	-	8	N
bang	banga	----	-	-	-	-	a	-	3	N
barley	bærlic	barli	•	-	-	•	a	1	9	N
barn	bern	barn	•	-	S	-	e	-	8	N
beard	beard	berd	•	•	-	-	e	-	5	N
behind	be-hindan	behinde	•	•	S	-	i	-	1	P
behold	behaldan	biholden	•	•	-	-	a	-	4	V
belong	langian	(bi) longen	-	-	-	-	o	-	3	V
bend	bendan	benden	-	-	-	-	e	-	1	V
bind	bindan	binden	•	•	-	-	i	-	1	V
bird	bird	brid/bird	•	-	-	-	i	-	5	N
birth	ȝebird	bird	•	-	L	-	i	-	5	N
blend	blandan	blenden	-	-	L	-	a	-	1	N
blind	blind	blind	•	•	L	-	i	-	1	A
board	bord	bord	•	•	L	-	o	-	5	N

Abbreviations and symbols:
L = the ModE item has a long nucleus; **H** = the ModE long nucleus is due to **HOL**; **O** = vowel quantity as suggested by Orrm's spelling; **σ₂** = the second syllable is stable **W** = weight of the final syllable; **V** = vowel in σ₁; **C** = type of coda at the end of σ₁ (1 = /nd/, 2 = /mb/, 3 = /ŋg/, 4 = /ld/, 5 = /rd/, 6 = /rð/, 7 = /rz/, 8 = /rn/, 9 = /rl/); **S** = syntactic category

ModE	OE	ME	L	H	O	σ₂	V	W	C	S
bold	bald	bald/bold	•	•	L	-	a	-	4	A
bond	band	band	-	-	L	-	o	-	1	N
bond	bonda	bond	-	-	-	-	o	-	1	N
bound	bunden	bunden	•	•	L	-	u	-	1	V
bourn	beornan	burnen	•	•	-	-	u	-	8	V
brand	brand	brand	-	-	-	-	a	-	1	N
bring	bringan	bringen	-	-	S	-	i	-	3	V
build	byldan	bilden	-	-	-	-	i	-	4	V
bundle	byndelle	bundel	-	-	-	•	u	1	1	N
burden	byrðen	birden	•	-	-	•	u	1	5	N
burn	beornian	burnen	•	-	L	-	u	-	8	V
byrnie	byrne	burne/brinie	•	-	-	•	u	1	8	N
candle	candel	candel	-	-	-	•	a	1	1	N
carl	carl	carl	•	-	-	-	a	-	9	N
ceorl	ceorl	carl	•	-	-	-	a	-	9	N
charlock	cerlic	carloc	•	-	-	-	e	-	9	N
chield	child	sheld	•	•	-	-	e	-	4	N
child	child	child	•	•	L	-	i	-	4	N
churl	ceorl	cherl	•	-	L	-	e	-	9	N
cinder	sinder	sinder	-	-	-	•	i	1	1	N
climb	climban	climben	•	•	L	-	i	-	2	V
cling	clingan	clingen	-	-	-	-	i	-	3	V
clung	clungen	clungen	-	-	L	-	u	-	3	V
cold	cald	cold	•	•	L	-	a	-	4	A
comb	camb	comb	•	•	L	-	o	-	2	N
coomb	cumb	cumb	•	•	-	-	u	-	2	N
corn	corn	corn	•	-	L	-	o	-	8	N
cringe	cringan	cringen	-	-	-	-	i	-	3	V
curse	cursian	cursien	•	-	S	-	u	-	6	V
darn	dyrnan	dernen	•	-	-	-	e	-	8	V
December	December	Decembre	-	-	-	•	e	1	2	N

ModE	OE	ME	L	H	O	σ2	V	W	C	S
dern	dierne	derne	•	-	-	-	e	-	8	N
dreng	dreng	dreng	-	-	-	-	e	-	3	N
dumb	dumb	domb	-	-	-	-	u	-	2	N
dung	dung	dong	-	-	-	-	u	-	3	N
earl	eorl	eorl	•	-	L	-	e	-	9	N
earn	earnian	ernen	•	-	-	-	e	-	8	V
earnest	eornost	ernest	•	-	-	•	e	3	8	A
earth	eorðe	erthe	•	-	L	-	e	-	7	N
eld	eldo	eld	-	-	-	-	e	-	4	A
eldest	eldest	eldest	-	-	-	•	e	3	4	A
end	ende	ende	-	-	L	-	e	-	1	N
erne	earn	ern	•	-	-	-	e	-	8	V
faldstool	fælde-stol	falde-stol	•	-	-	•	a	3	4	N
fang	fang	fang	-	-	-	-	a	-	3	N
fern	fearn	fern	•	-	-	-	e	-	8	N
field	feld	feld	•	•	L	-	e	-	4	N
find	findan	finden	•	•	L	-	i	-	1	V
finger	finger	finger	-	-	-	•	i	1	3	N
fling	flinga (N)	flingen	-	-	-	-	i	-	3	V
fold	faldan	folden	•	•	-	-	a	-	4	V
ford	ford	ford	•	-	L	-	o	-	5	N
found	funden	funden	•	•	L	-	u	-	1	V
furlong	furlang	furlong	•	-	-	•	u	2	9	N
further	furðor	forther	•	-	S	•	u	1	7	A
gang	gang	gang	-	-	-	-	a	-	3	N
garth	geard	garth	•	-	-	-	a	-	5	N
geld	geld	geld	-	-	-	-	e	-	4	N
geld	gelda (N)	ȝeld	-	-	-	-	e	-	4	N
gild	gildan	gilden	-	-	L	-	i	-	4	V
ginger	gingifer	ginger	-	-	-	•	i	1	3	N
gird	gyrdan	girden	•	-	-	-	i	-	5	V

ModE	OE	ME	L	H	O	σ2	V	W	C	S
girdle	gyrdel	girdel	•	-	S	•	i	1	5	N
gold	gold	gold	•	•	L	-	o	-	4	N
grind	grindan	grinden	•	•	L	-	i	-	1	V
ground	grunden	grunden	•	•	L	-	u	-	1	V
groundsel	grunde-swelge	grounde-swel	•	•	-	•	u	-1	1	N
guild	gield	gilde	-	-	-	-	i	-	4	N
hand	hand	hand	-	-	-	-	a	-	1	N
handle	handel	handdlen	-	-	S	•	a	1	1	V
hang	hangian	hangen	-	-	-	-	a	-	3	V
hard	heard	hard	•	-	S	-	a	-	5	A
heard	hierde	herde	•	-	-	-	e	-	5	V
herd	heord	herd	•	-	-	-	e	-	5	N
herd	hierd	herd	•	-	-	-	e	-	5	N
hind	hind	hinde	•	•	-	-	i	-	1	N
hoard	hord	hord	•	-	L	-	o	-	5	N
hold	healdan	halden	•	•	L	-	a	-	4	V
horn	horn	horn	•	-	-	-	o	-	8	N
hornet	hyrnet	hornet	•	-	-	•	o	2	8	N
hound	hund	hound	•	•	L	-	u	-	1	Y
hundred	hund	hundred	-	-	-	•	u	2	1	A
hung	hungen	hungen	-	-	-	-	u	-	3	V
hunger	hungor	hunger	-	-	S	•	u	1	3	N
hurdle	hyrdel	hirdel	•	-	-	•	i	1	5	N
heards	heordan	herde	•	-	-	-	e	-	5	N
kernel	cyrnel	kirnel	•	-	-	•	i	1	8	N
kind	cynd	kinde	•	•	L	-	i	-	1	A
kind	ge-cynde	cinde	•	•	-	-	i	-	1	N
lamb	lamb	lamb	-	-	L	-	a	-	2	N
land	land	lond	-	-	L	-	a	-	1	N
learn	leornian	lernen	•	-	L	-	e	-	8	V
linger	lengan	leng(er)en	-	-	-	•	e	1	3	V

ModE	OE	ME	L	H	O	σ2	V	W	C	S
long	lang	longe	-	-	-	-	o	-	3	A
long	langian	longen	-	-	-	-	o	-	3	V
lung	lungen	longe	-	-	-	-	u	-	3	N
mild	milde	milde	•	•	L	-	i	-	4	A
mildew	mildeaw	mil-deu	-	-	-	•	i	2	4	N
mind	gemynd	minde	•	•	L	-	i	-	1	N
mingle	mengan	mengen	-	-	-	•	e	1	3	V
monger	mangere	monger	-	-	-	•	a	1	3	N
mould	molde	molde	•	•	-	-	o	-	4	N
mourn	murnan	murnen	•	•	-	-	u	-	8	V
murder	morðor	morther	•	-	-	•	u	1	5	N
old	ald	old	•	•	L	-	a	-	4	A
pard	pard	parde	•	-	-	-	a	-	5	N
pound	pund	pound	•	•	-	-	u	-	1	N
pound	pund	pund	•	•	-	-	u	-	1	N
rand	rand	rand	-	-	-	-	a	-	1	N
rend	rendan	renden	-	-	-	-	e	-	1	V
rind	rind	rind	•	•	-	-	i	-	1	N
ring	hring	(h)ring	-	-	-	-	i	-	3	N
ring	hringan	(h)ringen	-	-	L	-	i	-	3	V
rung	hrung	(h)rungen	-	-	-	-	u	-	3	V
sand	sand	sand	-	-	L	-	a	-	1	N
seldom	seldan	seldom	-	-	L	•	e	2	4	A
send	sendan	senden	-	-	S	-	e	-	1	V
shard	sceard	scarth	•	-	-	-	a	-	5	N
shield	sceld	sheld	•	•	-	-	e	-	4	N
should	solde	sholde	-	-	S	-	u	-	4	V
shoulder	sculder	shuldre	•	-	S	•	u	1	4	N
sing	singan	singen	-	-	-	-	i	-	3	V
singe	sengan	sengen	-	-	-	-	e	-	3	V
sling	slingan	slingen	-	-	-	-	i	-	3	V

ModE	OE	ME	L	H	O	σ2	V	W	C	S
sold	sealde	salde	•	•	L	-	a	-	4	V
song	sang	song	-	-	L	-	o	-	3	N
sound	gesund	sund	•	•	L	-	u	-	1	A
sound	sund	sund	•	•	-	-	u	-	1	N
spangle	spang	spangel	-	-	-	•	a	1	3	N
sponge	sponge	sponge	-	-	-	-	o	-	3	N
sprang	sprang	sprang	-	-	L	-	a	-	3	V
spring	springan	springen	-	-	L	-	i	-	3	V
sprung	sprungen	sprungen	-	-	L	-	u	-	3	V
spurn	spurnan	spurnen	•	-	-	-	u	-	8	V
stand	standan	standen	-	-	S	-	a	-	1	V
stern	stirne	stürne	•	-	L	-	i	-	8	A
sting	stingan	stingen	-	-	L	-	i	-	3	V
strand	strand	strand	-	-	-	-	a	-	1	N
string	streng	streng	-	-	-	-	e	-	3	N
strong	strong	stronge	-	-	L	-	o	-	3	A
stung	stungen	stungen	-	-	L	-	u	-	3	V
sunder	sundor	sunder	-	-	-	•	u	1	1	N
sung	sungen	sungen	-	-	L	-	u	-	3	V
sward	sweard	swarde	•	-	-	-	a	-	5	N
swing	swingan	swingen	-	-	-	-	i	-	3	V
swinge	swengan	swengen	-	-	-	-	e	-	3	V
sword	sweord	swerd	•	-	L	-	o	-	5	N
swung	swungen	swungen	-	-	-	-	u	-	3	V
thing	ðing	ðing	-	-	L	-	i	-	3	N
third	ðirda	ðirde	•	-	-	-	i	-	5	A
thong	ðwong	ð(w)ong	-	-	L	-	o	-	3	N
thorn	ðorn	ðorn	•	-	S	-	o	-	8	N
throng	geðrang	ðrang	-	-	-	-	a	-	3	N
timber	timber	timber	-	-	S	•	i	1	2	N
tinder	tynder	tinder	-	-	-	•	i	1	1	N

ModE	OE	ME	L	H	O	σ2	V	W	C	S
told	talde	talde	●	●	L	-	a	-	4	V
tongs	tang	tange	-	-	-	-	a	-	3	N
tongue	tunge	tunge	-	-	L	-	u	-	3	N
trend	trendan	trenden	-	-	-	-	e	-	1	V
trundle	tryndel	trindel	-	-	-	-	u	1	1	N
tumble	tumbian	tumben	-	-	-	●	u	1	2	V
turd	tord	tord	●	-	-	-	u	-	5	N
turn	tyrnan	turnen	●	-	S	-	u	-	8	V
twinge	twingan	twingen	-	-	-	-	i	-	3	V
under	under	under	-	-	S	●	u	1	1	P
wand	vond (on)	wand	-	-	L	-	a	-	1	N
ward	weard	warde	●	-	-	-	a	-	5	N
ward	weardian	wardien	●	-	-	-	a	-	5	V
warn	wearnian	warnien	●	-	-	-	a	-	8	V
weld	wealde	weld	-	-	-	-	e	-	4	N
wend	wendan	wenden	-	-	-	-	e	-	1	V
wield	wealdan	welden	●	●	S	-	e	-	4	V
wild	wild	wilde	●	●	L	-	i	-	4	A
wilderness	wildeornes	wildernesse	-	-	-	●	i	-	4	N
wind	wind	wind	-	-	L	-	i	-	1	N
wind	windan	winden	●	●	S	-	i	-	1	V
window	vind-ouga	windowe	-	-	-	●	i	2	1	N
wing	veng	winge	-	-	-	-	e	-	3	N
wold	wald	wold	●	-	-	-	o	-	4	N
womb	wamb	wambe	●	●	L	-	o	-	2	N
wonder	wundor	wunder	-	-	S	●	u	1	1	N
word	word	word	●	-	L	-	o	-	5	N
worse	wyrsa	wurs	●	-	S	-	u	-	6	A
worth	weorðan	wurðen	●	-	-	-	o	-	7	V
worthy	weorðe	wurði	●	-	-	●	o	1	7	A
wound	wunde	wunde	●	●	L	-	u	-	1	N

ModE	OE	ME	L	H	O	σ₂	V	W	C	S
wring	wringan	wringen	-	-	-	-	i	-	3	V
wrong	wrang	wrang	-	-	S	-	a	-	3	A
wrung	wrungen	wrungen	-	-	-	-	u	-	3	V
would	wolde	wolde	-	-	S	-	u	-	4	V
yard	geard	yard	•	-	S	-	a	-	5	N
yard	gerd	jerde	•	-	-	-	e	-	5	N
yarn	gearn	yarn	•	-	-	-	a	-	8	N
yearn	giernan	jernen	•	-	L	-	e	-	8	V
yield	geldan	jelden	•	•	L	-	e	-	4	V
young	geong	junge	-	-	L	-	u	-	3	A

Appendix III: SHOCC*

ME	No	ModE	EL	S	V	+	O	CCs	Σ	CT
adiȝte	1	-	-	-	i	-	-	-	2	FP
arme	1	-	-	-	a	-	-	-	2	LN
atprenche	2	-	-	-	e	-	-	-	2	NA
bichermet	1	-	-	-	e	-	-	-	2	LN
biclopt	1	-	-	-	o	•	-	-	1	PP
cheste	5	-	-	-	e	-	•	-	2	FP
chirme	1	-	-	-	i	-	-	-	2	LN
custe	3	-	-	-	u	-	•	-	2	FP
diht	1	-	-	-	i	-	-	-	1	FP
eft	9	-	-	-	e	-	-	-	1	FP
fulste	1	-	-	-	u	-	-	-	2	LFP
gengþ	1	-	-	-	e	-	-	-	1	NBF
hiȝteþ	1	-	-	-	i	-	-	-	2	FP
hoȝfule	1	-	-	-	o	•	-	-	3	FF
houhsiþe	1	-	-	-	o	•	-	-	3	FF
hunke	1	-	-	-	u	-	-	-	2	NP
ibolwe	1	-	-	-	o	-	-	-	2	LF

Abbreviations and symbols:
EL = etymologically long; S = short(ened); V = vowel type; + = cluster contains a boundary; O = the cluster is a potential onset; CCs = there is still a cluster in Modern English (options: Y = yes, N = no, E = a vowel has come to be epenthesized, V = one constiutent of the cluster has come to be vocalized, V^r = one of the constituents is /r/ and has been vocalized in non-rhotic dialects, $V^{(0)}$ = one of the constituents is optionally vocalized, Y^*= the cluster is preserved, but its second constituent has come to act as syllabic nucleus); Σ = number of σ in the foot; CT = type of consonant cluster: L = liquid; N = nasal; F = fricative; B = voiced stop; P = voiceless plosive.

* Based on *The Owl and the Nightingale*

ME	№	ModE	EL	S	V	+	O	CCs	Σ	CT
idorue	1	-	-	-	o	-	-	-	2	LF
ilke	2	-	-	-	i	-	-	-	2	LP
iworpe	1	-	-	-	o	-	-	-	2	LP
iworþe	1	-	-	-	o	-	-	-	2	LF
meoster	1	-	-	-	e	-	•	-	2	FP
misrempe	2	-	-	-	e	-	-	-	2	NP
misstorte	1	-	-	-	o	-	-	-	2	LP
nawiht	1	-	-	-	i	-	-	-	1	FP
nost	1	-	-	-	o	•	•	-	1	FP
nowiȝt	2	-	-	-	i	-	-	-	2	FP
nusteþ	1	-	-	-	u	•	•-	N		FP
orfe	1	-	-	-	o	-	-	-	2	LF
schirme	1	-	-	-	i	-	-	-	2	LN
shafte	1	-	-	-	a	-	-	-	2	FP
sothede	2	-	-	-	o	•	-	-	3	PF
tort	1	-	-	-	o	-	-	-	1	LP
totwichet	1	-	-	-	i	-	•	-	2	A
þarf	1	-	-	-	a	-	-	-	1	LF
þeostre	1	-	-	-	e	-	•	-	2	FPL
þilke	1	-	-	-	i	-	-	-	2	LP
unker	7	-	-	-	u	-	-	-	2	NP
unwiȝt	2	-	-	-	i	-	-	-	1	FP
unwiȝtis	1	-	-	-	i	-	-	-	2	FP
unwreste	3	-	-	-	e	-	•	-	2	FP
uorcrempeþ	1	-	-	-	e	-	-	-	2	NP
warp	2	-	-	-	a	-	-	-	1	LP
weolcne	1	-	-	-	e	-	-	-	2	LPN
wiȝt	5	-	-	-	i	-	-	-	1	FP
wiȝte	4	-	-	-	i	-	-	-	2	FP
wiȝtes	2	-	-	-	i	-	-	-	2	FP
worp	1	-	-	-	o	-	-	-	1	LP
worpe	1	-	-	-	o	-	-	-	2	LP
worpeþ	1	-	-	-	o	-	-	-	2	LP
worþ	1	-	-	-	o	-	-	-	1	LF
wurþe	4	-	-	-	u	-	-	-	2	LF

ME	No	ModE	EL	S	V	+	O	CCs	Σ	CT
after	11	after	-	-	a	-	-	Y	2	FP
Aluered	1	Alfred	-	-	a	-	-	Y	3	LF
alured	11	Alfred	-	-	a	-	-	Y	2+	LFL
alswa	2	also	-	-	a	-	-	Y	2+	LFG
alswo	3	also	-	-	a	-	-	Y	2+	LFG
ongred	1	angered	-	-	o	-	-	Y	2	NBL
andsuare	3	answer	-	-	a	-	-	Y	3	NBFG
andswere	2	answer	-	-	a	-	-	Y	3	NBFG
ansvere	2	answer	-	-	a	-	-	Y	3	NFG
answare	5	answer	-	-	a	-	-	Y	3	NFG
ondsware	2	answer	-	-	a	-	-	Y	3	NBFG
ondswere	1	answer	-	-	e	-	-	Y	3	NBFG
art	21	art	-	-	a	-	-	Y	1	LP
nart	11	art (not)	-	-	a	-	-	Y	1	LP
niʒtes	4	at night	-	-	i	-	-	V	2	FP
best	2	best	-	-	e	-	•	Y	1	FP
bituxen	1	betwixt	-	-	u	-	•	Y	2	PF
burʒ	1	borough	-	-	u	-	-	E	1	LF
iborʒe	1	borrow	-	-	o	-	-	E	2+	LF
aboʒte	1	bought	-	-	o	-	-	V	2	FP
berste	1	burst	-	-	e	-	-	Y	2	LFP
to-berste	1	burst	-	-	e	-	-	Y	2	LFP
tobursteþ	1	burst	-	-	u	-	-	Y	2	LFP
canst	6	can	-	-	a	•	-	Y	1	NFP
const	2	can	-	-	o	•	-	Y	1	NFP
cartare	1	carter	-	-	a	-	-	V^r	3	LP
castel	1	castle	-	-	a	-	•	Y	2	FP
Certes	1	certain	-	-	e	-	-	V^r	2	LP
childre	2	children	-	-	i	-	-	Y	2	LBL
children	2	children	-	-	i	-	-	Y	2+	LBL
chirche	3	church	-	-	i	-	-	V^r	2	LA
chirche	1	church	-	-	i	-	-	V^r	2	LA
chirche-bende	1	church	-	-	i	-	-	V^r	2	LA
chirche-song	1	churchsong	-	-	i	-	-	V^r	3	LA
darst	2	dare	-	-	a	•	-	N	1	LFP

ME	No	ModE	EL	S	V	+	O	CCs	Σ	CT
dai-liȝt	1	daylight	-	-	i	-	-	V	1	FP
duntes	1	dints/dunts	-	-	u	-	-	Y	2	NP
orþliche	1	earthly	-	-	i	-	-	Vʳ	3	LFL
efne	1	even-ly	-	-	e	-	-	E	2	FN
faukun	3	falcon	-	-	a	-	-	V⁽ᵒ⁾	2	LP
fals	1	false	-	-	a	-	-	Y	1	LF
faste	1	fast	-	-	a	-	•	Y	2	FP
uastre	1	faster	-	-	a	-	•	Y	2	FPL
fiȝt	3	fight	-	-	i	-	-	V	1	FP
viȝte	7	fight	-	-	i	-	-	V	2	FP
fiȝtinge	1	fighting	-	-	i	-	-	V	3	FP
fihtlac	1	fighting(þ)	-	-	i	-	-	V	2+	FPL
fihs	1	fish	-	-	i	-	-	S	1	FF
folc	1	folk	-	-	o	-	-	V	1	LP
folȝeþ	1	follow	-	-	o	-	-	E	2+	LF
folȝi	1	follow	-	-	o	-	-	E	2+	LF
forme	1	former	-	-	o	-	-	Vʳ	2	LN
auorþ	1	forth	-	-	o	-	-	Vʳ	1	LF
uorþ	6	forth	-	-	o	-	-	Vʳ	1	LF
fort	3	forto/until	-	-	o	-	-	Vʳ	1	LP
uaȝt	1	fought	-	-	a	-	-	V	1	FP
fox	3	fox	-	-	o	-	-	Y	1	PF
foxes	1	fox's	-	-	o	-	-	Y	2	PF
forþure	1	further	-	-	o	-	-	Vʳ	3	LF
gente	1	gentle	-	-	e	-	-	Y	2	NP
golfinc	1	goldfinch	-	-	o	•	-	Y	2+	LF
gult	1	guilt	-	-	u	-	-	Y	1	LP
gulte	2	guilt	-	-	u	-	-	Y	2	LP
halue	2	half	-	-	a	-	-	V	2	LF
uthalue	1	half	-	-	a	-	-	V	2	LF
hong	1	hang	-	-	o	-	-	Y	1	NB
hard	1	hard	-	-	a	-	-	Y	1	LB
harm	4	harm	-	-	a	-	-	Y	1	LN
harpe	4	harp	-	-	a	-	-	Y	2	LP
heorte	4	heart	-	-	e	-	-	Y	2	LP

ME	№	ModE	EL	S	V	+	O	CCs	Σ	CT
horte	11	heart	-	-	o	-	-	Y	2	LP
helpe	9	help	-	-	e	-	-	Y	2	LP
helpþ	1	helps	-	-	e	-	-	Y	1	LPF
halt	2	hold	-	-	a	-	-	Y	1	LP
holʒ	2	hollow	-	-	o	-	-	E	2+	LF
holi-chirche	1	holy church	-	-	o	-	-	Vʳ	2	LA
hors	2	horse	-	-	o	-	-	Vʳ	1	LF
hundred	1	hundred	-	-	u	-	-	Y	2+	NBL
houene-liʒte	1	hvn's light	-	-	o	-	-	V	2	FP
ich	1	I	-	-	i	-	•	V	1	A
king	4	king	-	-	i	-	-	N	1	NB
londfolc	1	landfolk	-	-	o	-	-	Y	1	NBF
lahfulnesse	1	lawfulness	-	-	a	•	-	V	4	FF
lenst	1	lend	-	-	e	-	-	Y	1	NFP
lengþe	1	length	-	-	e	-	-	Y	2	NBF
unlengþe	1	length	-	-	e	-	-	Y	2	NBF
liʒt	3	light	-	-	i	-	-	V	1	FP
liʒte	5	light	-	-	i	-	-	V	2	FP
lusteþ	1	listen	-	-	u	-	•	N	2	FP
litle	1	little	-	-	i	-	-	Y*	2	PL
lutle	9	little	-	-	u	-	-	Y*	2	PF
lutli	1	(be)little V	-	-	u	-	-	Y*	2	PF
long	6	long	-	-	o	-	-	Y	1	NB
leng	4	longer	-	-	e	-	-	Y	1	NB
luste	4	listen	-	-	u	-	•	N	2	FP
luste	3	lust	-	-	u	-	•	Y	2	FP
lust	6	lust	-	-	u	-	•	Y	1	FP
lust	5	lost	-	-	u	-	•	Y	1	FP
lustes	2	lusts	-	-	u	-	•	Y	2	FP
mer5e	1	marsh	-	-	e	-	-	Vʳ	2	NF
merci	1	merci	-	-	e	-	-	Vʳ	2	LF
middel-niʒte	1	mid of night	-	-	i	-	-	V	4	FP
miʒtest	1	might(st)	-	-	i	-	-	V	2	FP
mildre	1	milder	-	-	i	-	-	Y	2	LBL
milse	1	mildness	-	-	i	-	-	Y	2	LF

ME	№	ModE	EL	S	V	+	O	CCs	Σ	CT
milc	1	milk	-	-	i	-	-	Y	1	LP
murȝþe	6	mirth	-	-	u	-	-	V^r	2	LFF
miste	1	missed	-	-	i	-	•	Y	2	FP
a-morȝe	1	morrow	-	-	o	-	-	E	2+	LF
most	1	must	-	-	o	-	•	Y	1	FP
moste	1	must	-	-	o	-	•	Y	2	FP
nest	7	nest	-	-	e	-	•	Y	1	FP
neste	6	nest	-	-	e	-	•	Y	2	FP
netle	1	nettles	-	-	e	-	-	Y*	2	PL
aniȝt	6	night	-	-	i	-	-	V	1	FP
niȝt	6	night	-	-	i	-	-	V	1	FP
niȝte	5	night	-	-	i	-	-	V	2	FP
niȝtingale	24	nightingale	-	-	i	-	-	V	4	FP
nihtegale	6	nightingale	-	-	i	-	-	V	4	FP
norþ	1	north	-	-	o	-	-	V^r	1	LF
oft	7	often	-	-	o	-	-	Y$^{(o)}$	1	FP
ofte	5	often	-	-	o	-	-	Y$^{(o)}$	2	FP
ofne	1	oven	-	-	o	-	-	E	2	FN
oxe	1	ox	-	-	o	-	•	Y	2	PF
pulte	2	pelt	-	-	u	-	-	Y	2	LP
poure	1	poor	-	-	o	-	-	V	2	FL
Portesham	1	Portesham	-	-	o	-	-	V^r	3	LP
Porteshom	1	Portesham	-	-	o	-	-	V^r	3	LP
red-purs	1	purse	-	-	e	-	-	V^r	1	LF
rente	3	rent	-	-	e	-	-	Y	2	NP
rest	1	rest	-	-	e	-	•	Y	1	FP
reste	1	rest	-	-	e	-	•	Y	2	FP
ariȝt	5	right	-	-	i	-	-	V	1	FP
rehte	1	right	-	-	e	-	-	V	2	FP
riȝt	21	right	-	-	i	-	-	V	1	FP
riȝte	31	right	-	-	i	-	-	V	2	FP
rihtne	1	right	-	-	i	-	-	V	2	FPN
þarrihte	1	...right	-	-	i	-	-	Y	2	FP
salue	1	salve	-	-	a	-	-	Y	2	LF
isihst	3	see	-	-	i	•	-	N	1	FFP

ME	№	ModE	EL	S	V	+	O	CCs	Σ	CT
sichst	1	see	-	-	i	●	-	N	1	FFP
seolfe	1	self	-	-	e	-	-	Y	2	LF
seolue	2	self	-	-	e	-	-	Y	2	LF
solue	2	self	-	-	o	-	-	Y	2	LF
sulf	1	self	-	-	u	-	-	Y	1	LF
sulfe	1	self	-	-	u	-	-	Y	2	LF
sulue	3	self	-	-	u	-	-	Y	2	LF
serueþ	1	serve	-	-	e	-	-	Y	2	LF
setle	1	settle	-	-	e	-	-	Y*	2	PL
scharp	2	sharp	-	-	a	-	-	V^r	1	LP
scharpe	3	sharp	-	-	a	-	-	V^r	2	LP
short	1	short	-	-	o	-	-	V^r	1	LP
seoluer	1	silver	-	-	e	-	-	Y	2	LF
singþ	1	sing	-	-	i	-	-	Y	1	NBF
singst	8	sing	-	-	i	-	-	Y	1	NBFP
softe	3	soft	-	-	o	-	-	Y	2	FP
softest	1	soft	-	-	o	-	-	Y	2+	FP
sumne	2	some	-	-	u	●	-	N	2	NN
song	31	song	-	-	o	-	-	N	1	NB
seorhe	1	sorrow	-	-	e	-	-	E	2+	LF
sorȝe	2	sorrow	-	-	o	-	-	E	2+	LF
ispild	1	spilt	-	-	i	●	-	Y	1	LB
a-stable	1	stable	-	-	a	-	●	Y*	2	BL
bistant	1	stand	-	-	a	-	-	Y	1	NP
astorue	1	starve	-	-	o	-	-	V^r	2	LF
fast-rede	1	steadfast	-	-	a	-	●	Y	3	FPL
unstrengþe	1	strength	-	-	e	-	-	Y	2	NBF
isuolȝe	1	swallow	-	-	o	-	-	E	2+	LF
telst	1	tell	-	-	e	●	-	N	1	LFP
þonc	2	thank	-	-	o	-	-	Y	1	NP
þonkes	1	thanks	-	-	o	-	-	Y	2	NP
þar-after	3	thereafter	-	-	a	-	-	Y	2	FP
þar-among	1	thereamong	-	-	o	-	-	N	1	NB
þing	21	thing	-	-	i	-	-	Y	1	NB
þencheþ	2	think	-	-	e	-	-	Y	2	NA

ME	No	ModE	EL	S	V	+	O	CCs	Σ	CT
þincþ	3	think	-	-	i	-	-	Y	1	NPF
þincþe	1	think	-	-	i	-	-	Y	2	NPF
þinche	1	think	-	-	i	-	-	Y	2	NA
þincheþ	1	think	-	-	i	-	-	Y	2	NA
þinchest	1	think	-	-	i	-	-	Y	2	NA
þingþ	1	think	-	-	i	-	-	Y	1	NBF
þuncþ	3	think	-	-	u	-	-	Y	1	NPF
þuncheþ	1	think	-	-	u	-	-	Y	2	NA
þungþ	1	think	-	-	u	-	-	Y	2	NBF
biþenche	4	think	-	-	e	-	-	Y	2	NA
biþenchest	1	think	-	-	e	-	-	Y	2	NA
iþenche	1	think	-	-	e	-	-	Y	2	NA
þenche	2	thinkl	-	-	e	-	-	Y	2	NA
þurʒ	13	through	-	-	u	-	-	V	1	LF
þurʒut	2	throughout	-	-	u	-	-	V	2+	LF
toward	4	toward	-	-	o	-	-	Vʳ	2	LB
turf	1	turf	-	-	u	-	-	Vʳ	1	LF
turnþ	1	turn	-	-	u	-	-	Vʳ	1	LNF
unriʒt	6	unright	-	-	i	-	-	V	1	FP
unrihtfulnesse	1	unright...	-	-	i	-	-	V	4	FPF
unwurþ	1	unworthy	-	-	u	-	-	Vʳ	1	LF
iwarnesse	1	awareness	-	-	a	•	-	Vʳ	2+	LN
warm	1	warm	-	-	a	-	-	Vʳ	1	LN
warme	1	warm	-	-	a	-	-	Vʳ	2	LN
waste	1	waste	-	-	a	-	•	Y	2	FP
weste	2	waste	-	-	e	-	•	Y	2	FP
wepne	1	weapon (s)	-	-	e	-	-	E	2	PN
west	1	west	-	-	e	-	•	Y	1	FP
a-winter	3	winter	-	-	i	-	-	Y	2	NP
a-wintere	1	winter	-	-	i	-	-	Y	3	NP
wintere	1	winter	-	-	i	-	-	Y	3	NP
winteres	1	winter's	-	-	i	-	-	Y	3	NP
wicchecrefte	1	witchcraft	-	-	i	-	•	Y	4	A
wiecche-crafte	1	witchcraft	-	-	i	-	•	Y	4	A
witles	1	witless	-	-	i	•	-	Y	2+	PL

ME	No	ModE	EL	S	V	+	O	CCs	Σ	CT
wulues	1	wolves	-	-	u	-	-	Y	2	LF
word	11	word	-	-	o	-	-	V^r	1	LB
wirche	1	work	-	-	i	-	-	V^r	2	LA
wurchen	1	work	-	-	u	-	-	V^r	2	LA
a-worlde	1	world	-	-	o	-	-	V^r	2	LLB
worlde	1	world	-	-	o	-	-	V^r	2	LLB
wormes	1	worms	-	-	o	-	-	V^r	2	LN
wurs	2	worse	-	-	u	-	-	V^r	1	LF
wurþschipe	1	worship	-	-	u	-	-	V^r	3	LFF
wurþsipe	1	worship	-	-	u	-	-	V^r	3	LFF
wurschipe	1	worship	-	-	u	●	-	V^r	3	LF
alre-vurste	1	worst	-	-	u	-	-	V^r	2	LFP
alre-worste	1	worst	-	-	o	-	-	V^r	2	LFP
wurþ	6	worth	-	-	u	-	-	V^r	1	LF
forworþe	3	worth	-	-	o	-	-	V^r	2	LF
wurþful	1	worthy	-	-	u	-	-	V^r	2+	LFF
woldest	1	would	-	-	o	●	-	V	2	LB
unwrenche	2	wrench (?)	-	-	e	-	-	Y	2	NA
ȝerd	1	yard (???)	-	-	e	-	-	V^r	1	LB
ȝolst	1	yell	-	-	o	●	-	N	1	LFP
ȝeilpest	1	yelp	-	-	ei	-	-	Y	2	LP
ȝelpst	1	yelp	-	-	e	-	-	Y	1	LPFP
ȝeolpest	1	yelp	-	-	e	-	-	Y	2+	LP
ȝulpest	2	yelp	-	-	u	-	-	Y	2+	LP
ȝunglinge	1	youngling	-	-	u	-	-	Y	3	NBL
ȝunling	1	youngling	-	-	u	-	-	Y	2+	NL
aȝte	2	-	●	-	a	-	-	-	2	FP
aht	3	-	●	-	a	-	-	-	1	FP
amanset	1	-	●	-	a	-	-	-	2+	NF
atwist	1	-	●	-	i	●	●	-	1	FP
bisne	2	-	●	-	i	-	●	-	2	FN
eiȝte	1	-	●	-	ei	-	-	-	2	FP
este	5	-	●	-	e	-	●	-	2	FP
golnesse	5	-	●	-	o	●	-	-	3	LN
godhede	1	-	●	-	o	●	-	-	3	BF

ME	No	ModE	EL	S	V	+	O	CCs	Σ	CT
ȝephede	1	-	•	-	e	•	-	-	3	PF
lerdest	1	-	•	-	e	•	-	-	2+	LB
liste	4	-	•	-	i	-	•	-	2	FP
mansing	1	-	•	-	a	-	-	-	2+	NF
mansinge	1	-	•	-	a	-	-	-	3	NF
redles	1	-	•	-	e	•	-	-	2+	BL
þuster	3	-	•	-	u	-	•	-	2	FP
þusternesse	1	-	•	-	u	-	•	-	4	FP
þustre	1	-	•	-	u	-	•	-	2	FPL
utheste	1	-	•	-	e	-	•	-	2	FP
wanst	1	-	•	-	a	•	-	-	1	NFP
ax	1	ask	•	-	a	-	-	Y	1	PF
axest	1	ask	•	-	a	-	-	Y	2	PF
axestu	1	ask	•	-	a	-	-	Y	2	PF
askedest	1	asked	•	-	a	-	•	Y	2	FP
oȝt	2	aught	•	-	o	-	-	V	1	FP
ibroȝt	2	brought	•	-	o	•	-	V	1	FP
upbroȝte	1	brought up	•	-	o	-	-	V	2	FP
chist	1	chide	•	-	i	•	•	N	1	FP
deoulene	1	devil	•	•	e	-	-	E	3	FL
dest	4	dost (V, 2sg)	•	•	e	•	•	Y	1	FP
dost	2	dost (V, 2sg)	•	•	o	•	•	Y	1	FP
euch	2	each	•	-	e	-	•	Y	1	A
east	1	east	•	-	e	-	•	Y	1	FP
Engelonde	1	England	•	•	e	-	-	Y	4	NB
ȝaure	1	ever	•	•	a	-	•	E	2	FL
eure	11	ever	•	•	e	-	•	E	2	FL
eurich	11	every	•	•	e	-	•	Y	2	FL
uint	1	find	•	-	i	-	-	Y	1	NP
fust	1	fist	•	•	u	-	•	Y	1	FP
gost	3	ghost	•	-	o	-	•	Y	1	FP
gest	3	go	•	-	e	•	•	N	1	FP
Goddspel	1	Gospel	•	•	o	-	-	Y	2	BFP
Goddspelle	1	Gospel	•	•	o	-	-	Y	3	BFP

ME	No	ModE	EL	S	V	+	O	CCs	Σ	CT
gostes	1	gost's	•	-	o	-	•	Y	2	FP
Henri	1	Henry	•	•	e	-	-	Y	2	NL
alre-hecst	2	highest	•	-	e	•	-	V	1	PFP
hexst	1	highest	•	-	e	•	-	V	1	FFP
hord	2	hoard	•	-	o	-	-	V^r	1	LB
Irlonde	1	Irland	•	-	i	•	-	V^r	2+	LL
lefdi	1	lady	•	-	e	-	-	V	2	FB
ilast	1	last	•	-	a	-	•	Y	1	FP
ilest	2	last	•	-	e	-	•	Y	1	FP
ileste	1	last	•	-	e	-	•	Y	2	FP
ilesteþ	1	last	•	-	e	-	•	Y	2	FP
last	2	last	•	-	a	-	•	Y	1	FP
lest	1	last	•	-	e	-	•	Y	1	FP
list	1	lie (LOC)	•	-	i	•	•	N	1	FP
liʒtliche	2	lightly	•	-	i	-	-	V	2+	FPL
lihtlich	2	lightly	•	-	i	-	-	V	2+	FPL
lodlich	3	loathly	•	-	o	•	-	Y	2	BL
Maister	2	master	•	-	ai	-	•	Y	2	FP
Maistre	1	master	•	-	ai	-	•	Y	2	FPL
menst	1	mean	•	-	e	•	-	N	1	NFP
alre-mest	1	most	•	-	e	-	•	Y	1	FP
mest	1	most	•	-	e	-	•	Y	1	FP
neure	3	never	•	•	e	-	-	E	2	FL
alre-necst	1	next	•	•	e	•	-	Y	1	PFP
alre-nest	1	next	•	•	e	•	•	Y	1	FP
nabuʒþ	1	obey	•	-	u	•	-	V	1	GF
oþre	2	other	•	•	o	-	•	E	2	FL
oþres	1	others	•	•	o	-	•	E	2+	FL
readliche	1	readily	•	•	a	•	-	E	3	BL
techest	1	teach	•	-	e	-	•	Y	2	A
þoʒtest	1	thought	•	-	o	•	-	V	2	FP
tacninge	1	token	•	-	a	-	•	e	2	PN
wenst	1	ween	•	-	e	•	-	Y	1	NFP

Appendix IV: TRISH*

ME wordform	N	ModE	EL	S	C	ə#	{1}	W	V	Con
engeles	1	angels	-	-	HC	-	-	-	e	-
answare	5	answer	-	•	CC	•	•	-	a	-
ansvere	2	answer	-	•	CC	•	•	-	a	-
andsware	3	answer	-	•	CC	•	•	-	a	-
andswere	2	answer	-	•	CC	•	•	-	a	-
ondsware	2	answer	-	•	CC	•	•	-	o	-
ondswere	1	answer	-	•	CC	•	•	-	o	-
axestu	1	ask	•	-	CC	-	-	-	a	-
askedest	1	asked	•	-	CC	-	-	-	a	-
bataile	1	battle	-	•	C	•	•	-	a	-
betere	10	better	-	•	C^c	•	•	-	e	-
kanunes	1	canons	-	•	C	-	-	-	a	-
cartare	1	carter	-	-	CC	•	•	-	a	-
chaterest	1	chatter	-	•	C^c	-	-	-	a	-

Abbreviations and symbols:
N = frequency of wordform; EL = etymological long vowel; S= shortened in ModE; C = coda type (C = one consonant, CC = more than one consonant, C^c = one consonant, but a cluster may be created through the deletion of an intermediate vowel, HC = homorganic cluster); ə# = the third syllable is /ə/ and may be lost; {1} = without internal morpheme boundaries; W = the item tends to occur unstressed; V = vowel in σ1; **Con** = trisyllabic on the following conditions: - = no conditions; i = if /iV/ sequences are analysed as disyllabic; s = if final \<e\> is regarded as silent; **si** = if both of the last two conditions hold.

* Based on *The Owl and the Nightingale*

ME wordform	N	ModE	EL	S	C	ə#	{l}	W	V	Con
chatere	1	chatter	-	•	C^C	•	•	-	a	-
chatering	1	chattering	-	•	C^C	-	-	-	a	-
clennesse	1	cleanness	•	-	CC	•	-	-	e	-
cradele	1	cradle	-	•	C^C	•	•	-	a	-
kukeweld	1	cuckold	-	•	C^C	-	-	-	u	-
(a)kursedest	1	curse	-	•	HC	-	-	-	u	-
deoulene	1	devil	•	•	CC	•	-	-	e	-
Dorsete	1	Dorset	-	-	HC	•	•	-	o	-
drunnesse	1	drunkenness	-	•	CC	•	-	-	u	-
orþliche	1	earthly	-	•	CC	•	-	-	o	-
etestu	1	eat	-	-	C^C	-	-	-	e	-
erende	1	errand	•	•	C^C	•	•	-	e	-
euening	1	evening	•	-	C^C	-	•	-	e	-
eauere	1	ever	•	•	C^C	•	•	-	e	-
eauereeuch	1	every	•	•	C^C	-	•	•	e	-
eauereuch	2	every	-	•	C^C	-	•	•	e	-
euereuch	4	every	•	•	C^C	-	•	•	e	-
uuele	2	evil	-	-	C^C	•	•	-	u	-
vuele	5	evil	-	-	C^C	•	•	-	u	-
falewi	1	fallow	-	•	C^C	-	-	-	a	-
fiȝtinge	1	fighting	-	-	CC	•	-	-	i	-
uindestu	1	find	-	-	HC	-	-	-	i	-
uoreward	2	foreward	-	-	C^C	-	-	-	o	-
fuliche	1	foully	•	-	C	•	-	-	u	-
fulliche	1	foully	•	-	CC	•	-	-	u	-
fuȝele	1	fowl	-	-	C^C	•	•	-	u	-
fuheles	1	fowl(s)	-	-	C^C	-	-	-	u	-
fuȝeles	2	fowl(s)	-	-	C^C	-	-	-	u	-
forþure	1	further	-	-	HC	•	-	-	o	-

ME wordform	N	ModE	EL	S	C	ə#	{l}	W	V	Con
gabbinge	1	gabbing	-	•	C	•	-	-	a	-
(to)gadere	1	(to)ge/ather	-	•	Cᶜ	•	•	-	a	-
gidie	1	giddy(-ness)	-	•	C	•	•	-	i	-
gladdere	1	gladder	-	•	Cᶜ	•	-	-	a	-
grettere	1	greater	•	-	Cᶜ	•	-	-	e	-
grimliche	1	grimly	-	•	CC	•	-	-	i	-
grisliche	1	grizzly	•	•	CC	•	-	-	i	-
hareme	1	harm	-	•	Cᶜ	•	•	-	a	-
hauestu	1	have	-	•	Cᶜ	-	-	•	a	-
nauestu	1	have	-	-	Cᶜ	-	-	•	a	-
neuestu	1	have	-	•	Cᶜ	-	-	•	e	-
hauekes	1	hawk	-	•	Cᶜ	-	-	-	a	-
houene	5	heaven	-	•	Cᶜ	•	•	-	o	-
heouene	1	heaven	-	•	Cᶜ	•	•	-	e	-
kunrede	1	kindred	-	•	CC	•	-	-	u	-
lauedi	2	lady	•	-	CC	-	•	-	a	-
liȝtliche	2	lightly	•	-	CC	•	-	-	i	-
lilie	1	lily	-	•	C	•	•	-	i	-
linnene	1	linen	•	•	C	•	•	-	i	-
longinge	2	longing	-	•	HC	•	-	-	o	-
lauerdes	1	lord's	•	-	Cᶜ	-	-	-	a	-
louerdes	1	lords	•	-	C	-	-	-	o	-
manie	1	many	-	•	C	•	•	-	a	-
monie	2	many	-	•	C	•	•	-	o	-
murie	3	merry	-	•	C	•	•	-	u	-
miȝtistu	1	might	-	-	CC	-	-	-	i	-
mureȝþe	1	mirth	-	•	Cᶜ	•	-	-	u	-
munekes	1	monks	-	•	Cᶜ	-	-	-	u	-
murninge	1	mourning	-	-	HC	•	-	-	u	-

ME wordform	N	ModE	EL	S	C	ə#	{l}	W	V	Con
muchele	2	much	-	•	C^C	•	•	-	u	-
narewe	2	narrow	-	•	C^C	•	•	-	a	-
neuere	1	never	•	•	C^C	•	•	-	e	-
Nichole	3	Nicholas	-	•	C	•	•	-	i	-
oþeres	2	others	•	•	C^C	-	-	•	o	-
utlete	1	outlet	•	-	CC	•	-	-	u	-
ahene	2	own	•	-	C^C	•	•	-	a	-
oȝene	3	own	•	-	C^C	•	•	-	o	-
pipinge	3	piping	•	-	C	•	-	-	i	-
Portesham	1	Portesham	-	-	CC	-	-	-	o	-
Porteshom	1	Portesham	-	-	CC	-	-	-	o	-
raddere	1	rather	-	-	C^C	•	-	-	a	-
raþere	1	rather	-	-	C^C	•	•	-	a	-
Scotlonde	1	Scotland	-	•	CC	•	-	-	o	-
utschute	1	shout out (?)	•	-	CC	•	-	-	u	-
seolliche	1	silly	•	•	CC	•	-	-	e	-
sunegeþ	1	sin	-	•	C^C	-	-	-	u	-
sunegi	1	sin	-	•	C^C	-	-	-	u	-
sunfulle	1	sinful	-	•	CC	•	-	-	u	-
singinde	1	singing	-	•	HC	•	-	-	i	-
sulieþ	1	soil/sully (?)	-	-	C	-	-	-	u	-
speddestu	1	sped	-	•	C^C	-	-	-	e	-
sumeres	1	summer	-	•	C^C	-	-	-	u	-
sumere	4	summer	-	•	C^C	•	•	-	u	-
tacninge	1	taking	-	-	C	•	-	-	a	-
þarafter	3	thereafter	•	-	C	-	-	-	a	-
þarinne	1	therein	•	-	C	•	-	-	a	-
þarouer	1	thereover	•	-	C	-	-	-	a	-
þiderward	1	thitherward	-	•	C	-	-	-	i	-

ME wordform	N	ModE	EL	S	C	ə#	{l}	W	V	Con
tiþinge	2	tiding	•	-	C	•	-	-	i	-
(i)warnesse	1	wariness	-	-	CC	•	-	-	a	-
Wenestu	1	ween	-	-	C^C	-	-	-	e	-
whonene	1	whence	-	•	C^C	•	•	-	o	-
hwarfore	1	wherefore	•	-	CC	•	-	-	a	-
winteres	1	winter	-	•	CC	-	-	-	i	-
(a-)wintere	2	winter	-	•	CC	•	•	-	i	-
wisdome	3	wisdom	•	•	CC	•	-	-	i	-
wisure	2	wiser	•	-	C	•	-	-	i	-
wimmane	1	women	-	•	C	•	•	-	i	-
Wundere	1	wonder	-	•	HC	•	•	-	u	-
wurschipe	1	worship	-	•	CC	•	-	-	u	-
wurþsipe	1	worship	-	•	CC	•	-	-	u	-
wurþschipe	1	worship	-	•	CC	•	-	-	u	-
wraslinge	1	wrestling	-	•	C	•	-	-	a	-
wrechede	2	wretched	-	•	C	•	-	-	e	-
ȝulinge	1	yelling	-	•	C	•	-	-	u	-
ȝunglinge	1	youngling	-	•	CC	•	-	-	u	-
areȝþe	2	--------	-	-	C^C	•	-	-	a	-
areme	1	--------	-	-	C^C	•	•	-	a	-
aþele	1	--------	-	-	C^C	•	•	-	a	-
(a-)bisemar	1	--------	-	-	C^C	-	•	-	i	-
boldhede	1	--------	•	-	CC	•	-	-	o	-
dernliche	1	--------	-	-	CC	•	-	-	e	-
diȝele	1	--------	•	-	C^C	•	•	-	i	-
duȝeþe	1	--------	-	-	C^C	•	-	-	u	-
dweole-song	1	--------	-	-	C	-	•	-	e	-
ereming	1	--------	-	-	C^C	-	-	-	e	-
godede	1	--------	-	-	C	•	-	-	o	-

ME wordform	N	ModE	EL	S	C	ə#	{l}	W	V	Con
godhede	1	--------	-	-	CC	•	-	-	o	-
golnesse	5	--------	•	-	CC	•	-	-	o	-
hiderward	1	--------	-	-	C	-	-	-	i	-
hoȝfule	1	--------	-	-	CC	•	-	-	o	-
houhsiþe	1	--------	-	-	CC	•	-	-	o	-
hwatliche	1	--------	-	-	CC	•	-	-	a	-
ȝarewe	1	--------	-	-	C^C	•	•	-	a	-
ȝephede	1	--------	•	-	CC	•	-	-	e	-
ȝomere	1	--------	•	-	C^C	•	•	-	o	-
licome	1	--------	•	-	C	•	-	-	i	-
mansinge	1	--------	•	-	CC	•	-	-	a	-
noþerward	1	--------	•	-	C	-	-	-	o	-
oreue	1	--------	-	-	C^C	•	•	-	o	-
readliche	1	--------	-	-	CC	•	-	-	e	-
(a)schewele	1	--------	•	-	C^C	•	•	-	e	-
sheueles	1	--------	•	-	C^C	-	-	-	e	-
skentinge	4	--------	-	-	CC	•	-	-	e	-
sothede	2	--------	-	-	CC	•	-	-	o	-
soþ-sawe	1	--------	•	-	CC	•	-	-	o	-
steuene	7	--------	-	-	C^C	•	•	-	e	-
svikedom	1	--------	-	-	C^C	-	-	-	i	-
svikeldom	1	--------	-	-	C	-	-	-	i	-
taueleþ	1	--------	-	-	CC	-	-	-	a	-
þarone	1	--------	•	-	C	•	-	-	a	-
þuuele	1	--------	•	-	C^C	•	•	-	u	-
utheste	1	--------	•	-	CC	•	-	-	u	-
(at)uitestu	2	--------	-	-	C^C	-	-	-	i	-
(att)witestu	1	--------	-	-	C^C	-	-	-	i	-
woninge	1	--------	•	-	C	•	-	-	o	-

ME wordform	N	ModE	EL	S	C	ə#	{l}	W	V	Con
fulieþ	1	foul (v)	•	-	C	-	-	-	u	i
hatiet	1	hate	-	-	C	-	-	-	a	i
luuie	2	love	-	•	C	•	-	-	u	i
luuieþ	2	love	-	•	C	-	-	-	u	i
luuien	1	love	-	•	C	-	-	-	u	i
makie	1	make	-	-	C	•	-	-	a	i
Schamie	1	shame	-	-	C	•	-	-	a	i
schuniet	1	shun	-	•	C	-	-	-	u	i
shunieþ	1	shun	-	•	C	-	-	-	u	i
werieþ	1	wear	-	-	C	-	-	-	e	i
ȝonie	1	yawn	-	-	C	•	•	-	o	i
erien	1	--------	-	-	C	-	-	-	e	i
foliot	1	--------	-	-	C	-	-	-	o	i
fundieþ	1	--------	-	-	HC	-	-	-	u	i
(over)quatie	1	--------	-	-	C	•	•	-	a	i
wlatie	1	--------	-	-	C	•	•	-	a	i
wonie	1	--------	•	-	C	•	•	-	o	i
baldeliche	1	boldly	-	-	HC	-	-	-	a	s
boldeliche	1	boldly	-	-	HC	-	-	-	o	s
chateringe	2	chattering	-	-	C	-	-	-	a	s
chirche-songe	1	churchsong	-	-	CC	-	-	-	i	s
Engelonde	1	England	-	•	HC	-	-	-	e	s
Galeweie	1	Galloway	•	•	C	-	•	-	a	s
gideliche	1	giddily	-	-	C	-	-	-	i	s
Goldeforde	1	Guildford	-	•	HC	-	-	-	u	s
hardeliche	1	hardly	-	•	HC	-	-	-	a	s
holinesse	1	holiness	•	-	C	-	-	-	o	s
lahfulnesse	1	lawfulness	-	-	CC	-	-	-	a	s

ME wordform	N	ModE	EL	S	C	ə#	{l}	W	V	Con
manifolde	1	manifold	-	-	C	-	-	-	a	s
modinesse	1	moodiness	●	-	C	-	-	-	o	s
modinesse	1	moodiness	●	-	C	-	-	-	o	s
nihtegale	6	nightingale	-	-	CC	-	●	-	i	s
niȝtingale	15	nightingale	-	-	CC	-	-	-	i	s
Noreweie	1	Norway	-	-	C^C	-	-	-	o	s
opeliche	1	openly	-	-	C	-	-	-	o	s
þareuore	2	therefore	●	-	C^C	-	-	-	a	s
wareuore	3	wherefore	●	-	C^C	-	-	-	a	s
wildernisse	1	wilderness	-	-	HC	-	-	-	i	s
wiecche-crafte	1	witchcraft	-	-	C^C	-	-	-	i	s
wicchecrefte	1	witchcraft	-	-	C^C	-	-	-	i	s
wudewale	1	witwall (bird)	-	-	C^C	-	●	-	u	s
ateliche	1	-------	-	-	C	-	-	-	a	s
chokeringe	1	-------	-	-	C	-	-	-	o	s
copenere	1	-------	●	-	C^C	-	-	-	o	s
heriinge	1	-------	●	-	C	-	-	-	e	s
ȝoȝelinge	1	-------	-	-	CC	-	-	-	o	s
sikerhede	1	-------	-	-	C	-	-	-	i	s
sikerliche	1	-------	-	-	C	-	-	-	i	s
svikeldom	1	-------	-	-	C	-	-	-	i	s
swikelede	1	-------	-	-	C	-	-	-	i	s
writelinge	1	-------	●	-	C	-	-	-	i	s
wrouehede	1	-------	●	-	C^C	-	-	-	o	s
þusternesse	1	-------	●	-	C	-	-	-	u	s
wunienge	1	-------	-	-	C	-	-	-	u	si

Notes

1 Approaching the changes

1 Nach meiner ansicht beruhen die großen Quantitätsveränderungen, welche in spät-altenglischer und früh-mittelenglischer zeit in der tonsilbe zu tage treten, auf der tendenz, die silbenquantität auf ein normalmass, und zwar ein gewisses durchschnittsmass zu bringen. ... ich meine weiter, wir müssen da unterscheiden zwischen silben, die für sich das wort ausfüllen, und solchen, auf welche noch eine oder zwei unbetonte folgen. Das scheint mir der springende punkt zu sein.

Wir haben meines erachtens drei quantitätsstufen anzusetzen:
1. stufe: kurzer vokal in offener silbe: a-;
2. stufe: kurzer vokal + kurzem konsonanten   ab;
       langer vokal in offener silbe: a-;
3. stufe: kurzer vokal + langem konsonanten: ab;
       kurzer vokal + zwei konsonanten: abt;
       langer vokal + kurzem konsonanten: ab;

... Ich behaupte nun: die stufe 3 ist das normalmass im einsilbigen wort, die stufe 2 im zweisilbigen, die stufe 1 im dreisilbigen einfachen wort, und alle grossen quantitätsveränderungen ergeben sich aus dem (natürlich unbewußten) streben, diese normalmasse zu erreichen. Die silben ..., welche diese masse nicht haben, werden so weit als möglich auf sie gebracht, teils durch längung, teils durch kürzung. (Luick 1898: 336f.)

2 However, the terminology employed by scholars such as Luick was also highly metaphorical and, in certain respects, rather mystifying. See below, pp. 5ff.

3 If one consults contemporary handbooks on historical English linguistics, one will find that attitudes towards the problem differ considerably, although the question is seldom addressed explicitly and never answered fully. On the one hand, there are accounts which suggest – at least implicitly – that the four processes had little to do with each other: sometimes the changes are listed under a single heading, but without any comment on their relations to one another. See, for example, Fernandez (1982), who includes all changes except the first lengthening in one chapter on Middle English shortenings and lengthenings (pp. 128–30);

Welna (1978), whose approach is similar; or Mossé (1952: 16–19)); and sometimes they are simply described separately (this is the case in Brunner 1960, or Pinsker 1974). On the other hand, there are authors who do suggest that there is a connection between the changes, but they offer no detailed descriptions and express their hypotheses with great caution and in rather general terms. (Thus, Berndt (1960) argues that the changes conspired to transform 'das Quantitätssystem des Ae. ..., das im wesentlichen die in der Grundsprache herrschenden Verhältnisse fortsetzt' (p. 17) into a new system, which was 'phonetic' rather than 'etymological' (cf. p. 20); Berndt (1984), then, follows Lass (1974) and suggests that 'the series of shortenings and lengthenings ... all formed part of a trend 'to dephonologize quantity' (Berndt 1984: 183); Strang (1970: 250) senses 'a persistent tendency ... to deploy long vowels in open syllables, short ones in closed syllables (except in polysyllables, where the tendency – ... never fully realized – has been towards the abolition of long vowels)'. She also argues that the 'general pattern was that two or more consonants following a vowel would inhibit lengthening or cause shortening' (1970: 293), but notes that 'like later quantitative changes this tendency was disturbed, impeded or reversed' (1970: 293); and Jordan (1974: 46) refers to Eliason (1948), who argued that the lengthenings and shortenings were 'related processes' and depended crucially on syllable structure.)

4 For a brief history of earlier syllable research see Awedyk 1975; for an insight into its status within contemporary theories see, for instance, Vennemann 1972a, Kahn 1976, Selkirk 1982, Clements and Keyser 1983, Anderson 1986, Nespor and Vogel 1986 or Vennemann 1986 and 1988.

5 The most prominent proponents of this view are Chomsky and Halle (1968).

6 It should suffice here to note that since 1898 the study of speech sounds has successively come to be reformed by such phonological theories as structuralism – both Prague School and taxonomic – generativism, and more recently by natural phonology and by various sorts of non-linear theories, such as CV-phonology, metrical phonology, dependency phonology and many others.

7 Thus, structuralism introduced the distinction between the systemic length of a vowel and its actual duration. Chomsky and Halle (1968) then argued that the concept of length played hardly any role at all in the description of (English) vowels, but should be replaced by tenseness. Also, it has always been controversial how length should be represented within

a phonological theory. It would go far beyond the scope of this study to give even a rough survey of the various approaches towards vowel length that have been taken since Luick's days.

8 See, for instance, Weinreich, Herzog and Labov 1968 or Labov 1982.

9 The same interpretation can also be given to arrows or similar symbols in schemes such as the following:

[–long]→[+long]

V→VV

{a,e,o}→{aː, eː, oː}.

10 More exactly, two interpretations of 'sound change' are possible:

Given two situations (S) and (S'), where (S) and (S') can be characterized as follows:

> (S) A group of people, who constitute a speech community (C_1), normally fulfil a (set of) communicative function(s) (X_1) by directing their speech organs to perform an articulatory gesture with the feature (A), which is intended to be different in one or more ways from gestures with a feature (~A).
>
> (S') Another group of people, who constitute a speech community (C_2) reflecting speech community (C_1), fulfil a (set of) communicative function(s) (X_2), which corresponds to the (set of) communicative function(s) (X_1) of speech community (C_1) by directing their speech organs to perform a gesture with the feature (B), which is intended to be different from gestures with a feature (~B), where A implies (~B).

The concept **sound change** stands:

> A. for all **factors** that **cause** a situation such as (S) to be succeeded by a situation such as (S');
>
> B. and/or for the mere fact that the situations are isomorphous (have the same structure) and that therefore feature (B) can be regarded as the (functional) counterpart of (A).

11 As a matter of fact, linguistic analyses of OSL, while pretending to deal with a well-defined phenomenon, have been quite idiosyncratic in their choice of the language systems they actually described. Thus, studies of OSL have been based both on comparisons of English spoken immediately before and after the lengthening supposedly took place (e.g. Luick 1914/21), and on comparisons of Old or Early Middle English, and Modern English (e.g. Minkova 1982).

12 In fact these arguments are common handbook knowledge. See, for instance, Lyons (1981), who argues that 'dialects of spoken English were less homogeneous and less neatly separable one from another than traditional accounts of the history of English present them as being; ...

if we had a full historical record of any one spoken dialect, ... we should be unable to identify any definite time at which the dialect in question suddenly changed from being that of one period to being that of another' (p. 183).

13 It deserves to be noted that this discussion leaves a factor aside that seems to complicate things even further, namely the coexistence of, in Modern English varieties, short and long counterparts of one and the same Old English form. An example would be *besom*, for which the *OED* lists both /biːzəm/ and /bezəm/ as possible pronunciations. The problem one faces here, however, is essentially the same as with the more straightforward cases of the *Latin/make* type: do the different pronunciations stem from different dialects, or do both forms go back to a single variety in which the lengthening did not affect *besom* as fully as *maken,* i.e. left half of its occurrences unlengthened, if such a simplistic concept may be introduced for the sake of the argument.

14 Never mind – at this point – that the list does not include any words with high vowels.

15 Example (4) is based on a list of potential inputs to OSL drawn up by Minkova (1982). The Romance items are from Bliss (1952/3).

16 Of course, the Modern English words do not have [+long] vowels, but – in most of the cases – diphthongs. This, in turn, permits the assumption that they must have had [+long] vowels as counterparts at some earlier stage. See, for instance, Prins 1974: 158–60.

17 The examples are practically all taken from Minkova 1982, although, on top of that, they include a small number of words which I happened to come across during my own studies.

18 Some scholars oppose this view and speak of **Open Syllable Tensing** instead. See, for instance, Malsch and Fulcher 1975, or Stockwell 1985. However, the arguments behind this disagreement are not relevant to the problem we are presently dealing with.

19 Recently, however, this view has come to be challenged and I will deal with this problem in greater detail below. For the time being, however, I shall follow the established practice and speak of OSL as a lengthening of vowel segments.

20 Of course, statement (6) cannot be regarded as a prediction proper, since it does not refer to the future but only 'post-dicts', so to say, events that came to happen in the past. Also, operating with a theoretically finite set of data (written corpora), any 'post-diction' that is (successfully) tested against all available data will afterwards be absolutely immune to falsification. Practically, however, this is not such a great problem, for nobody has ever yet managed to go through

all the records that exist to serve as data. So it does not amount to a very big exaggeration to say that the set of potential data for historical linguist is as good as open anyway.

21 Although *alder* does seem to have a long vowel in Modern English, it is not the OSL one. Rather, the long open /ɔː/ goes back to an /au/ diphthong which developed out of /a/ before /l/ plus consonant, in this case epenthetic /d/. The latter was inserted between *l* and *r* in the oblique case *alr-*

22 Another possibility – which was actually suggested by Karl Luick – would be that in some dialects certain words did not have the structure which triggered the lengthening (cf. Luick 1914/21: 402f.). Thus ME *nare* existed beside *narowe* (through *o*-epenthesis) 'narrow', and *rekenen* beside *reknen* (through syncope) 'reckon'.

23 As a matter of fact, I feel that it must have the very denial that they could serve this purpose that has made Luick's quantity changes practically immune to falsification and thus prolonged their life to the present day.

24 Alternatively, the process might have been implemented through the addition of a rule such as

$$[-\text{long}] \rightarrow [+\text{long}] \, / X$$

in post-OSL phonology. For more ways in which phonological processes may 'denaturalize' see Dressler 1982.

25 For instance: if the lengthening behind OSL had affected stressed vowels in all speech styles and in all phonological environments equally, one might speculate that diachronically it would have resulted not in target re-interpretations but in the addition of a rule such as

$$[-\text{long}] \rightarrow [+\text{long}] \, / \begin{bmatrix} --- \\ +\text{stress} \end{bmatrix} x.$$

26 The plausibility of the assumption needs to be justified empirically, of course. As it is, its value relies on its intuitiveness. I am painfully aware of this fact.

27 Before continuing, it probably ought to be clarified what it means to say that something is twice as likely as something else. Obviously, it makes no sense to say that doubling a chance means multiplying it by 2. That would mean that a doubled 2/3 chance was a 4/3 chance, which is logically impossible, of course. One cannot have four favourable out of three possible cases. Therefore, take the classic example of white and black balls in a bag. Doubling the chance of picking a ball of one colour can be achieved in two ways. Either one doubles the number of balls of that colour, while leaving the number of balls of the

other colour unchanged, or one takes half the balls of the other colour away without altering the number of balls of the colour one intends to pick. Thus, if there are two white balls and eight black ones in the bag (which amounts to a 2/10 chance of picking a white ball), the chance of picking a white one can be regarded as doubled either if two more white balls are put into the bag (which amounts to a 4/12 chance of picking a white ball), or if half the black balls (i.e. 4) are taken away (which amounts to a 2/6 chance). In this sense, then, doubling a 1/5 (= 2/10) chance yields a 1/3 (4/12 = 2/6) chance.

28   In fact, there are only two conceivable exceptions to this assumption, and both are fairly improbable. First, the way in which dialects mix might be correlated to phonological structures after all. Dialect A might contribute to a mixture only words that end in voiceless consonants, for example, while dialect B contributes all others. If B lengthens all vowels and A none, the distribution in the mixed dialect will seem to reflect a process that was blocked before voiceless consonants, which would not be true. Fortunately, though, I have never heard that such a situation ever existed in any language.

Second, two dialects might constrain processes in opposite ways. Thus, dialect A might lengthen vowels only before liquids and nasals, while dialect B lengthens vowels only before obstruents. The resulting picture we might get in the mixed variety would then suggest that phonological environment had no impact on vowel lengthening, while in fact it did have. – Although this scenario might appear less implausible than the first one, I would still regard it as relatively improbable, to say the least, and know of no evidence that it should have been relevant for vowel lengthening in English.

29   Of course, very much like a 'sound change', such a reconstructed state is an interpretation of evidence rather that part of objective reality. It is therefore equally problematic as data of an investigation. However, contrary to 'sound changes', reconstructions of historical language systems are normally relatively immediate interpretations of real evidence. It can be assumed that approximative descriptions, such as a cautious interpretation of the evidence yields, can be taken as the safest starting point possible in historical linguistic research. In any case, we have no alternative: unless we make it the point of our own investigation to reconstruct 'pre-OSL English', we have to rely on generally accepted descriptions of historical language systems – at least to begin with. If our investigations should yield arguments for modifying or elaborating the generally accepted view of the system that we shall be dealing with, we will of course do so.

30 If non-structural parameters are accessible, however, they will be taken into account. This is true of an item's etymological origin, for example, which might be expected to correlate with register.

31 It is disputable whether /ɪ/ and /ʊ/ ought to be regarded as high vowels at all. Phonetically, all arguments seem to speak against this, because /ɪ/ and /ʊ/ are centralized, mid rather than high in the strict sense of the word. In more abstract and holistic models of vowel space, however, particularly in dependency and natural phonology, where *i*, *u* and *a* mark extreme points of vowel quality, /ɪ/ and /ʊ/ are seen as the vowels closest to *i* and *u* if the other vowels in the system are /e/, /o/ and /a/, for example. It is in this – admittedly slightly misleading way – that /ɪ/ and /ʊ/ can be regarded as the 'high' vowels in the system.

32 Although, /ɪ/ and /ʊ/ are also problematic in that they seem to have been lowered to /eː/ and /oː/ when they were lengthened, we shall, for the sake of clarity, separate the lowering from the lengthening, and come back to the problem only after an exhaustive description of OSL as a sound change affecting the quantity of vowels.

33 Before proceeding, one important point should be made: representation (28) is not intended to suggest that those Modern English words that do not reflect OSL have never in the history of English had counterparts that did reflect it. It must not be interpreted to mean something like 'OSL applied with a probability of about 30 per cent'. Such an interpretation would involve assumptions about historical pronunciation in the same way as the classical proposal that OSL lengthened *all* items that had the structure on which it worked. Therefore it should be avoided. Rather, scheme (28) should be understood as absolutely neutral as to what might have happened to in-dividual words in the time between the twelfth and the twentieth cen-turies. It simply relates pre- and post-quantity-change English, as defined above on page 23, and therefore neither rests on nor excludes the possibility that at some stage during the late thirteenth century OSL might indeed have been reflected throughout the vocabulary. The question is as irrelevant for our purposes as it is impossible to answer.

The neglect of intermediate stages is not a drawback, even if there was at some period in the history of English a dialect in which OSL was reflected by 100 per cent of the relevant words, so that Luick's version could be regarded as making correct predictions about this variety. Because even in this highly improbable case the Modern English situation would remain to be accounted for. Mere reference to 'dialect mixture' and to 'analogical levelling' cannot be regarded as a satisfactory solution, but if one assumes that there were such cases of form co-occurrence, one will have to state in how many of those cases the form reflecting OSL has been adopted into Modern English, and in how many cases a rivalling form with a short vowel has survived. Now, this is exactly where representation (28) would come in as an adequate description. Also, since we have decided to regard the → symbol as representing the mere fact that there is a correspondence between two language systems, we need not worry whether 'dialect mixture' or 'analogical levelling' were involved in bringing this correspondence about.

2 Reconstructing OSL

1 For evidence suggesting that final schwa was being lost at about the same time when OSL took place, see for instance Minkova 1982, 1983 and 1991.

2 The behaviour of such auxiliaries as *have* or *were* is only indirectly syntactically conditioned, because it results from the weak sentence stress that auxiliaries tend to carry.

3 All the credit for the discovery of this relation is due to Donka Minkova, of course.

4 Note that the syllables called 'light' are implied to be stable. It is on this dimension that they differ from unstable syllables, which are of course also 'light', strictly speaking.

5 As already indicated, I shall return to this problem and deal with it in greater detail below. Also, the special role postvocalic sonorants have played with regard to Open Syllable Lengthening is a well-known and widely studied phenomenon. Attempts at integrating it in an explanation of OSL, such as that of Malsch and Fulcher 1975 have not really been successful, however.

6 Although there is little disagreement about the relative sonority of the consonant classes involved here, it probably ought to be mentioned that I am referring to a sonority hierarchy as employed in Vennemann 1988 (cf. p. 9).

3 Widening the meaning of OSL

1 These examples are not unproblematic because in ModE *where* and *there* length is neutralized before the /r/. However, the quality of the vowels suggests that they were lengthened prior to the quantity neutralization, since otherwise one would expect ModE */wɑː/ and */ðɑː/.

2 This is only true of Open Syllable Lengthening, of course; not of Homorganic Lengthening. Remember, though, that we are not yet concerned with the latter at this point.

3 As I intend to show, however, the relations that underlie those rules can be incorporated into slightly altered versions of the rules on the number of Cs following V and the weight of the syllable following V, respectively.

4 Apart from being a mere assumption whose implicit predictions have not been tested against the HOL data or other quantity changes, this type of account has another weakness that might seem disturbing to many. Thus, it can convey only an incomplete and rather vague picture of the 'lengthenings' related to OSL and does not admit the derivation of the absolute probability of lengthening to occur in any particular item. All it states is whether a vowel in a particular item was relatively likely or relatively unlikely to undergo diachronic lengthening. Statements that go beyond that, such as the 'prediction'

$$V \rightarrow [+\text{long}]/\# \begin{bmatrix} ----- \\ +\text{stress} \\ -\text{high} \end{bmatrix} \S\sigma\text{unstable}\#$$

have not been (and cannot be) derived from the rules proposed above. They have simply been gained from counting a sample of data, carried out – in this case – by Donka Minkova.

However, incorporating results such as Minkova's into the tendency rules I am proposing would make them blatantly circular. This would deprive them of the little explanatory value they have, so that it seems one has to choose between circularity and vagueness. As far as I am concerned, there is no way I would opt for the former.

4 A suprasegmental view of OSL

1 Even though it can be explained on account of linguistic tradition, because OSL has been regarded as an essentially segmental phenomenon ever since it was first observed.

2 Of course, it has always been known that certain phonological phenomena can be expressed on more than one level. Thus, realizing that

Laute, Silben, Sprechtakte, ... Wörter und Wortgefüge ... sich manchmal decken (viele Wörter sind auch Sprechtakte) und im übrigen ineinander enthalten sind [und daß] eine vollständige Darstellung der Veränderungen jedes dieser Sprachbestandteile zu fortwährenden Wiederholungen führen [würde] (p. 2).

Karl Luick argued that 'jede Veränderung immer nur einem bestimmten Sprachbestandteil eigen [ist], in dem Sinne, daß sie mit dessen Eigenart zusammenhängt und daher als seine Veränderung schlechthin zu fassen ist' (p. 2). However, – in spite of his undeniable awareness both of the problem of descriptive levels and of the syllabic aspects of OSL – Karl

Luick did not break with the common practice of his days to approach practically all phonological phenomena on the segmental level. Therefore, he treated OSL as an essentially segmental phenomenon as well.

3 Thus, she argues that OSL

> was triggered off by the disturbance of the balance within the foot created by the loss of an unstressed syllable immediately adjacent to a foot-initial light syllable. [It] ... is interpreted as the acquisition of additional rhythmical weight by the foot initial syllable ..., so that the overall weight of the word is preserved; there is no difference of morae before and after the change.

In a paper based on Minkova's study, Lass (1985) was even more explicit and called OSL a phenomenon of *foot* resolution.

4 See, for instance Leben 1980, Stemberger 1983 or Vago 1987, but also most of the studies cited in the following note.

5 Anderson 1986, Awedyk 1975, Bell 1979, Bell 1987, Booij 1983, Cairns and Feinstein 1982, Clements and Keyser 1983, Couper-Kuhlen 1986, Giegerich 1985, Goldsmith 1976, Hayes 1981, Hogg and McCully 1987, Kahn 1976, Kaye 1981, Kiparsky 1981, Laubstein 1987, 1988, Lutz 1986, McClenon 1981, Murray and Vennemann 1982, Nespor and Vogel 1986, Selkirk 1980, Vennemann 1972a, 1988, Vincent 1986, Wiese 1986.

6 There are a few exceptions to this rule of thumb, notably /st/ clusters.

7 Also, syllabicity seems to be a linguistic universal: every conceivable utterance can be parsed into syllables and every natural language has them as well.

8 This is regarded as plausible on account of such evidence as 'poetry (alliteration of onsets vs. rhyming of rhymes), [or] the most frequent type of contaminations, where the onset of one source word is conjoined with the rhyme of the other source word (e.g., *sm/oke* and *fl/og* → *sm/og*), etc.' (Dressler 1985: 35). However, there are linguists (e.g. Clements and Keyser 1983) who doubt the conclusiveness of this evidence.

9 Thus, the ModE words *fast, hat, sea, it* or *I* would be attributed syllable structures in the following way:

O	R	
	N	C
f	aː	st
h	æ	t
s	iː	
-	i	t
-	ai	-

10 For an exhaustive list of syllable types, see Vennemann (1988: 5–10).

11 For example, some autosegmental theories (for instance, Clements and Keyser 1983) operate with a so-called CV tier onto which segments are projected as either Cs or Vs according – basically – to whether they are more vocalic or more consonantal. It is this tier, then, that syllable structure refers to. There, ModE *hat* would be analysed as follows:

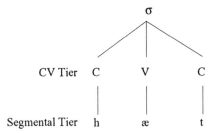

This kind of notation has no explicit labels for such constituents as **rhyme** or **onset**. Implicitly, at least some of them are present, of course: thus, onsets will be the leftmost Cs in a syllable. With the other intrasyllabic constituents things are not quite as easy, however. See Clements and Keyser 1983.

Dependency phonology, on the other hand, represents segments as being made up of different gestures, and only one of them, namely the categorial gesture, which specifies the relative sonority of the segments in terms of infrasegmental dependencies between C and V elements, plays a role in syllable structure assignment. Thus, it resembles, albeit faintly, the CV tier in autosegmental phonologies. A dependency representation of *hat* would be:

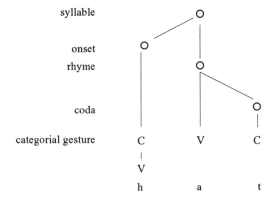

Of course, there are other theoretical and/or notational frameworks, but since this study is not intended as a state-of-the-art report, none of them will be presented.

12   Of course, there is nothing essentially new about this view. It goes back at least to Jacobson. However, traditional phonological notations offered few real alternatives to representing length on the segmental level. For recent approaches see Leben 1980, Prince 1980 and Vago 1987.

13   Since the distinction between the two syllable types is relevant in a large number of languages, it would also generally have to be regarded as undesirable if it could only be expressed with reference to intrasegmental qualities.

14   However, I shall come back to the representation of length and deal with it in greater detail below.

15   Given the many different vanriants of /r/, can there be a single place for a phoneme /r/ on a sonority scale at all? And, therefore: should sonority be regarded as a property of phonemes at all?

16   This example illustrates the notation that we shall henceforth employ for the representation of suprasegmental phonological structure: for the sake of clarity, we shall label all constituents, although there might be more elegant or economic options. Units in suprasegmental structure will be represented as ●s.

17   Unfortunately, this approach is difficult to reconcile with the idea that stress placement can be predicted on the basis of syllable structures derived through general maximal syllabification, because the re-syllabification rules by which general maximal syllables are created depend themselves on predetermined stress location. This argument does not weigh very heavy, however, because the question whether stress placement should be at all handled by phonological rules in all cases is not really settled.

18   The term 'word' is not to be taken too seriously here. Obviously, the isolated and strongly stressed syllables in question neither have lexical meanings nor seem to satisfy such basic phonotactic well-formedness conditions as the one ruling out fully stressed CV words in English.

19   Never mind the crossing branches. The purpose of the employed notation is just to make clear that each of the elements in the intermediate cluster 'belongs' both to the first and the second syllables.

20   Some recent publications on the topic include Basbøll 1988, Auer 1989, Hayes 1989 or Tranel 1991.

21   Note that this way of determining syllable weight depends crucially on the representation of long vowels as two elements. Note, further, that Vennemann's instructions for the calculation of syllable weight are

rather vague with regard to such questions as which elements should be counted (probably not segments) or why all elements contribute equally to syllable weight.

22 The same generalization would also cover the fact that the Middle English counterparts of Old English monosyllables of the structure onset+V would *always* have a long vowel in their nucleus position. This could be captured in a statement such as

> The probability of a monomoric syllable's getting a counterpart with a long vowel equals 1.

23

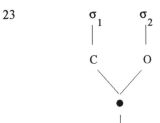

#X[SONORANT]Y#

24 Of course, their behaviour seems idiosyncratic only from the point of view being taken in this study, namely that it would be normal for sonorants to increase the probability of vowel lengthening rather than make it zero. Thus, if no explanation for the idiosyncrasy of sonoronts can be given, one might have to conclude that it is my standpoint which gives a distorted view of what is normal or not.

25 Another example which illustrates the principle that the syllabic function of a segment determines its shape may be seen in the fact that even in some non-rhotic dialects of Modern English 'linking' /r/s surface in prevocalic environments such as *for a change*: there, one might argue, it is not vocalized/deleted because the (consonantal aspect of) /r/ is required to function as the onset of the following syllable.

26 Note that my phrasing implies a functional view of syllable structure, and I am aware that this involves an interpretation of current models of syllable structure which goes a step further than viewing them in terms of essentially spatial relations. Thus, what I call the unfolding of a sonorant's vocalicity in an adaptation to its nuclear function might be described more straightforwardly as the movement of a vocalic offspring of the sonorant into the nucleus domain. While my interpretation is not undisputable, of course, it also has some advantages. See the following note, for example.

27 Viewing the relation of a segment to syllable structure as a role that is
played rather than a position that is taken has the advantage of making
it easier to grasp the idea that one element might oscillate between two
or more constituents in suprasegmental structure (ambisyllabicity),
because the idea that something might fulfil two purposes at the same
time is much more familiar to the traditional way of thinking than the
notion of something being at two places simultaneously. Thus, it is not
problematic to think of the underlying /l/ in ModE *full* as functioning
both as a part of the (vocalic) nucleus and as the (consonantal) coda
(and – potentially – as the onset of a following syllable), while the idea
of the [l] 'being' in 'both syllables at the same time' might tend to
make at least those linguists uncomfortable who appreciate boundaries
between elements to be clear cut.

28 One great disadvantage of our proposal is that the role which sonorants
seem to play with regard to vowel lengthening differs so much from
that which obstruents play, that it looks deplorably unlikely that the
elegant solution of making the chance vowel lengthening dependent on
the sonority of the following consonant can be maintained: if words
cannot simply be ordered on a scale of coda sonority, and if a
fundamental difference must be made between sonorant codas and
obstruent codas, we would need two Middle English Lengthening
Laws, so that our attempts at unifying our account would be doomed to
failure.

However, it is not impossible that a scalar parameter – such as that
of sonority or vocalicness – should yield classes that behave in such
markedly different manners that the scalar nature of the parameter on
which they differ is obscured: thus, in English only sonorants and
vowels can act as syllabics and it seems that the best way of expressing
this was by introducing the digital distinction between [+syllabic] and
[–syllabic] segments. Yet, it cannot be denied that the ability of a
segment to function as a nucleus depends on its position on the
sonority scale.

29 Coda deletion resulted from later weakening processes. (cf. Luick,
1914/21: 1053ff., 1056ff., 1119ff.)

30 Obviously, the principle that ●-nodes that are attached to onsets cannot
be attached to V-gestures at the same time hardly needs to be justified.
It is generally acknowledged that vowels cannot act as syllable onsets,
because even where they seem to, they are phonetically preceded by
glottal stops, which are fully consonantal, of course.

31 This view is not uncontroversial. I shall not go into any theoretical
detail, however.

32 'Diese Dehnung ist an Starkton gebunden: bei gemindertem Ton wurde die Kürze bewahrt.' (Luick 1914/21: 399)

33 While this generalization could theoretically also be expressed without reference to foot structure, the foot-based version is easier to accommodate within a wider explanatory framework. First of all, (39) seems to be motivated by the principle of foot isochrony: if feet tend to last about equally long, then it is logical that longer feet will tend to be reduced while shorter feet will tend to get lengthened. Any version of (39) that is not foot-based will therefore have to be translated into terms of foot structure when it comes to explaining it, for which reason it is more economical to express it in terms of feet in the first place. At the same time, the fact that foot structure depends on the relative prominence of one syllable explains why, if a foot expands for reasons of isochrony, it will be the head rather than one of the weak syllables that gets lengthened, because lengthening, and thus foregrounding, of a weak syllable would level out prominence distinctions.

5 Summary: OSL refined

1 Thus, it could be argued that x must be greater than y, because a strong syllable is not as likely as a weak syllable to be reduced in pronunciation, so that the average time consumed by strong syllables will be greater than that consumed by weak syllables of equal weight. Thus, one could also handle the fact that monosyllabic CVC items are normally supposed not to have been affected by any lengthening at all, although their overall foot weight seems to have been smaller than that of CVCV items. In my framework, a CVC item would weigh 2 moras, a CVCV item 2½. So unless x were greater than y, my vowel lengthening formula (1) would imply that CVC items ought to lengthen at least as often as CVCV items, which does not seem to be true.

Bear in mind, however, that this argument is just meant to illustrate the way in which – at least relative – values for a–z could be provided. Its correctness is not my concern at this point.

2 Although – for practical purposes – its binary character is drawn into question by the fact that certain items have a significant tendency to occur in unstressed position (e.g. *have*; cf. Luick 1914/21: 399). If this is taken into account, *stress* may be taken as a scalar feature as well.

3 This is indicated by both rhyme and spelling evidence (cf. Lieber 1979: 7).

4 In terms of conventional generative phonology, such a rule could be formalized as

$$V \rightarrow \left[+\text{tense}\right] / \left[\begin{array}{c} ----- \\ +\text{long} \end{array}\right]$$

5   Therefore, Lass (1984) has even argued that the feature pair TENSE–LAX
    should be abandoned altogether, because whatever it expresses can also
    be expressed in terms of height and frontness and backness.

6 Homorganic Lengthening

1   The corpus referred to in Minkova and Stockwell's 1992 article on HOL
    differs from mine in two ways. First, it is based on Bosworth and Toller's
    Anglo Saxon Dictionary rather than the *Oxford Etymological Dictionary*;
    second, it is more restrictive with regard to possible HOL inputs. Thus,
    rl, rs, rð are excluded. A detailed comparison was not possible, however,
    because Minova and Stockwell's corpus has not, to my knowledge, been
    published in its fullness.

2   It needs to be said that if one maintains that homorganic clusters
    favoured lengthening because they were highly sonorous and at the same
    time 'monomoric', as I do, one creates an interesting problem. After all,
    homorganic clusters caused lengthening also in monosyllables, and if
    they did so because they were sonorous and monomoric, why didn't
    single word final nasals, too, for example? Why, in other words, did
    words of the *child* type seem to lengthen more easily than words of the
    kin type? Apparently formula (1) of chapter 5 does not handle this fact
    too well. However, this does not imply that the correlations it expresses
    are wrong. Rather, it may just need further specification. As far as the
    case in point is concerned, for example, the apparently contradictory
    behaviour of words of the *kin* and *child* types may simply be due to the
    fact that, in the former, the final *n* represents the only coda constituent,
    whereas the *l* in *child* does not. The sonorants in words of the *kin* type
    may thus be under greater pressure to behave consonantally than the ones
    in words of the *child* type, which may therefore associate more easily
    with the preceding nuclei and thus result in such quasi-nuclear vowel–
    sonorant configurations as outlined above on page 66. In principle, it
    ought to be possible to quantify a a concept such as 'minimal required
    consonantality' and add it as a paramater to formula (1) of chapter 5.
    Without further empirical investigation and conceptual refinement, how-
    ever, any conclusions to this effect would be rash.

7 Shortenings

1   The fact that the change involves two types of synchronic processes is
    not problematic: first, the implicit assumption that there should be a one-
    to-one relation between synchronic process types and diachronic
    correspondences (= 'changes') is *ad hoc* and theoretically unfounded;
    and, second, the processes involved in our case, albeit not identical, are
    not unrelated at all, but are in fact fully isomorphous.

2 Recall our discussion of language change in sections 1.3 and 1.4. If socio-stylistic variation is taken into account – which our approach does – such phenomena could be accounted for quite easily: ambivalent environments would lead to lengthening, if other factors (such as style or tempo) support lengthening, and to shortening, if those factors should favour shortening. Since language learners will build their phonologies from a mixture of varieties only probabilistic predictions can be made about which of the outputs will play a more prominent role in that process.

3 The data on which the following sections are based are taken primarily from handbooks. They are not as numerous as the data on which our investigations on the lengthening processes were based. There are good reasons for this, however.First of all, it can be shown by purely deductive means that, as far as the majority of parameters of rule (1) of chapter 5 is concerned, the shortenings behave exactly as predicted. However, a pilot investigation, in which *The Owl and the Nightingale* was searched for potential inputs to the two shortening rules, showed that it would be extremely difficult to collect a sample that was representative enough to perform such statistical investigations as we did with the lengthenings.

As far as Trisyllabic Shortening is concerned, there are very few Early Middle English words that have counterparts in Modern English to which they could be compared. This is due both to the fact that trisyllabic wordforms were very rarely morphologically simple (thus, they cannot be taken as real counterparts of Modern English base forms, which are simple) and to the fact that practically no Early Middle English trisyllabic item has kept all of its three syllables. (It is significant, however, that this is not true of Romance loans. With regard to the latter, Trisyllabic Shortening has come to play a rather special role with which we shall deal below.)

As far as Shortening before Consonant Clusters is concerned, at least the first argument is true of most potential inputs to the change as well: most of the Early Middle English items in which a long vowel was followed by two consonants were morphologically complex word-forms that do not have any real counterparts in Modern English with its simplified morphology. Apart from this, certain cluster types have come to be simplified through vocalization (in EME *leoht* 'light', for example), so that the Modern English counterparts of potential inputs to Shortening before Consonant Clusters do not serve as evidence either.

In other words, there is no point in attempting to prove the obvious. Hence, I will spare myself the trouble of doing so.

In order to complement handbook evidence where such proof was deemed necessary, *The Owl and the Nightingale* (a typical example of an

Early Middle English text, of which a machine-readable version was available to me) was searched for items that would fulfil the conditions for being affected by Trisyllabic Shortening and Shortening before Consonant Clusters and the items found in this way were used to obtain additional insight into the scope and the implementation of the sound changes in question.

The program used to carry out the actual search was MICRO OCP.

4 See p. 96 for my doubts concerning the concept of sound-change triggers.

5 It is a general Neogrammarian practice to introduce the concepts of form co-occurrence and analogy when their rules fail, but to disregard these concepts completely when they would make things difficult for them. This is what happens in the present case too.

6 Note, however, that none of the arguments that have been presented against the assumption of TRISH as a separate sound change are meant to imply that a rule that deserves the name TRISH did not at any time become relevant to the phonology of English. It did in fact, but not as the diachronic implementation of a natural process, but rather as a morphonological rule resulting from a re-interpretation of the shortening process as an index of derivation on the basis of Romance word-formation patterns; thus, when pairs like *divine–divinité* came to be integrated into the English vocabulary, the stressed vowels were analysed as having those underlying quantities that they would have in native words of corresponding structures, so that *divíne* (being stressed on the second /i/ in Anglo-Norman) would get a long vowel, while *divinité* (which was originally stressed on the final /e/) would get a short /i/. After some time two things are likely to have happened: first, the position of main stress in words such as *divinité* was eventually moved from the final syllable to the antepenultimate one, and second the number of loans reflecting the same pattern of derivation became large enough for the derivation to acquire a new sort of transparency. This means that pairs such as *divine – divinity* could be analysed as having the same underlying 'stem', probably #*divín#*, and the short /i/ in *divinity* could be derived by means of a rule of TRISH that was restricted to a few foreign suffixes such as *-ity*, *-ion*. In Modern English, things have been obscured even more, of course (through such changes as the Great Vowel Shift, and others, which affected consonants), so that many alternations that might have been accounted for by TRISH for a short period must today probably be seen as cases of allomorphy, although the rule could still be used for alternations such as

tenacious – tenacity, sane – sanity, sincere – sincerity, saline – salinity, brief – brevity, serene – serenity, vain – vanity, obscene – obscenity, opaque – opacity, austere – austerity, profound – profundity, conspire – conspiracy, supreme – supremacy, despise – despicable, creed – credible, divide – devisible, flame – flammable, placate – placable, mode – modify, type – typify, sole – solitude, grade – gradual, rite – ritual, derive – derivative, appeal – appellative, define – definitive, evoke – evocative, provoke – provocative, repeat – repetitive, type – typical ... (cf. Myers 1987: 494f.)

8 Epilogue: explaining Middle English Quantity Adjustment

1 The relevance of acoustics is restricted to phenomena that influence the auditory reception of speech. Therefore, one might argue that the role which acoustics plays in the study of human speech is a relatively indirect one.

2 For ample evidence see, for example, Donegan 1978.

3 This is reflected, for instance, in the asymmetricity of the Great Vowel Shift or in the articulatory positions of ModE /e/ vs. short /ɒ/.

4 The following references are taken from Hubmayer (1986: 224).

5 In the sense that they must be assumed to exert their influence whenever human beings communicate with each other with their mouths and ears.

6 This notion is not absurd: if Quantity Adjustment crucially involves socio-stylistic factors (e.g. casual and rapid speech favouring shortenings, and formal and slow speech favouring lengthenings) the universality of Quantity Adjustment is a direct consequence of the universality of socio-stylistic variation.

7 In fact, this question is just one particular version of the more general argument that is always raised against 'natural' or 'universalist' approaches to sound change: why, if the laws governing sound change are universal, have not all languages come to develop identical sound systems.

8 *I*-umlaut was no longer a productive phonological rule, but purely morphologically conditioned.

9 Neglecting the zero allomorph that might be assumed to mark the nom./acc. sg. of *cyme.*

10 However, handbooks do not really commit themselves, and an empirical investigation of this question would have exceeded the scope of this study by far.

11 The role which the restructuring of English morphology played in the implementation of phonological processes in newly emerging base forms may serve to indicate, at the same time, why the phonological development of inflectional endings did not have any major impact at least on the long-term effects of Quantity Adjustment.

12   Diagram (11) is based on a computer-aided investigation of three text samples of 10,000 items each. The first sample comprises *The Battle of Maldon* and excerpts from *Beowolf*, the second most of *The Owl and the Nightingale*, and the third *The General Prologue* and parts of *The Prologue of the Wife of Bath* from Chaucer's *Canterbury Tales*. All text samples were analysed and indexed morphologically and syllabically. The analysis was surface-oriented, which means that only such morphemes were indexed as were recoverable from surface forms. Syllable boundaries were inserted on the principle of general maximal syllabification. Appendix V shows excerpts of the indexed samples. The actual counting of items was then performed with the help of the Oxford Concordance Program.

13   Polysyllabic feet are 'better' than monosyllabic ones, because the latter violate the general semiotic principle of figure and ground: a stressed syllable needs to be in the environment of unstressed ones in order to be perceived as stressed.

References and further reading

Abercrombie, David. 1964. A phonetician's view of verse structure. *Linguistics* 6: 5–13.

Acobian, Richild (ed.). 1979. *Festgabe für Hans Pinsker zum 70. Geburtstag.* Vienna.

Adamson, Sylvia. Vivien Law, Nigel Vincent and Susan Wright (eds.). 1988. *Papers from the Fifth International Conference on English Historical Linguistics.* Amsterdam.

Aitchison, Jean. 1974. Phonological change: some causes and constraints. In Anderson and Jones, vol. II: 1–15.

Andersen, Henning. 1972. Diphthongization. *Language* 48: 11–50.

1973. Abductive and deductive change. *Language* 49: 765–93.

Anderson, John M. 1973. Syllable structure and gemination in Old English. *Edinburgh Working Papers in Linguistics* 3: 100–5.

1985. Structural analogy and dependency phonology. *Acta Linguistica Hafnienis* 19: 5–45.

1986. Suprasegmental dependencies. In Durand (ed.): 55–135.

Anderson, John M. and Jacques Durand. 1986. Dependency phonology. In Durand (ed.): 1–54.

Anderson, John M. and Charles Jones (eds.). 1974. *Historical linguistics.* Amsterdam.

1977. *Phonological structure and the history of English.* Amsterdam.

Anderson, John M., Ewen, Colin and Staun, Jorgen. 1985. Phonological structure: segmental, suprasegmental and extrasegmental. *Phonology Yearbook* 2: 203–24.

Atkins, J.W.H. (ed.). 1922. *The Owl and the Nightingale.* New York.

Auer, Peter. 1989. Some ways to count morae: Prokosch's Law, Streitberg's Law, Pfalz's Law, and other rhythmic regularities. *Linguistics* 6: 1071–1102.

Awedyk, Wieslaw. 1975. *The syllable theory and Old English phonology.* Wroclaw.

Bach, Emmon and R.T. Harms (eds.). 1968. *Universals in linguistic theory.* New York.

Bailey, Charles–James N. 1972. The integration of linguistic theory. internal reconstruction and the comparative method in descriptive analysis. In Stockwell and Macaulay (eds.): 23–31.

Basbøll, Hans. 1988. The Modern Danish Stød and phonological weight. In Bertinetto and Loporcacro (eds.): 119–52.

Bauer, Gerd. 1956. The problem of short diphthongs in Old English. *Anglia* 74: 427–37.

Bauer, Gero. 1979. Zum Problem der Rekonstruktion von Lautwerten im älteren English. In Acobian (ed.): 16–32.

Beade, Pedro. 1975. Vowel length in Middle English: continuity and change. *Leuvense Bijdragen* 64: 313–20.

Behrens, Susan J. 1985. The perception of stress and lateralization of prosody. *Brain and Language* 26: 332–49.

Bell, Alan. 1979. The syllable as constituent versus organizational unit. In Chyne, Hanks and Hofbauer (eds.): 11–20.

  1987. The articulatory syllable. *Colorado Research in Linguistics* 9: 9–19.

Bell, Alan and Joan Bybee Hooper (eds.). 1978. *Syllables and segments.* Amsterdam.

Berg, Thomas. 1985. Is voice a suprasegmental? *Linguistics* 23: 883–917.

Berndt, Rolf. 1960. *Einführung in das Studium des Mittelenglischen.* Halle.

  1984. *A history of the* English *language.* 2nd edn. Leipzig.

Bertinetto, Pier Marco and Loporcacro, Michele (eds.). 1988. *Certamen Phonologicum.* Turin.

Bliss, Alan J. 1952/3. Vowel-quantity in Middle English borrowings from Anglo-Norman. *Archivum Linguisticum* 4: 121-47 and 5: 22-47.

  1955. Quantity in Old French and Middle English. *Archivum Linguisticum* 7: 71–86.

  1969. Vowel-quantity in Middle English borrowings from Anglo-Norman. In Lass (ed.): 164–207.

Booij, Geert. 1983. Principles and parameters in prosodic phonology. *Linguistics* 21: 249–80.

Brook, George Leslie. 1957. *English sound-changes.* Manchester.

Bruck, Anthony, Roberta A. Fox and Michael W. La Galy (eds.). 1974. *Papers from the parasession on natural phonology.* Chicago.

Brunner, Karl. 1953. The Old English vowel phonemes. *English Studies* 34: 247–51.

1960. *Die englische* Sprache. *Ihre geschichtliche Entwicklung.* 2nd edn. Tübingen.

Cairns, Charles E. and Mark H. Feinstein. 1982. Markedness and the theory of syllable structure. *Linguistic Inquiry* 13: 193–226.

Campbell, Alistair. 1959. *Old English grammar.* Oxford.

Catford, John C. 1982. *Fundamental problems in phonetics.* Edinburgh.

Chen, Matthew. 1970. Vowel length variation as a function of the voicing of the consonant environment. *Phonetica* 22: 129–59.

1972. The time dimension: contribution toward a theory of sound change. *Foundations of Language* 8: 457–98.

1973a. On the formal expression of natural rules in phonology. *Journal of Linguistics* 9: 223–49.

1973b. Predictive power in phonological description. *Lingua* 32: 173–91.

1974. Natural phonology from the diachronic vantage point. In Bruck, Fox and La Galy (eds.): 43–80.

Chen, Matthew and William S.Y. Wang. 1975. Sound change: actuation and implementation. *Language* 51: 255–81.

Chomsky, Noam and Morris Halle. 1968. *The sound pattern of English.* New York.

Christie, W.M. (ed.). 1976. *Current progress in historical linguistics.* Amsterdam.

Chyne, Paul R., William F. Hanks and Carol L. Hofbauer (eds.). 1979. *The elements. Papers from the parasession on linguistic units and levels.* Chicago.

Clements, Georg N. and Samuel Jay Keyser. 1983. *CV-phonology: a generative theory of the syllable.* Cambridge, MA.

Connine, C.M., C. Clifton and A. Cutler. 1987. Effects of lexical stress on phonetic categorization. *Phonetica* 44: 133–47.

Couper-Kuhlen, Elizabeth. 1986. *An introduction to English prosody.* Tübingen.

Crystal, David. 1985. *A dictionary of linguistics and phonetics.* 2nd edn. Oxford.

Cutler, Ann. 1991.Why not abolish psycholinguistics?. In Dressler *et al.* (ed.): 77–87.

Cutler, Ann, Jacques Mehler, Dennis Norris and Juan Segui. 1986. The syllable's differing role in the segmentation of French and English. *Journal of Memory and Language* 25: 385–401.

Danchev, Andrei. 1980. On vowel quantity in Old English. *English Studies (Sophia University)*: 62–78.

Davenport, Michael, Erik Hansen and Hans Friede Nielsen (eds.). 1982. *Current topics in English historical linguistics. Proceedings of the Second International Conference on English Historical Linguistics held at Odense University 8–15 April 1981*. Odense.

De Chene, Brent and Stephen R. Anderson. 1979. Compensatory lengthening. *Language 55*: 505–35.

Dobson, Eric J. 1962. Middle English lengthening in open syllables. *Transactions of the Philological Society*. 124–48.

Dogil, Grzegorz. 1988. Phonological configurations: natural classes, sonority and syllabicity. *Wiener Linguistische Gazette* 40/1: 93–102.

Donegan, Patricia Jane. 1976. Raising and lowering. In Mufwene, Walker and Steever (eds.): 145–60.

1979. *On the natural phonology of vowels*. Ann Arbor.

Dressler, Wolfgang U. 1978. *How much does performance contribute to phonological change?* In Fisiak (ed.): 145–58.

1982. A semiotic model of diachronic process phonology. In Lehmann and Malkiel (eds.): 93–132.

1985. *Morphonology: the dynamics of derivation*. Ann Arbor.

Dressler, Wolfgang U., Oskar E. Pfeiffer and John R. Rennison (eds.). 1981. *Phonologica 1980* (= Innsbrucker Beiträge zur Sprachwissenschaft 36). Innsbruck.

Dressler, Wolfgang U., Hans C. Luschützky, Oskar E. Pfeiffer and John R. Rennison (eds.). 1987. *Phonologica 1984*. Cambridge.

1991. Phonologica *1988*. Cambridge.

Durand, Jacques (ed.). 1986. *Dependency and non-linear phonology*. London.

Eckhardt, Eduard. 1916. Die neuenglische Verkürzung langer Tonsilbenvokale in abgeleiteten und zusammengesetzten Wörtern. *Englische Studien 50*: 199–299.

1936. Die Quantität einfacher Tonvokale in offener Silbe bei zwei- oder dreisilbigen Wörtern französischer Herkunft im heutigen Englisch. *Anglia 60*: 49–116.

Eilers, Friedrich. 1907. *Die Dehnung vor dehnenden Konsonantenverbindungen im Mittelenglischen*. Halle an der Saale.

Ekwall, Eilert. 1975. *A history of Modern English sounds and morphology*. London.

Eliason, N.E. 1948. Old English vowel lengthening and vowel shortening before consonant groups. *Studies in Philology* 1: 1–20.

Elsendoorn, Ben A.G. 1985. Production and perception of Dutch foreign vowel duration in English monosyllabic words. *Language and Speech* 28: 231–55.

Erdmann, Peter H. 1971. *Tiefenphonologische Lautgeschichte der englischen Vokale.* Frankfurt-on-Main.

Ewen, Colin J. 1980. Aspects of phonological structure, with particular reference to English and Dutch. Ph.D. thesis. University of Edinburgh.

Fernandez, Francisco. 1982. *Historia de la lengua inglesa.* Madrid.

Fery, Caroline. 1988. Review of Heinz Giegerich, 1985. 'Metrical phonology and phonological structure. German and English'. *Beiträge zur Geschichte der deutschen Sprache und Literatur* 110: 106–14.

Fintoft, K. 1961. The duration of some Norwegian speech sounds. *Phonetica* 7: 19–36.

Fisiak, Jacek (ed.). 1978. *Recent developments in historical phonology.* The Hague.

1980. *Historical morphology.* The Hague.

Flasdieck, Hermann M. 1954. Pall Mall. Beiträge zur Etymologie und Quantitätstheorie. *Anglia* 72: 129–383.

Foley, James. 1977. *Foundations of theoretical phonology.* Cambridge.

Fries, Udo and Heusser, Martin. 1988. *Meaning and beyond. Ernst Leisi zum 70. Geburtstag.* Tübingen.

Fry, Dennis B. 1979. *The physics of speech.* Cambridge.

Fujimura, Osamu and Julie B. Lovins. 1978. Syllables as concatenative phonetic units. In Bell and Hooper (eds.): 107–20.

Giegerich, Heinz J. 1985. *Metrical phonology and phonological structure.* Cambridge.

Gil, David. 1986. A prosodic typology of language. *Folia Linguistica* 20: 165–233.

Goldsmith, John A. 1976. *Autosegmental phonology.* Bloomington.

Goman, Roderick David. 1979. *Consonants in natural phonology.* Ann Arbor.

Gonzo, Susan Thiede. 1978. *English historical phonology: some issues in the theory of phonological change.* Ann Arbor.

Hackmann, Gottfried. 1908. *Kürzung langer Tonvokale vor einfachen auslautenden Konsonanten im Alt-, Mittel- und Neuenglischen.* Halle an der Saale.

Halle, Morris. 1962. Phonology in a generative grammar. *Word* 18: 54–72.

1977. Tenseness, vowel shift, and the phonology of the back vowels in Modern English. *Linguistic Inquiry* 8: 611–25.

Halle, Morris and Kenneth N. Stevens. 1967. On the mechanisms of glottal vibration for vowels and consonants. *Quarterly Progress Report of the Research Laboratory of Electronics, Massachusetts Institute of Technology* 83: 105–13.

Harris, John. 1987. A hierarchical model of length variation in vowels. In Dressler *et al.* (eds.): 95–103.

Hayes, Bruce Philip. 1981. *A metrical theory of stress rules.* Bloomington.

1989. Compensatory lengthening in moraic phonology. *Linguistic Inquiry* 20: 253–306.

Heald, A.R.B. 1965. *Some graphic evidence for vowel length in three Old English manuscripts.* University of Texas.

Herbert, Robert K. 1986. *Language universals, markedness theory, and natural phonetic processes.* Berlin, New York and Amsterdam.

Hock, Hans Henrich. 1986a. Compensatory lengthening: in defense of the concept 'mora'. *Folia Linguistica* 20: 431–461.

1986b. *Principles of historical linguistics.* Berlin, New York and Amsterdam.

Hockett, Charles F. 1959. The stressed syllabics of Old English. *Language* 35: 575–97.

Hogg, Richard and C.B. McCully. 1987. *Metrical phonology: a coursebook.* Cambridge.

Holthausen, Ferdinand. 1933. Zu ae. *i* für *e. Beiblatt zur Anglia* 1: 26–27.

Hooper, Joan Bybee. 1972. The syllable in phonological theory. *Language* 48: 525–40.

1976. *An introduction to natural generative phonology.* New York.

Hubmayer, Karl. 1986. *'Natürliche Diachronie': Untersuchungen zur phonetischen Motivation historischer phonologischer Prozesse im Englischen.* Salzburg.

Hyman, Larry M. 1977a. On the nature of linguistic stress and accent. In Hyman (ed.): 37–82.

(ed.). 1977b. *Studies in stress and accent.* Los Angeles.

Jakobson, Roman and Morris Halle. 1956. *Fundamentals of language.* The Hague.

Jassem, W. 1953. Regular changes of vocalic quantity in Early New English. *College English* 12: 149–78.

Javkin, H. 1978. Phonetic universals and phonological change. Ph.D. thesis. University of Berkeley.

Jespersen, Otto M. 1928. *Monosyllabism in English.* London.

Joerden, Otto. 1915. Das Verhältnis von Wort-, Satz- und Versakzent in Chaucers Canterbury Tales. *Englische Studien* 54: 111–16.

Jones, Charles. 1972. *An introduction to Middle English.* New York.

1986. A dependency approach to some wellknown features of historical English phonology. In Durand (ed.): 257–69.

1989. *A history of English phonology.* London and New York.

Jordan, Richard. 1974. *A handbook of Middle English* (translated and revised by Eugene Joseph Crook). The Hague and Paris.

Kahn, Daniel. 1976. *Syllable based generalizations in English phonology.* Bloomington.

Kaisse, Ellen M. 1985. *Connected speech: the interaction of syntax and phonology.* Orlando.

Kastovsky, Dieter. 1984. Typological changes in the nominal inflectional system of English and German. Unpublished University of Vienna paper.

1988. Typological changes in the history of English morphology. In Fries and Heusser (eds.): 159–78.

1989. Typological changes in the history of English word-formation. In Müllenbrock and Noll-Wieman (eds.): 287–93.

1990. The typological status of Old English word-formation. In Adamson *et al.* (eds.): 205–23.

Kaye, Jonathan D. 1981. Syllable structure and markedness theory. In Belletti *et al.* (eds.): 287–315.

Keating, Patricia A. 1985. Linguistic and nonlinguistic effects on the perception of vowel duration. *UCLA Working Papers in Phonetics* 60: 20–40.

Keller, W. 1919. Mittelenglische lange Vokale und die altfranzösische Quantität. *Englische Studien* 54: 111–17.

Keyser, Samuel J. and Morris Halle. 1966. Chaucer and the study of prosody. *College English* 28: 187–219.

Kinkade, M. Dale. 1985. More on nasal loss on the North West coast. *International Journal of American Linguistics* 51: 478–80.

Kiparsky, Paul. 1968. Linguistic universals and linguistic change. In Bach and Harms (eds.): 171–205.

1970. Historical linguistics. In Lyons (ed.): 302–15.

1979. Metrical structure assignment is cyclic. *Linguistic Inquiry* 10: 421–42.

1981. Remarks on the metrical structure of the syllable. *Phonetica* 27: 245–56.

Kiparsky, Paul and W. O'Neill. 1976. The phonology of Old English inflections. *Linguistic Inquiry* 7: 527–57.

Knieza, Veronika. 1977. The development of the Old English long vowel system and diphthongs. *Annales Universitatis Scientiarum Budapestinensis* 8: 55–64.

Kristensson, Gillis. 1979. On the evidence for phonemic change. *Neuphilologische Mitteilungen* 80: 304–7.

Kurlowicz, Jerzy. 1973a. Contributions à la theorie de la syllabe. In Kurylowicz (ed.) vol. I: 193–220.

(ed.). 1973b. *Esquisses linguistiques*. Munich.

Labov, William. 1972. The internal evolution of linguistic rules. In Stockwell and Macaulay (eds.): 101–72.

1982. Building on empirical foundations. In Lehmann and Malkiel (eds.): 17–92.

Lakoff, Robin. 1972. Another look at drift. In Stockwell and Macaulay (eds.): 172–99.

Lass, Roger (ed.). 1969. *Approaches to English historical linguistics*. New York.

1974. Linguistic orthogenesis? Scots vowel quantity and the English length conspiracy. In Anderson and Jones (eds.): 335–68.

1976. *English phonology and phonological theory*. Cambridge.

1978. Mapping constraints in phonological reconstruction on climbing down trees without falling out of them. In Fisiak (ed.): 245–86.

1984. *Phonology*. Cambridge.

1985. Minkova noch einmal: MEOSL and the resolved foot. *Folia Linguistica Historica* 6: 245–65.

1986. Conventionalism, invention and 'historical reality': some reflections on method. *Diachronica* 3: 15–43.

Lass, Roger and John M. Anderson. 1975. *Old English phonology*. Cambridge.

Laubstein, Anne Stuart. 1987. Syllable structure: the speech error evidence. *Canadian Journal of Linguistics* 32: 339–65.

1988. *The nature of the 'production grammar' syllable.* Bloomington.

Leben, William R. 1980. A metrical analysis of length. *Linguistic Inquiry* 11: 497–509.

Lehiste, Ilse 1970. *Suprasegmentals.* Cambridge, MA.

Lehmann, Winfred and Yakov Malkiel (eds.). 1968. *Directions for historical linguistics.* Austin, Texas.

1982. *Perspectives on historical linguistics.* Amsterdam and Philadelphia.

Liberman, Mark and Alan S. Prince. 1977. On stress and linguistic rhythm. *Linguistic Inquiry* 8: 249–336.

Lieber, Rochelle. 1979. On Middle English lengthening in open syllables. *Linguistic Analysis* 5: 1–27.

Lüdtke, Helmut 1980a. Sprachwandel als universales Phänomen. In Lüdtke (ed.): 1–20.

(ed.). 1980b. Kommunikationstheoretische *Grundlagen des Sprachwandels.* Berlin and New York.

Luick, Karl. 1898. Beiträge zur englischen Grammatik III: Die Quantitätsveränderungen im Laufe der englischen Sprachentwicklung. *Anglia* 20: 335–62.

1914/21. *Historische Grammatik der englischen Sprache.* Oxford and Stuttgart.

1921. Über die Betonung der französischen Lehnwörter im Mittelenglischen. *Germanisch-Romanische Monatsschrift* 9: 14–19.

Luschützky, Hans Christian. 1988. Sixteen possible types of natural phonological processes. *Wiener Linguistische Gazette.* 42/3: 79–105.

Lutz, Angelika. 1986. The syllabic basis of word division in Old English manuscripts. *English Studies* 67: 193–210.

Lyons, John (ed.). 1970. *New horizons in linguistics.* Harmondsworth.

1981. *Language and linguistics.* Cambridge.

Maling, J.M. 1971. Sentence stress in Old English. *Linguistic Inquiry* 3: 379–99.

Malone, Kemp. 1926. Studies in English phonology. *Modern Philology* 23: 483–90.

Malsch, Derry Lawrence. 1971. *Redundancy rules and phonological change in the history of English.* Ann Arbor.

1976. Syllable, mora, and length in the development of English. In Christie (ed.): 83–93.

Malsch, Derry Lawrence and R. Fulcher. 1975. Tensing and syllabification in Middle English. *Language* 51: 303–14.

Markus, Manfred (ed.). 1989. *Historical English. On the occasion of Karl Brunner's 100th birthday.* (= Innsbrucker Beiträge zur Kulturwissenschaft. Anglistische Reihe 1). Innsbruck.

McClenon, Charles Lee. 1981. *Toward an interactive phonology of the English syllable.* Ann Arbor.

Mcintosh, Angus. 1956. The analysis of written Middle English. In Lass (ed.) 1969: 35–57.

Meyer, E. 1903. *Englische Lautdauer.* Uppsala.

Miller, Patricia Donegan. 1972. Some context-free processes affecting vowels. *Ohio State Working Papers in Linguistics* 11: 136–67.

Minkova, Donka. 1981. Middle English final -e from a phonemic point of view. In Davenport *et al.* (eds.): 191–209.

    1982. The environment for open syllable lengthening in Middle English. *Folia Linguistica Historica* 3: 29–58.

    1985. Of rhyme and reason: some foot governed quantity changes in English. *Current Issues in Linguistic Theory* 41: 163–79.

    1991. *A history of unstressed vowels.* Berlin, New York and Amsterdam.

Minkova, Donka and Robert P. Stockwell. 1992. Homorganic clusters as moric busters in the history of English: the case of -*ld*, -*nd*, -*mb*. In Rissanen *et al.* (eds.): 191–207.

Mitchell, Bruce and Fred C. Robinson (eds.). 1987. *A guide to Old English.* 4th edn. Oxford and New York.

Mohr, B. 1971. Intrinsic variations in the speech signal. *Phonetica* 23: 65–93.

Moore, Samuel. 1969. *Historical outlines of English sounds and inflections.* Ann Arbor.

Mossé, Fernand. 1952. *A handbook of Middle English* (translated by James A. Walker). London.

Mufwene, Salikoko S., Carol A. Walker and Sanford B. Steever (eds.). 1976. *Papers from the twelfth regional meeting of the Chicago Linguistic Society.* Chicago

Müllenbrock, Heinz Joachim and Renate Noll-Wieman (eds.). 1989. *Anglistentag 1988 Göttingen. Vorträge.* Tübingen.

Murray, Robert W. and Theo Vennemann. 1982. Sound change and syllable structure [: problems] in Germanic phonology. *Language* 59: 514–28.

Myers, Scott. 1987. Vowel shortening in English. *Natural Language and Linguistic Theory* 5: 485–518.

Nespor, Marina and Irene Vogel. 1986. *Prosodic phonology.* Dordrecht.

Ohala, John J. 1974. Experimental historical phonology. In Anderson and Jones, vol. II: 353–91.

Ohala, John J. and Haruko Kawasaki. 1984. Prosodic phonology and phonetics. *Phonology Yearbook* 1: 113–27.

O'Neill, W. 1970. Explaining vowel gradation in Old English. *General Linguistics* 10: 149–63.

Phillips, Betty. 1981. The phonetic basis of a Late Old English sound change. In Dressler *et al.* (eds.): 337–41.

Pilch, Herbert. 1968. Altenglische historische Lautlehre als phonologisches Problem. *Word* 24: 350–70.

　　1970. *Altenglische Grammatik.* Munich.

Pillinger, O.S. 1981. Towards an autosegmental analysis of syllable strcture. *Occasional Papers of the Department of Language and Linguistics at the University of Essex* 24: 54–66.

Pinsker, Hans Ernst. 1974. *Historische englische Grammatik.* 4th edn. Munich.

Plotkin, V.Y. 1972. *The dynamics of the English phonological system.* The Hague.

Prince, Alan S. 1980. A metrical theory for Estonian quantity. *Linguistic Inquiry* 11: 511–62.

Prins, A.A. 1974. *A history of English phonemes from Indo-European to present-day English.* Leiden.

Rakerd, B., W. Sennet and C.A. Fowler. 1987. Domain-final lengthening and foot-level shortening in spoken English. *Phonetica* 44: 147–56.

Reitemeyer, L. 1911. *Die Qualität der betonten langen e-Vokale in den französischen Lehnwörtern des Mittelenglischen.* Halle an der Saale.

Richardson, John F., Mitchell Marks and Amy Cluterman (eds.). 1983. *Papers from the parasession on the interplay of phonology, morphology and syntax.* Chicago

Rissanen, Matti, Ossi Ihalainen, Terttu Nevalainen and Irma Taavitsainen (eds.). 1992. *History of Englishes.* Berlin and New York.

Ritt, Nikolaus. 1986. Aspekte der englischen Silbengeschichte: Zur Dehnung vor homorganen Gruppen. *Klagenfurter Beiträge zur Sprachwissenschaft* 13/14: 507–25.

　　1988. Old and Middle English changes of vowel quantity. *Wiener Linguistische Gazette.* Suppl. 6: 64–7. Vienna.

1989. The processes amounting to MEOSL and its exceptions. In Markus (ed.): 153–65.

Robinson, Fred Norris (ed.). 1957. *The works of Geoffrey Chaucer*. 2nd edn. Oxford.

Russ, C.V.J. 1976. The data of historical linguistics: sources for the reconstruction of pronunciation from written records. *York Papers in Linguistics* 6: 65–73.

Saltarelli, Mario. 1983. The mora unit in Italian phonology. *Folia Linguistica* 17: 7–24.

Samuels, Michael L. 1969. Some applications of Middle English dialectology. In Lass (ed.): 404–18.

Sankoff, David (ed.). 1978. *Linguistic variation: models and methods*. New York.

Schane, Sanford A. 1972. Natural rules in phonology. In Stockwell and Macaulay (eds.): 199–230.

Selkirk, Elisabeth O. 1980. The role of prosodic categories in English word stress. *Linguistic Inquiry* 11: 563–605.

1982. The syllable. In Van der Hulst and Smith (eds.): 337–85.

Sievers, Eduard. 1901. *Grundzüge der Phonetik zur Einführung in das Studium der Lautlehre der indogermanischen Sprachen*. Leipzig.

Spencer, A. 1986. Vowel harmony, neutral vowels and autosegmental theory. *Lingua* 69: 3–23.

Spenser, A. 1986. Towards a theory of phonological development. *Lingua* 68: 3–39.

Stampe, David. 1979. *A dissertation on natural phonology*. Bloomington.

Stampe, David and Patricia Jane Donegan. 1983. Rhythm and the holistic organization of language structure. In Richardson, Marks and Cluterman (eds.): 337–49.

Stemberger, Joseph Paul. 1984. Length as a suprasegmental. *Language* 60: 895–913.

Steriade, Donca. 1988. Review of Clements and Keyser 1983. *Language* 64: 118–30.

Sternefeld, Wolfgang. 1986. Rewiew of Giegerich 1985. *Studium Linguistik* 20: 75–81.

Stockwell, Robert Paul. 1958. The phonology of Old English. *Studies in Linguistics* 13: 13–24.

1961. The Middle English 'long close' and 'long open' mid vowels. *University of Texas Studies in Literature and Language* 2: 529–38.

1985. Assessment of alternative explanations of the Middle English high vowel lowering when lengthened in the open syllable. *Current Issues in Linguistic Theory* 41: 303–19.

Stockwell, Robert Paul and Ronald Macaulay (eds.). 1972. *Linguistic change and generative theory*. Bloomington and London.

Strang, Barbara Mary Hope. 1970. *A history of English*. London.

Strangert, Eva. 1987. Speech rate and the temporal structure of stressed and unstressed syllables in Swedish. *Reports from the Uppsala University Department of Linguistics* 17: 22–9.

Suzuki, S. 1985. The role of syllable structure in Old English poetry. *Lingua* 67: 97–121.

Sweet, Henry, 1888. *A history of English sounds*. Oxford.

Tranel, Bernard. 1991. CVC light syllables, geminates and moraic theory. *Phonology* 8: 291–303.

Treimann, Rebecca. 1986. The division between onsets and rimes in English syllables. *Journal of Memory and Language* 25: 476–92.

Trilsbach, Georg. 1905. *Die Lautlehre der spätwestsächsischen Evangelien*. Bonn.

Vachek, Joseph. 1975. Problems of phonological interpretation of past stages of language. *Prague Studies in English* 16: 15–22.

Vago, Robert M. 1987. On the representation of length. In Dressler *et al.* (eds.): 189–92.

Van der Hulst, Harry and Norval Smith (eds.). 1982. *The structure of phonological representations*. Dordrecht.

Vennemann, Theo. 1972a. On the theory of syllabic phonology. *Linguistische Berichte* 18: 1–18.

1972b. Sound change and markedness theory: on the history of the German consonant system. In Stockwell and Macaulay: 230–75.

1986. *Neuere Entwicklungen in der Phonologie*. Berlin, New York and Amsterdam.

1988. *Preference laws for syllable structure and the explanation of sound change*. Berlin, New York and Amsterdam.

Vincent, Nigel. 1986. Constituency and syllable structure. In Durand (ed.): 305–19.

Weimann, Klaus. 1982. *Einführung ins Altenglische*. Heidelberg.

Weinreich, Uriel, William Labov and Marvin Herzog. 1968. Empirical foundations for a theory of language change. In Lehmann and Malkiel: 95–195.

Welna, Jerzy. 1978. *A diachronic grammar of English.* Warsaw.

Wieden, Wilfried. 1981. *Elemente der temporalen Organisation von englischer connected speech.* Salzburg.

Wiese, Richard. 1986. Zur Theorie der Silbe. *Studium Linguistik* 20: 1–16.

Wittig, Kurt. 1951. Über die mittelenglische Dehnung in offener Silbe und die Entwicklung der *er*-Laute im Frühneuenglischen. *Anglia* 70: 47–69.

Wrenn, Charles Leslie. 1944. The value of spelling as evidence. *Transactions of the Philological Society*: 14–39.

Wrenn, Charles Leslie (ed.). 1973. *Beowulf.* 3rd edn. London.

Wright, Joseph. 1928. *An elementary Middle English grammar.* 2nd edn. London.

Wurzel, Wolfgang Ulrich. 1980. Ways of morphologizing phonological rules. In Fisiak (ed.): 443–463.

Zimmermann, S. and S. Sapon. 1958. A note on vowel duration seen crosslinguistically. *The Journal of the Acoustic Society of America* 30: 152–3.

Zwicky, Arnold M. 1972. Note on a phonological hierarchy in English. In Stockwell and Macaulay (eds.): 275–301.

1986. Forestress and afterstress. *Ohio State Working Papers in Linguistics* 32: 46–62.

Index

Abercrombie, David, 69
Ablaut, 66
absolute chronolgy of HOL and OSL, 92–3
allomorphy rule, 114
ambisyllabicity, 52, 53, 54, 55, 60, 61, 63, 64, 84, 96, 102, 105
Anderson, John M., 54, 56, 65, 67, 72
assimilation, 91
autosegmental phonology, 49

backgrounding: of syllables, 38
backness of vowels, 110
base form, 116, 117, 118, 121
Bliss, Alan J., 29

casual speech, 16, 17, 20, 21, 24
Catford, John C., 110
Chaucer, Geoffrey, 90, 122
Chen, Matthew, 111
chronology of HOL and OSL, 88
coda, 48, 49, 52, 54, 55, 59, 63, 65, 66, 68, 75, 76, 84, 85, 86, 87, 88, 89, 96, 102, 104, 105, 112
coda reduction, 89
coda sonority, 86, 87, 111
coda weight, 102
compensatory lengthening, 68, 89
consonantality, 65
constraints on quantity changes, 15, 16, 17, 18, 20, 22, 23, 24, 27, 30, 32, 35, 37, 45, 72, 81, 84, 85, 88, 95, 97, 100, 107, 108, 109, 110, 112, 122
coronal obstruents, 90
Couper-Kuhlen, Elizabeth, 69, 109

CV syllables, 54
CVC syllables, 54

data, 8; modern, 11; Modern English data as evidence, 10–11, 12; Modern English evidence, 15; the search for suitable data, 8–11; theory-neutral data, 5; uncritical use of, 4
denaturalization, 114
dependency phonology, 49
dialect mixture, 11–23, 12, 15, 23, 24, 25
Dressler, Wolfgang U., 15, 48, 55, 109, 112, 117

epenthesis, 68, 69, 89
etymological origin, 29
explanation: circularity, 75, 108; definition of, 107
explanation of QUAR, 107–23

fast speech, 16, 17, 20, 21
final /b/: deletion of, 90
Fintoft, K., 111
foot, 69; definition of, 69; foot structure and vowel lengthening, 72–3; foot vs. wordform. 70, 71–2, 122; representation of, 70
foot weight, 73, 78
formal speech, 17, 20, 24
frontness of vowels, 110

goal conflict, 112

.